Two-Way Story

Two-Way

Story

An Autobiography by
Cliff Michelmore
and

Jean Metcalfe

Elm Tree Books . London

First published in Great Britain 1986
by Hamish Hamilton Ltd/Elm Tree Books Ltd
27 Wrights Lane London W8 5TZ

British Library Cataloguing in Publication Data

Michelmore, Cliff
　Two-way story: an autobiography.
　1. Metcalfe, Jean　2. Broadcasters—Great
　Britain—Biography　3. Michelmore, Cliff
　4. Broadcasters—Great Britain—
　Biography
　I. Title　II. Metcalfe, Jean
　791.44′092′4　　　PN990.72.M4

　　ISBN 0–241–11852–2

Photoset, printed & bound in Great Britain by
Redwood Burn Limited, Trowbridge, Wiltshire.

Contents

Acknowledgements

The authors wish to thank the following for the use of copyright photographs:

page 5, tea in the BBC canteen, 1944, with GFP listeners from the RAF, RNVR and Canadian Army, photograph by Saidman; BBC wartime fan-mail card: BBC; page 6, Cliff as commentator for the BFN in Hamburg: British Crown copyright reserved; picture of Jean: BBC; page 8, the wedding: Belgrave Press Bureau; page 9, Jean interviewing Jack Hawkins on *Woman's Hour*: BBC; with General Sir Brian Horrocks, Robert Reid, Brian Johnston and Henry Riddell, British Crown copyright reserved; page 10, the fireman's lift, 1955: Syndication International; page 11, the first *Tonight* studio at St Mary Abbott's Place: BBC; an Isle of Wight newspaper comments on Cliff's Tussauds figure, 1959: Tom Smitch; page 12, Guy and Cliff on Cowes Esplanade, 1959: Associated Newspapers; page 13, Sir Matt Busby on *With Michelmore*, and Prince Charles' first interview: BBC; page 14, Cliff, 1968, © David Bailey; page 15, picture of Jean by Karsh, Camera Press/Woodfin Camp; page 16, Cliff with Bruce Forsyth, Alan Shepard, the astronaut and Burt Lancaster: Ian Joy; *en famille* in Inverness: James Anderson; and Nottingham: Nottingham Trader.

Thanks also to the BBC Written Archives Centre for their help in providing copyright material.

Front jacket photograph by Nic Barlow
Back jacket photograph of Cliff with the *Tonight* team, Alasdair Milne, Grace Wyndham Goldie and Derek Hart, copyright © BBC; photograph of Jean by courtesy of Associated newspapers
Jacket design by Don Macpherson

1/JEAN

You Must Be Cliff...

Isn't it strange, the things you remember, the pinpricks which leave a lasting mark? To this day I'd swear there's a side-ways parting across the top of my head, the merest cut-and-blow away from view, put there forty years ago by a pair of heavy metal head-phones. The Home Perm had not been invented which could withstand their weight. Continuity announcers wore them for hours on end as part of the job of knitting a radio service into a whole, darning the gaps, seaming the programmes together. I was working on the Light Programme in 1949 and the Continuity head-phones had settled into their customary furrow among the corrugated waves, when the door from the Control Cubicle was pushed open by a tall man in a sharp grey three-piece suit. 'You must be Jean' he said, and I replied 'You must be Cliff.'

If only I'd seen him coming, what a glamorous exchange that could have been. At school we had wasted much logarithm time planning the moments when we would enslave the men of our dreams. They were situations born in Hollywood, bred by Metro-Goldwyn-Mayer out of the Majestic cinema down the road. Our Rinso-clean heroes always had glittering names like Errol, or Navarro. 'Arrowsmith' was the one I fancied – Ronald Colman must have had something to do with that – and the manoeuvre to enslave him would be a Norma Shearer swoon in a sea of sinking, billowing taffeta. The possibility that 'Arrowsmith' might simply step over me never crossed my mind.

When the time came in 1939 to leave school and go to work on The Plan, to perm the hair and dab the 'Californian Poppy', I had lived long enough to learn that swooning frequently involves a certain amount of throwing-up and the exposure of none-too-enticing, sensible underwear. It was wartime. Not too many 'Arrowsmiths' around then. Nor, with clothes rationing and Utility labels, unlimited amounts of billowing taffeta.

So here I am, one Wednesday afternoon in April 1949, harnessed by the headphones to the Light Continuity announcer's desk in the basement of Broadcasting House. And here he is, my co-presenter on *Two-Way Family Favourites*, face to face for the very first time.

Two-Way had been part of my regular duties ever since I joined the Light Programme two years earlier. It is difficult to appreciate now how avant-garde it was at the time: unscripted, after years of wartime censorship; broadcast simultaneously in Britain and in Germany; and, perhaps its most unusual feature, allowing a male and female presenter to exchange informal, friendly conversation week after week, Sunday after Sunday. A number of people had handled the German end of the programme, all of them servicemen doing their conscripted time with the British Forces Network in Hamburg. Derek Jones put in the longest spell but he was suddenly taken ill and replaced at the last moment by the Deputy Station Director.

When I came on duty that Sunday, the name 'Michelmore' had been inked on to the running order without warning, and I remember wondering how it should be pronounced. Hurried calls were made between the Broadcasting House Control Room and the engineer in Hamburg. Should it be Michael-more, Mishelmoor or Mitchell-more? In the event, the programme went well. Our patterns of speech fell into place like a well-made jigsaw and we seemed to have the same feeling for varying pace and length of announcements. Evidently Alec Sutherland, the Station Director in Germany, thought so too because Cliff remained on the programme and we quickly became friends, though in voice only.

There was a telephone link between London and Hamburg for ten minutes before we went on the air to enable presenters to make any last-minute alterations in the record order or message details. Soon we were using every bit of that time – it was already paid for, after all – for more personal, day-to-day, conversation. Members of BFN staff ('visiting firemen') on leave from Germany called in at Broadcasting House as a goodwill gesture. One, Peter Page, brought me a present from Cliff, a bottle of Benedictine casually wrapped in a copy of BFN's programme sheet which happened to include a modest, blurred picture of my opposite number's face. I wrote Cliff a somewhat flirtatious letter of thanks and received

2

four friendly pages from him in reply. They contained this significant anecdote:

'I was at a very sedate sort of party the other day, thrown by a relatively senior officer. One husband introduced me to his wife who greeted me with "Cliff Michelmore! Well, how is your wife?" After I was lifted from the floor she said "But everybody knows that you are Jean Metcalfe's husband." To this day [it was March 14th] a certain lady does not believe that we have never even met!' Cliff says he still remembers the name of the lady in question. I can only imagine she possessed 'second sight' because, at that point, the only facts I knew about him were that he was an RAF Squadron Leader and had a voice quite unlike most broadcasters of the day. Their accents were upper-crust, polished and la-di-da. His crackled with vitality and had a hint of the countryman about it. We were still playing a lot of Ivor Novello music in those days and he always said 'We'll gather lie-lacs', which was intriguing.

But nothing had prepared me for this unexpected meeting. Certainly not those schoolgirl dreams of 'Arrowsmith' and Norma Shearer. His civilian suit was made by a German tailor. My dress was early C&A. 'You must be Jean,' he said and when he spoke I recognised the voice... 'You must be Cliff.'

The pause which followed had never occurred in any of my romantic scenarios. What do you say to an old friend you have never seen before? Remark on the sharp suit? Talk about the weather? Fool that I was, I fastened on to his outstandingly tanned complexion, little knowing it resulted from childhood years spent on a farm, by the sea. Like dye on leather that sort of conditioning lasts a lifetime. 'My word,' I said, plunging on, 'my word, you do look well.' 'It's funny you should say that,' he replied, 'because I've been sent home on sick leave.' This was not in the script I had been writing for so long. It seems the more you plan and mark out your route, the more guide lines there are to trip over. We'd stumbled at the start but Cliff manfully forgave me and suggested dinner that evening. Now here was another hiccup in the story-line. I had promised to go with my father to the finals of the Railway Firemen's Boxing Competition. They were being held at the Seymour Street Baths and Father, a deeply loyal servant of the Southern Railway and a push-over to the end of his days for a free corned beef sandwich, would be disappointed if I let him down. It was clutch-at-straws-time before 'Arrowsmith' walked off into someone else's sunset. I remembered hearing that Cliff was making quite a mark as a sports commentator in Hamburg, with prize fights in the Max Schmeling class under his belt. Tentatively

3

I asked . . . if by chance . . . provided he wasn't doing anything else . . . there was the slightest possibility . . . that he might care to join us at the Railway Firemen's Boxing instead? Without visibly flinching, he agreed.

As a lifelong shrinking violet, you can imagine how much I had been looking forward to the prospect of all those grunting, bleeding stokers slugging away at each other. Hadn't I waged a childhood campaign against the cruelty-to-insects of our scullery fly paper? Never mind that the creatures I rescued looked none too healthy after I'd pulled them off the stickiness. It's the thought that counts, and those thoughts still lingered when it came to anticipating Father's boxing finals that evening. But, by the time we were all at the ringside, the need to impress the splendid fellow sitting next to me was a blessed anaesthetic against the ugly details of the sport we'd come to see. Truth to tell, I don't remember the boxing at all. It was the interval which made its mark and sealed my fate.

Hollow with hunger because lunch had not come my way that day, I longed for something warm and soothing to muffle the inner rumblings. Hot coffee, even khaki-coloured, cardboard-tasting coffee, would have been manna in the wilderness but Father, intent on his free beer and corned beef sandwiches, led the way to a dismal bar. He dismissed the crowd round the steaming urns. 'You'll never get through that scrum. Look at them. Ten deep. Pushing and shoving. Better have a beer with us.' That was when Michelmore played his ace. 'I'll get you a coffee,' he said and my newly found 'Arrowsmith', my champion, my knight in shining German tailoring, disappeared into enemy territory.

So, on our first date, Father came too. And the boxing firemen. And the corned beef sandwiches. It was a long way from billowing taffeta but that would have been worn out and threadbare decades ago. This memory has lasted for thirty-six years and there's a lot of mileage in it yet.

In spite of the gloom of the boxing baths, Cliff came back for more. We went out to dinner two nights later to take the nasty taste away. This time the setting was the Brylcreem-shiny Café Anglais in Leicester Square. The owner-driver of this baroque little folly was the bandleader Harry Roy, whom I had announced on many of his broadcasts. In the restaurant, every piece of iron which could be wrought, had been; every foldable napkin was a waterlily. Cliff bought me a corsage from the 'Tiller Girl' with a tray of flowers and we talked and talked and talked. Just as well really, because there was a tiny dance floor menacingly close to our table and I have always been a dreadful dancer. 'Please God' I prayed, 'don't let Cliff be a why-don't-we-roll-up-the-carpet-and-dance kind of fellow.' I was ready to slip the nearest waiter a fiver to break my leg for me. It wasn't necessary. To please the band, we shuffled modestly round the bit of polished floor, but there were no chassés or flashy quicksteps so I concluded he was no great whizz in that department either; something else we had in common. By the end of the evening, conversation between us had taken off its gloves and eased its shoelaces. We were more than friends. When Cliff returned to Germany a few days later we both knew with certainty that something very important was happening in our lives.

Now the phones rang between England and Germany and the letters flew between us like a continuing conversation. On May 6th – I was 'Dearest Jean' by now – Cliff wrote explaining the all-sorts nature of his job in Hamburg: 'I did an OB on Monday, a British Zone Finalists' Quiz on Wednesday, the *Anne Shelton Show* last evening and have just returned from a forty-minute commentary on the unveiling of a war memorial, XIth Hussars, by the Military Governor, General Robertson. I have to stay here tonight so that Ernest Bevin can broadcast from Wunstorf tomorrow, and, on top of all this, I have to spend next Wednesday night on the Helmstedt border waiting for the blockade to be lifted on Thursday – sometime!' This letter ends, very correctly with 'Regards to Father (and Mother despite the fact that we haven't met).'

Photographs of the Hamburg back streets beneath his office followed on May 13th. *Friday* the 13th, 'I'm superstitious,' he said 'and never leave a letter needing an answer on such a day.' On the 23rd he wrote about Hanover, 'a city hollowed out by bombing. The zoo is receiving its first consignment of animals but the high lions' hills are overgrown and the notices reading "EIN" badly need a coat of paint. The Observatory has a patchwork quilt stretched over the dome where the glass has gone.' Three days later BFN was in a turmoil of preparation 'for the impending visit of the Director General, Sir William Haley himself. We are busily scrubbing the marble staircase and giving Mozart and Brahms a bath.' Two British theatrical companies were visiting Hamburg at the time . . . 'the London Gate Theatre Company, sponsored by the Arts Council, performing *Hamlet* and a West End Company playing *Mountain Air*. In order to boost the latter an over-print was ordered reading "The funniest play ever seen in the Zone". These were given to the bill poster who stuck them on all the *Hamlet* notices.'

'The DG's visit went off well,' he wrote on May 29th. 'He said the BBC were taking over BFN next April except for a small local staff. This is all confidential at the moment – everybody knows about it!'

5

By now, all our letters were love letters. On *Two-Way Family Favourites* every hackneyed ballad was grand opera to our ears. When Cliff was about to return for his next leave in June, the record which ended the programme was 'I'll be seeing you'. Meeting again our relationship was quite different, buoyant with plans and the conspiratoral support of friends. On his first day home we lunched at the Mandeville Hotel off Wigmore Street, an elegant place where they warmed the serving spoons and the waiters moved as silently as skaters. I wore a hat – well, most of us did in those days – and Cliff gave me yellow roses to wear. There was no formal proposal but both of us knew that we would marry one day and all our plans were based on that assumption.

Before we met I had survived one passionately unhappy affair, a broken engagement and sundry, less serious flirtations. Cliff had made a brief and disastrous wartime marriage, so we were no longer skittish young things to be bowled over by a wink or a wiggle. True, I loved him for his fair hair and brown eyes, his broad shoulders and slim hips, but, with maturity, other qualities mattered more. I loved his voice, his sudden flashes of generous kindness, his humour, his well-trained disciplined mind. Mine was an entirely intuitive intelligence with almost no training at all. I even loved him for his quick temper which compensated for my pillow-soft placidity. He was competitive and determined while I was easily discouraged and diverted. He could be powerfully decisive whenever my opinions chopped and changed. I loved him because he wanted to make me happy. We had come to the point in our lives when we were looking for the same things in the future – stability, a home and family.

Decisive as ever, Cliff had determined to leave his Air Force career in order to break into broadcasting here at home. This was an immense relief because I was never cut out to be a Service wife, moving from house to house, limiting possessions to the easily packable and less easily broken. It takes an exceptional person to plant a rose for someone else to pick. I was willing to try, but with as much confidence as a novice on a high wire. So the good news was that he was coming over to my side of the fence, commuterland, and the cut and thrust of post-war broadcasting at the BBC. It was going to be very competitive with so many returning staff to be accommodated and multitudes of others who, having tasted the delights of Forces broadcasting during the war, wanted to make it a full-time career. But Cliff was determined to pack his old Air Force trunk for the last time and I couldn't wait to help him.

Then came the tricky bit. The BBC made it clear that there could be no question of making our liaison public, no formal engagement, while we worked together on *Two-Way*. Socially we were treated as a couple but had to behave like friendly business colleagues on our Sunday programmes. Discretion is difficult when you want nothing so much as a rooftop to shout from and a ring to wear on your third-finger-left-hand, but it was vital to keep up the façade if Cliff was ever to be welcomed into the close-knit prevailing monopoly of British broadcasting. *We* knew, our *friends* knew, even our *employers* knew but the *public* must not know until Cliff had left Hamburg. They might think we were using their programme to carry on our courtship. Of course they did, and of course, we were. 'The Peggy Lee record was just for you,' Cliff wrote in May. In June it was Jean Sablon singing 'Can I Forget You?' which was 'really a message from me to you.' July 4th: 'A request is to hand for anything by Harry Roy. There'll be a multitude of memories.' July 11th: 'Next Sunday's programme is designed for you. The others can listen if they like!' Our letters were full of all the things we could not put into words on the programme. But the BBC insisted, and the BBC must be obeyed, nothing must be said about our relationship – officially.

That summer in 1949, the Government lifted its ban on people from this country visiting Germany on holiday. Before you could say 'Nordwestdeutsche Rundfunk' plans were made for me to nip across and see Cliff's stamping ground for myself. This could only be a flying visit, fitted in between Sunday and Sunday, and never referred to on the air. My plane tickets cost me all my spare cash – £36 – but Cliff insisted on footing every other bill. My mother was uneasy about the trip, after all, she had never met the man and I had given her plenty of cause to worry in my twenty-six years. Forty years ago most of us lived at home until we married and boyfriends were introduced early for family approval. 'Home by midnight' was the rule, and in those pre-Pill days, 'never get drunk or you'll be pregnant in the morning.' No wonder she was concerned. But Cliff sent her a cable asking her permission and that seemed to do the trick. Bonnets were over the windmill and I was off to meet my 'intended'.

Aboard the BEA Viking I was determined to get my money's-worth. The stewardess brought round barley sugar. I accepted barley sugar. She brought round cottonwool earplugs. I had some of those too. By now we were airborne and swooping up and down like a rollercoaster at a funfair. I had never flown before and thought it was always as lively as this, gale or no gale, with seatbelts fastened all the way. Business men were greening and closing their eyes, briefcases clutched against stomachs for comfort. Funny people, I thought, when everyone else refused the coffee we were offered. I wasn't going to miss that bit of my £36. The stewardess was swaying on her feet as she poured most of it into my cup. I started to drink at the very moment the plane hit an air pocket and dropped hundreds of feet. My arm shot up in the air and stayed there like something raised on invisible wires. No matter how hard I tried to pull it down, the hand – it was no longer anything to do with me – remained, waving the cup above my head with the wild abandon of a wedding guest in a Breughel painting. When, at last, plane, hand and coffee cup levelled out, I heaped embarrassed apologies all over my poor neighbour who had been sheltering beneath his newspaper. His only response was a wary 'Bitte?', which did nothing to restore the poise I'd put on, like a best dress, back at Northolt.

One glance at Cliff's anxious face when we landed put everything right. He'd been worried by our late arrival and knew it had been an exceptionally rough ride, so I lapped up his concerned attention, adopting the pose of a world-weary traveller. No one should ever know that I thought it was always like that.

The next three days were a confusion of places and people, a lightning sketch of his most recent background. He was a distinguished officer in the RAF, used to hobnobbing with Generals and Air Chief Marshals. I was a BBC announcer following in the celebrated limelight of Alvar Lidell and Stuart Hibberd. We had a lot to live up to, a lot to hide. But by the end of that visit to Germany we had been able, on our own, to unroll our lives for each other, back to their beginnings. When the threads were unravelled and laid out for inspection they turned out to be made from very ordinary stuff indeed.

You Must Be Jean . . .

It is tempting to say that I remember everything about that day before Easter 1949. Honesty compels me to admit that my memory has lived up to its unreliable reputation and let me down. Mind you I should have known better and pocketed my much more trustworthy notepad. But you do not take a notepad along when you are about to have your very first meeting with someone you have long admired and have been angling to meet for months, do you? I had a strong, almost certain, feeling that I was going to be welcomed. I had a hope that I would get to know this girl with the lilt and smile in her voice. Servicemen across the world had fallen for her voice as she broadcast 'Thank you for your letters' and played record requests for them. Marjorie Anderson, Joan Griffiths, Jean Metcalfe and the rest were wife and girlfriend substitutes and home-coming soldiers, sailors and airmen often made their way up Regent Street to Portland Place bearing gifts for these unseen, but frequently heard girls-back-home.

After the war *Two-Way Family Favourites*, which linked the forces in the British Army of the Rhine and their families at home, became a part of a traditional Sunday. As the strings of Andre Kostelanetz swooped into 'With a Song in My Heart' one of radio's biggest audiences were setting about their Sunday lunch. Jean Metcalfe presented the programme from London and from the Musikhalle in Hamburg I had taken over, at short notice, from Derek Jones when he suddenly went into hospital.

At the British Forces Network in Germany everyone was expected to do everything – write scripts, handle request

9

programmes, act in plays, announce concerts or take their turn in the first floor continuity suite. So in addition to looking after the Variety Section and Outside Broadcasts and reading, in a countrified voice the 'Man with a spade' weekly garden talks, I had also done some request programmes. But broadcasting to millions on the Light Programme was a voice-quaking experience. It was the prestige, name-making programme. The one thing that helped me through that first day was the calming, comforting voice of Jean at the other end of the telephone. The presenters always had a word with each other before they began, to make certain that running orders had not changed or the censorious hand of BBC authority had not 'forbidden' a particular record or request. After that first programme and a few friendly words of advice from the Station Director, Alec Sutherland, I settled in, more and more enjoying the pre-broadcast phone link with London. As time went by did I detect a slightly flirtatious tone to the conversation? If this is to be told without exaggeration and extenuation then I must admit that I did. But what did Jean Metcalfe actually look like? Everyone knew what she sounded like. As time went by I found myself wanting to know all about this girl with so much charm in her voice.

Trevor Hill was an ex-BBC junior programme engineer who became one of the best producer-scriptwriters we ever had at BFN. In his office he had, under the glass-top of his desk, a collection of photographs of all the announcers with whom he had worked. There, in the near corner as you came in the door, I remember it well, was a photograph of Jean Metcalfe looking almost shy of the camera. It was only later that I was to discover just how shy she really was of cameras and that no photograph – not even one by Karsh of Ottawa – did her justice. But this was my first glance at the girl I talked with every Sunday and whose voice intrigued me. I liked what I saw.

'She has got the most lovely auburn hair,' said Trevor 'and she is such a lovely person.'

Another ex-BBC man, Peter Page, was about to go on leave and so unashamedly, wanting to ingratiate myself, I asked if he would be courier bearing an 'introductory' bottle. Benedictine was on offer at the NAAFI so that was it. Peter it was who wrapped the bottle in the single sheet BFN programme – which just happened to have my photograph on the front – and took it to Jean at Broadcasting House. A thank you letter came within a day. 'Sunday February 6th – My dear Cliff – you fabulous man! You fairy (in the nicest and least BBC sense!) godfather, you! ... Bless you Cliff, and here's to you – with all the goodwill "returning to base" a thousandfold in the years ahead. In a few weeks (oh, how omin-

10

ously few!) Metcalfe will be celebrating and *forgetting* birthday No. 26 and your Benedictine will be the highlight of the celebration. Cliff will be there in spirit.' And so the letter went on, talking of calling in when I came home and ending with 'See you one day we hope. Meanwhile, thank you over and over, With love, Jean.'

That was the last birthday Jean ever celebrated without me. The next twenty-six, and more, we were to spend together. But that letter was followed by another and a few weeks later I was to be on my way home for some leave. It had been a bad year until then. My mother had died from cancer, my lifelong friend had been killed in an aircrash and I had decided to get a divorce. A very brief wartime marriage with a nurse had ended almost as soon as it began with her going off with a Pole and having a baby by him. They had wanted to marry but stubborn, stupid, well-bruised pride had made me deny them the chance. Now, however, I felt I was going through a time of change so I set the law in motion. I had decided to leave the security of my RAF career and its distant prospect of a pension and was set on taking my chances in the eddying, unsteady waters of freelance broadcasting. I certainly did not have a BBC voice like Raymond Baxter who had returned from BFN to a job as a commentator with BBC Outside Broadcasts. So I must try other fields. When I was coming home on leave I got an introduction to one or two people in the Light Programme from Alec Sutherland and set off. I also had another objective. To meet Jean.

The voyage from the Hook of Holland was absolutely awful. Only the Medical Officer and one or two others of us made the Mess for breakfast – and those Dutch boats were renowned for serving the kind of wonderful breakfasts for which we had fought a war!

In London I stayed at the Mandeville Hotel. I had stayed there a number of times because it was handily just around the corner from Robert Adam Street where a former girlfriend lived. A young man newly out of the army by the name of Maxwell Joseph was in the process of rebuilding the Mandeville Hotel at that time; an operation he controlled from the small back room with a trestle table for a desk.

When I telephoned to make my appointments with John McMillan, the Deputy Head of the Light Programme and an ex-BFN Hamburg man, I casually asked if Jean Metcalfe happened to be on duty. At least I tried to sound casual about it but I was far from that. I had briefly mentioned the possibility of dropping in the Sunday before, when we talked on the phone between London and Hamburg and I found myself anxiously awaiting the reply. 'Yes she was due on duty any time now. She is on until six.'

11

First I went up on to the 2nd floor for my meetings which were unproductive and uneventful. The corridors of the BBC were crowded with aspiring freelance broadcasters at that time, all trying to make their mark with someone, I was just one of the many. They told me where to find Jean. Down in the basement in 'Light Con'.

On the left-hand side of the corridor was the door marked 'Light Continuity'. Inside and beyond the control room was the announcer's studio. It was rather like the one we had in Hamburg, all glass panels and double doors. She was writing. I told the control room engineer who I was. He put down his talkback switch. The hand waved me through the double doors and there I was with Jean for the first time. 'You must be Jean.' 'And you must be Cliff.'

This is the moment when I ought to have stored away every tiny important detail of what happened, what she was wearing, what we said and how I felt. The fact is that neither of us even remember the actual date! I do remember that lovely fall of auburn hair, the welcoming smile on her face as well as in her voice. It was late afternoon. I had two or three days to spend in London before going down to my home on the Isle of Wight. What was she doing that evening, would she like to come out to dinner?

She had already told her Father that she would go with him to the Railway Firemen's Boxing Championships at the Seymour Street Baths but then she asked if I would like to join them.

Sharing this new-found friend with thumping, heaving, sweating and grunting amateur boxers providing the romantic backcloth on our first evening out together was not exactly what I had in mind. And with her father too! But it was not an invitation I had any intention of refusing. If this was the only chance I'd take it.

There are some things I do remember about that evening very clearly indeed. It was raining quite gently as we walked out of the front of Broadcasting House and got a taxi. We met Father and were introduced to lines of his colleagues and bosses, all to a man, fans of Jean's. She was a celebrity. I was delighted to be in attendance but I was damned if I was going to be eased aside by General Managers, Senior Operating Managers, the Station Master of Waterloo or anyone else.

Of the evening's boxing matches not a flicker of a memory remains. I ought to have kept the programme but I did not. I ought to have done so many things that very special evening but I did not. One thing I did do, however, turned out to be *the* turning point in my life. I got Jean Metcalfe a cup of coffee, would you believe? It was the most important cup of coffee I have ever bought in my life.

Between bouts came time for refreshments and we stood together on the edge of the crowd struggling to get near the bar. Beer and sandwiches were on offer. The beer was warm and the sandwiches soggy, but both were free and Jean's father plunged in. Jean wanted coffee, so coffee she should have.

How the evening finished I have not the faintest idea, but I was by then even more determined that we should go out together without boxing firemen, Father or other adoring fans. We did.

There must have been a reason why we chose the Café Anglais for that first ever date (but neither of us knows to this day what it was). The photograph shows perfectly clearly that I was out to impress her. Wine, flowers, liqueurs, my new silk tie. She was unaffected, obviously friendly and even more amusing than she was on the radio and a delight to be with. It is too easy to recollect in the tranquillity of old age that I fell in love with her at that moment over dinner in the Café Anglais. The truth is, that I knew that I had already fallen in love with her voice and now I had fallen in love with her. We had talked to each other every Sunday with the world listening. We had been to a boxing match with her father and a few hundred railwaymen and their families. We had written a couple of letters to each other. We had now been out to dinner and even danced together once. We both knew that our friendship was now likely to take on a new look – and sound. *Two-Way Family Favourites*, Sundays and every day come to that, would take on a quite different meaning for me and I hoped for her too. They did.

As soon as I went back to Germany we started to write letters. Occasionally at first – that is, no more than two a week – but soon we were corresponding almost daily. Then came the telephone calls. The open line which we had on Sundays between London and Hamburg was really for talking about the programme and although we surreptitiously used it for quite other purposes, it was not as private as we were coming to want and need it to be. There were, however, such things as 'Social Calls' which could be made from the various Officers' Clubs and hotels. Six minutes was the allowance for a few marks. Each Wednesday I booked a call from wherever I happened to be in Germany, to Reigate 3111. The telephone calls and letters kept us going between the all too infrequent trips home.

'Tonight there'll be those precious couple of minutes. I shall be so strung up with waiting for the phone to ring, I shall leave everything unsaid or bungled or muttered, so that only the local Reigate operator can understand,' Jean wrote. Little did she know that I too got all strung up waiting to be called to the phone. I even put

13

down little notes so I would not forget what I wanted to tell her. They were precious minutes for me also.

'This *is* as absurdly like a magazine story as it looks to me isn't it? And it *is* true isn't it?' she asked. Yes, it was almost absurd and yes it was true.

'Did I ever tell you how much I liked you for unprotestingly getting me a coffee instead of beer at that boxing bar, when I hadn't had any tea? Silly, I don't think I did.' I said that it was the most important cup of coffee I ever bought.

'Have found a fascinating record, the most exciting thing since "Oye Negra" (only nothing will ever be quite as absurdly important as that's become). "Maladie d'amour" they call it. Henri Salvador. He sings in a sultry, slurred, French dialect, with a strangely echoing guitar – and there's a faintly silly naive bird that chirps away . . . must watch for a *loose* card to knot around it on *Two-Way Fam Favs* sometime. Just one person who leaves it to the "Dear Sir or Madam" that's all I want.'

'Ronnie Waldman yesterday, whom I haven't seen for years said "Your Fam Favs on Sunday is a fine show. When are you going to Hamburg? You should you know, good PR (me nodding like a demented mandarin)."' And then after a phone call a letter written very late at night. 'Exactly what we talked about I never can remember afterwards except that today it was something quite impossible about coming to Germany! Oh how I'd love to.'

Suddenly friends and relatives were to be allowed in to Germany for visits. British European Airways flew their propeller-driven Vickers Vikings. Jean insisted on paying her fare 'otherwise I would be a kept woman and I am not just yet'. The whole station looked forward to her coming because, by now, it was common knowledge that we were more than just friends. I was in a turmoil. I had fixed her a room in the hotel in which I had quarters, 'The Boccacio'. It was near to the station and had the reputation of having once been an SS brothel for high ranking officers. It was full of plush velvet settees, heavy curtains and enormous baths with their large wooden thermometers. I went out to the airport hours before the aircraft was due. The air traffic controller was a friend of mine. 'I'm afraid that they are a bit delayed. The weather is absolutely awful. Look, there is this deep front right across the channel and up into the North Sea.'

The relief on my face must have been all too obvious as I met her at the entrance to the terminal building. It had, according to the air steward, been 'one hell of a flight'.

For three short days we careered around Germany. Down the autobahn to Lubeck, and the seaside resort of Travemunde. The signs in German amused her 'I understand how you can *Aus*fahrt but how do you *Ein*fahrt?'

We certainly had immense faith in the capability of BEA to meet their schedules. Jean was booked on the early morning plane on Sunday, giving her little more than an hour to spare to get into the studio for our *Two-Way* programme at twelve. What our lords and masters would have said if she has missed getting there I shudder to think. It would have meant the sack at least.

By now I had made up my mind not to stay in Germany. The Station Director's job was up for a one-year contract, but that did not suit our plans at all. 'I keep an avid eye on the Post Vacant these days, just to get a line on the sort of things coming up', wrote Jean in late summer.

'I sat in the train tonight with a steel thread of hatred for London and its shoddy, shabby rush and tear twanging through my head and I imagined us *together*, working side by side. . . .'

There never was any formal asking her if she would marry me. We just assumed that as soon as I came back from Germany, I would get a place to stay for a while and then we would get married and live outside London. Jean's father had long since accepted the inevitable and her mother was soon to follow. 'Certainly not surprised . . . but highly delighted.'

By now we were working out where to live, when to marry and even what sort of engagement ring she would like.

'I told you about those lovely things in a Regent Street window a long time ago and I realised what an impression the unusual combination of pearl against diamond had made on my mind.'

The ring bought, not from Regent Street but from Mr William Hawkes in Chelsea, was a pearl and diamond cross-over – 'an unusual combination', as she had said. Getting to know families and backgrounds was a rushed affair, with only the odd week or two of leave in the whole of that eight months before I was to leave Hamburg for good.

'Our house is on a corner, a medium-sized, bargain-priced family residence as the estate agents say, with a bit of garden all round,' she wrote, preparing me for my first visit to the Reigate home.

It was four-square solid, with lots of intriguing nooks, corners and unexpectedly odd quirky bits added on. The house was almost the epitome of Jean's family and background. A background very different from mine, although we did share one thing. We both grew up in houses without bathrooms.

15

34 Howard Road

The Metcalfe's at No. 34 must have been in two minds about the arrival of their first-born in 1923. They had only been married a year and were just getting the hang of keeping appearances up and expenses down when I appeared to upset the apple-cart. My mother gave up hanging the front room curtains pattern side out to impress the neighbours and turned instead to patching sheets, sides to middle, until they blew away in shreds. We were heavy on economies like boiled mutton and eggs preserved in isinglass, not to mention dreadful, slippery junket. Junket was cheap because it was made from the second delivery milk, at noon. It makes me feel as old as Merrie England to realise I was alive when the milkman called more than once a day, tradesmen brought everything to the door, straw spread on the road meant someone was dying, and a row of drawn curtains meant someone was dead.

34 Howard Road was a rented semi-detached with the name 'Sunnylea' enamelled on glass above the door. It would have passed unnoticed among the redbrick terraces of Tooting but, because Father's job as a Southern Railway Clerk at Waterloo entitled him to free travel, he could push the privilege to its limits and live in the almost-country of Reigate, Surrey. No tramcars. No smuts. Every night he sponged his celluloid collar clean, ready for the morning, and stropped his safety razor on the strap hanging from the back of the scullery door. No bathroom of course. We were in the majority in those days. Look out of any railway carriage at the backs of houses and there they all were – the tin baths, stuck on the walls like barnacles. At least we didn't have to go

down the garden to the lavatory. Ours was very superior. Indoors, downstairs.

Next door at No. 36 lived my mother's sister Norrie, married to my father's brother Tom. Their marriage was childless which made my uncle and aunt almost as attentive as parents, so, together with a double ration of visiting grandparents, I spent my earliest years lolling about in a warm bath of adult adulation. But even the warmest bath can cool at times. With all those grown-ups around there was seldom a moment when at least one pair of eyes was not turned in my direction. I quickly learned that it paid to please. There was pocket money in it. But there were no bonuses for answering back or airing a cheeky childish opinion. I believe middle age had settled in before I ceased to mind even the mildest word of criticism or dared to query my change. As a child I made sure I was lovely to everyone, until my brother was born.

Poor old Colin. He arrived when I had enjoyed seven idolised years and put my nose right out of joint. All the lavender-scented old ladies poured over his pram and elderly gentlemen jangled their keys at him instead of offering me peppermint lumps. It was exceedingly good for me but smarted like a graze which wouldn't heal. As he grew and began to sit up and take 'solids', I was sometimes allowed to give him his dinner from a non-spill dish with a cow jumping over the moon round the rim. He had mashed potato with beef tea and I coveted it with all my greedy little guts. So while Mother was washing up in the scullery, Colin was strapped into his high-chair in the dining room – and totally in my power. I loaded his special spoon with the soft butter beefy potato and waved it slowly under his nose. His mouth opened like a baby sparrow's waiting to be fed, eyes on the spoon, head turning to follow it wherever I chose, until his face began to crumble for a cry. Then I'd pop a morsel in to keep him quiet and the 'game' began again. I ate more of the delicious stuff than he did. 'Two for me and one for you' was about right to maintain his silence. The memory of that wickednes returns to haunt me still whenever it's time to go on another diet. Nemesis is a calorie counter. I have apologised to him many times in the intervening years although, to be truthful, he's never shown any signs of being undernourished.

He was a beautiful child with a fine shaped head and delightful chuckle. I loved being able to make him laugh into his bib and, in later years, when the old lavender bags and key janglers had turned their attention elsewhere, we enjoyed ourselves greatly together in spite of the difference in our ages. He was the intelligent one, the university brain. I was the front-of-house lady, softening up the public; popular 'Pollyanna' who never said boo to a goose.

We had some good times as a family, Mother and Father, Aunt and Uncle, Colin and me. Uncle Tom worked for the Railway, like Father. The resultant privilege tickets all round enabled us to descend, *en masse*, on places as far afield as Cornwall, when most of our neighbours could only afford day trips, or a week in Bognor. We rented fishermen's cottages for a fortnight in the summer and lived on corned beef stew and fish, still stiff and bright from the harbour. The year we took a cottage at Looe, Prince George of Kent laid a foundation stone and Colin fell through a wall. My brother was little more than a year old so he was put to sleep in a camp bed, pushed up against the far side of the room, safely away from the window. Downstairs we could hear the sound of him crying but it was distant and muffled like a bird in a chimney. When we went to see what was wrong, the baby had disappeared. There was no sign of him anywhere. Just a flapping piece of wall-paper beside his bed. And then we realised . . . the landlord had de-cided, when he papered the room, to carry it on over an old fireplace. No plaster or hardboard, just slap and dash and Devil-take-the-grockles. There was Colin, black and wet with soot and tears, stuck in the grate behind the torn remnants of paper rosebuds and trellis.

At St An Pol in St Ives the doors were so low we pinned sheets of toilet roll on the lintels to remind the men to duck their heads. We played Bach's 'Air on a G String' morning, noon and night on the wind-up gramophone we had lugged all the way from Paddington on the train.

When we visited the Metcalfe grandparents in Fordingbridge, we paddled in a gravelly stream at Blissford and gorged on Grandma's lavish cooking. She tipped cream into everything but was far from fussy when it came to clearing up afterwards. Mother went round surreptitiously wiping down when her back was turned. On one occasion Grandpa Metcalfe took us to see the *Queen Mary* in dock at Southampton. He was a friend of the Chief Purser who showed us over the new and shining splendour of the thing. Grandpa had a lot of style – white whiskers, old Norfolk jacket – and stalked about as if he was inspecting his future State Room. But, walking back behind him down the gangway, we could see, where the heels of his socks should have been, two gleaming squares of skin. They were not domesticated, our country grandparents, but intensely interesting.

Ma and Pa Reed, Mother's side of the family, also loomed large in our lives. They were London based, in a tall Balham house with attics and a basement. It was full of shadowy corners, velour and flock wallpaper, but it brought many urban delights within reach.

The toy department at Gamage's for instance. There, at Christmas, a wheezy Santa Claus handed out parcels in vividly pink or blue paper. Balham was only a tram ride away from boating ponds in London parks and the moorish excesses of the Granada, Tooting. Paradise was a Picture Palace next door to a Lyon's Corner House.

Actually, paradise, in the sense of eternal rest, came too close for comfort several times in Balham. Nothing dramatic happened to me at home in Reigate, apart from falling out of my pram and swallowing wing-nuts off the push chair, but in Balham it was a different story. We were staying there during the General Strike in 1926 to be close to Father while he helped keep essential trains running. My grandparents had a fox terrier called Kip. He was old and sleeping on a chair, eye-high to a three-year-old child. I pushed my face against his pointed nose and he bit me, hard. Old and sleeping, I'd have done the same. Dr Brett was called to cauterise and stitch the wound, shaking his head at my good fortune not to have lost an eye. Another time I tried to copy Grandma's graceful trick with the candle-snuffer. Unwisely, I used a celluloid thimble. It flared instantly and melted into drops of flame. I would have suffered a similar fate if it hadn't been for the heavy plush tablecloth she threw over my hand. Miraculously I survived to give them all another fright in 1931. Again in Balham, outside Holdron's the drapers in the High Road, my appendix burst. That was serious in those pre-penicillin days and involved urgent ambulance bells, emergency treatment and a long stay in Bolingbroke Hospital. I can still remember the dreadful sound of the dressings trolley tinkling down the ward towards my bed, and the chilling words 'Be a brave girl'. Not any more if I can help it. Now, it's shoot the dental injections and pass the panacea.

No doubt that long separation from home, with only sparing visiting hours, had a lot to do with the limpet I've become, clinging at all costs to old, familiar rocks. That, and the holidays with the Whites in St Ives. They were generous, well-to-do people who paid for me to stay with them at the Porthminster Hotel. No matter how much I sobbed for months beforehand, my parents said it would be good for me, it would teach me independence and which knife and fork to use. They were right about the cutlery but I'm still a whimpering waif away from home. Not proud of it, you understand. Just whimpering.

It's odd that my father's daughter should have this patch of thin skin because he sailed buoyantly through life, not so much surmounting difficulties as refusing to acknowledge their existence. He was an open, friendly, immensely humorous man, given to warm-hearted gestures he could not afford in either time or money. He liked to be liked and his popularity lingers in a way which frequently takes me unawares. Often in some remote part of the country a stranger will come up to me and say 'I knew your father, Joe Metcalfe. He was a wonderful man.' He was not subtle, or tactful, but he was inexhaustibly kind.

Mother's gentle influence on us all can only be diminished by trying to put it into words. All her life she was convinced that she was fat and plain and commonplace but that genuine diffidence gave her a beauty of its own. Every line on her face turned comfortingly upwards and her eyes were never without the promise of a smile. Although she died almost thirty years ago, she is still too close and loved to be looked at with clarity, but none of us doubts that she was the backbone of the family, the axis round which we all revolved.

So there we were at 34 Howard Road, archetypal 'Ovaltiney' people with modest treats lighting a life of contented, conventional normality.

I went to the County School, Colin to the Grammar. I shone, worryingly, in all the ornamental subjects like art and elocution. For the rest, it was extra maths and tear-stained Latin. My flashy talents were worrying because the smartest girls always aspired to teaching or the Civil Service and neither profession appeared to set great store by verse-speaking or painting.

We all had our 'pashes' on prefects or staff. The object of my adoration was our English mistress, Miss Clutterbuck, because she was a long-necked, snappy dresser and favoured my floral style of prose. The day our compositions on blackberrying were marked, I sat back expecting to hear her read my piece out to the class. It began with the words 'O, Silver Birch, Queen of the Wood!' She'd be sure to like that. But she didn't. Ada Collier came top with a bit of plain speaking about brambles scratches on urchins' legs. It was Ada's finest hour. Miss C. was right of course, but I went off her after that. PE never earned more than a 'V Fair' on my reports and, regrettably, remains low on my list of favourite pastimes. On Sports Day everyone in the school was expected to enter at least one event, so I wore the loathsome black 'gym bags' for as long as it took to complete the egg and spoon race. In all my years of secondary education I never mastered the rules of hockey because of that unattractive phrase 'bully off'. My parents accepted their disappointing Diana with a good grace and saved their pride for school speech days instead.

These were prestigious occasions which called for a bit of borrowed musquash for Mother and the loan of a car for Father to drive for the night. The choir sang some very fancy folk songs, there was an art exhibition (a lot of me in that) and the elocution class (me again) gave their annual Sybil Thorndyke impersonation. For this we wore white dresses and stockings, and patent leather shoes. The year Mother made me a crêpe de chine dress I had a nosebleed all down the front of it just as we were leaving home. Nerves I expect. Aunt Norrie dabbed with cotton wool and cold water while Mother mopped it dry with a towel. Somehow they managed to clean it up in time but my Prize Giving frocks were always made of washing cotton after that. The school play was a bonus for them even though I spent a lot of time wrapped in a hearthrug as a goat herd. The year I gave my 'Queen Victoria' must have been their high-spot. I aged a treat in the later scenes, just like Anna Neagle, but she had Anton Walbrook for her 'Albert'. I had Jean Inglis.

There were 'Jeans' by the dozen at the County School. My best friend was Jean Sammes who lived round the corner in Glovers Road. We met each morning by the bus garage and walked to school through Church Fields. She strode, as she spoke, at speed. This extended me considerably both physically and mentally. Although our birthdays were only weeks apart Jean took me in hand and stirred into life the dormant parts of my brain which had been beyond reach of school teachers. When she left school she became a professional writer, married an American and went to live in Nyack, New York. Her letters about politics and people, children and grandchildren, are as animated and witty as her company was fifty years ago.

All through my growing years the wireless was my passion. From accumulator to aerial, slung on the roof like a hammock; cat's whisker to Bakelite Superhet; whatever they broadcast, I listened to it. Everyone did. It was the wonder of the age. C. H. Middleton talking about gardening, Christopher Stone on gramophone records, *Saturday Night Vaudeville, Sunday Night Chamber Music* ... it all went in one ear, and stayed there. Nothing changed my life so powerfully as *Children's Hour*. Those were the days of Commander Stephen King-Hall, Toy Town and birthday greetings. 'Hello-o-o Twins' they used to say in chorus and always there was someone called Eric or Maurice who was told to look behind the front room piano for his birthday present. I wrote to them once, those refined 'Uncles' and 'Aunts', to ask if I might be considered as a child actor but 'David', understandably, suggested I should try again when I had received some training. No one told me that the

21

little girls, Doris and Muriel, who broadcast 'Out with Romany', were in fact mature ladies of great experience. I wanted to *be* them and I couldn't wait. But Broadcasting House was as remote as Mecca. It had an almost mystical quality – Buckingham Palace and the Vatican rolled into one – and the people whose voices floated into our living rooms were not human beings like us. It was unthinkable that they ever took Syrup of Figs or wore smelly socks. They were celestial and godlike and, it seemed, unreachable.

Children's Hour ran a 'Radio Circle'. For a fee of ninepence a year which went to charity, its members could take part in competitions. Anyone who achieved three Winner's Certificates was invited to the studio to receive a silver plated pencil from the most senior god, Uncle Mac, and these rare and fortunate children actually spoke into the microphone. 'Thank you Uncle Mac' they said. I paid my ninepence and joined. I had only to be Best Child three times to breath the same air as Aunt Sophie and Uncle 'Caractacus', and to speak the magic words. Twice I was among the Competition Winners, once for a painting and once for a poem. I don't remember what those verses were about – perhaps it's just as well – but they contained the couplet 'Oh sir, how could you be so cruel? When, over the bridge there came a priest, Riding on a pure white mu-el'. The other entries can't have been up to much. Now I had two certificates. Only one to go. My Reigate County School Verse Speaking voice was poised and polished. I practised saying 'Thenk you Uncle Mec' like a posh person.

Then they stopped the competitions.

That was when I was thirteen. The next two years were sucked into the vortex of School Cert. examinations. My swotting was panic-stricken and uncomprehending. I learned my notes by heart in the hope that the examiners would not recognise the parrot echoes of my teachers. Unfortunately one lot, which I regurgitated word for word, contained misheard references to 'Walpole and the Corn Bores' and 'The South Sea Muddle'. Wax in my ears at the time? Or had Miss Burchell's diction been less than precise? Unlikely, because this greatly admired lady also took the elocution class. At all events, I was given the benefit of the doubt and, incredibly, snatched a Distinction in history. In spite of this confidence trick my results were nothing to write home about, with the exception of arty-farty subjects like English and art. Oh yes, and a surprisingly high mark for French aural, I remember. My hottest bit of vocabulary, nicely coming up to the boil as I went to 'converse' with the examiner in the school library, concerned The Countryside. She passed me a picture of The Seashore to describe. 'Au bord de la mer,' I said 'are many people who are on holiday from their homes à la campagne where they milk cows, live in cottages' and so on. She twinkled at me for a moment but gave me my head. From then on I was seduced by the power of a quick tongue to deceive the mind of a listener.

Maths and sciences came between me and Matriculation. Everyone else was disappointed and surprised but I always knew I was very average General School Certificate material.

Now it is 1939, the summer term, and realistic people are facing the certainty of war. To me, nurtured on talking pictures like *Hell's Angels* and *All Quiet on the Western Front*, it is all too awful to contemplate so I bury my nose in the saucier bits of 'The Home Doctor' which is given away free with Father's *Daily Express*. By the beginning of September an Anderson Shelter is waiting to be assembled outside, in preparation for the inevitable, and I decide to leave school.

'No good hoping to go to Art school now,' says Father. 'Even paper will be rationed. So why don't you learn shorthand and typing, then one day you can work for the Southern Railway like me? You'll get privilege tickets and, when you're sixty, a pension.' At the age of sixteen neither inducement had much appeal. I had set my heart on a high-heeled, red nailvarnished future and there wasn't a great deal of that to be seen in Father's office above Waterloo Station. However, six months later, when countless 'quick-brown-foxes' had jumped over 'lazy-dogs', I was an average typist with average shorthand, being whistled at from khaki convoys on my way home from Mrs Hobson's Secretarial School in Prices Lane. The red fingernails had yet to come but my heels were high and I was ready to tackle the world beyond Reigate.

Perhaps, before I applied to the Southern Railway for a job, it would be worth a shot at the BBC. There was one major hurdle to overcome. They were known to employ only the daughters of professional men – which I was not – on their secretarial staff. The cut-glass elegant wireless voices gave the clear impression that no one did it for the money. 'I am a person of Private Means' was implicit in every syllable but, if my gift of the gab got me through that French aural, might it not also sneak me in through the back door of Broadcasting House? *Children's Hour* hadn't wanted me. Perhaps the typing pool in General Office would.

I got myself up in my best tweed costume – men wore 'suits', ladies, 'costumes' – and answered their invitation to a test and interview. The latter I knew would be the greater challenge. Too many cats out of the bag about my social background and I was done for. The BBC was disinterestedly satisfied with my short-hand and typing, then sent me to be interviewed by Miss Cockle. She had the air of a country schoolmistress, hair netted in a dangling bun which crawled about the back of her neck. Her legs, in hand knitted stockings, were as burly as Jacobean furniture. First question: 'What does your father do for a living?' I was ready for her. 'A clerical worker for the Southern Railway' didn't sound sufficiently 'professional', but in his spare time he looked after a benevolent fund for gangers who were injured on the permanent way, and their dependents. He frequently went rushing off to bereaved families to make sure they had money for their immediate needs, the weekend joint, funeral expenses and so on. He was that sort of person. So, when Miss Cockle said 'What does your father do for a living?' I made him a Welfare Officer. It had the right vocational not-for-the-money ring about it. Miss C. looked quite relieved. 'Is that a family tradition?' she asked. 'Was your grandfather interested in social work?' My *grandfather*? I hadn't thought about poshing *him* up. I didn't think he would be needed.

Perhaps it has to do with the span of living memory but families often seem to go wrong at grandparent level. The healthy family tree stands soundly for generations then, where grandparents begin, along comes the rocky branch with Dutch Elm Disease. So it was with mine. Thinking fast as one does in a tight corner, I remembered Mother once telling me Great Grandfather Metcalfe was a doctor in Norfolk. There at last was my professional man, and it always sounds classy to live in Norfolk. Quick as a flash I moved him down a generation. Miss Cockle was pleased. She almost smiled as she said 'I see from your notes that you live in the country.' I sensed she hoped for rolling acres in reply. Anything but the single apple tree and plentiful golden rod in Howard Road. This was the moment when our lack of bathroom could exclude me forever from the ranks of well-plumbed gentlewomen who typed for the BBC. 'Oh yes' I said, hoping to fill her mind with visions of drives and paddocks and baths before dinner. 'It's lovely to have . . . an ORCHARD.'

Miss Cockle took off her glasses and welcomed me into the fold of the British Broadcasting Corporation. On August 14th a contract arrived for me to sign from the Women Staff Administrator. 'Your remuneration shall be at the rate of Two pounds, five shillings and six pence a week. You will also receive a cost of living bonus of one shilling and sixpence a week. . . . This engagement shall date from 19th August 1940. Should you wish to accept this offer will you please report to Miss Perry on Monday next at 10.0 a.m.' Should I? I was camping on the doorstep by half-past nine.

They called me 'Metcalfe' in General Office. No christian name or Miss, just Metcalfe or Richardson or Trotman as the case might be. I was quite adequate at the 'suburban' stuff, it was 'motorway' typing which scared me rigid. Give me a phone to answer, polite little letters and memos to type, and the world was my playpen, but whenever I was told by the Supervisor, in her all-seeing glass box, to take urgent Newsroom dictation on to the typewriter, my fingers froze in terror. Some interesting news items resulted, including one in which the letter 'c' turned up instead of the initial 'p' in 'population'. That must have brightened Bruce Belfrage's day.

They sent me out to work in the frightening Legal Department where erasers were not allowed. The day my desk drawer was discovered stuffed with spoiled stationery and half-eaten Lyons Fruity Buns I was returned – 'unsuitable'. Then there was a spell working for Sandy MacPherson who was a kind, quiet man. There was something hand-knitted about his gangling frame and the way his arms were always too long for his sleeves. But I wasn't even good enough for him, so it was back to General Office again. I lasted longer with Cecil Madden. There was nothing but air beneath my feet when he sent me to collect Emlyn Williams from Reception. Emlyn Williams! The prize signature in my autograph album! In person! The whiff of greasepaint which surrounded the eccentric Madden circus was intoxicating. When the office moved to the Criterion Theatre to accommodate the variety shows it produced round the clock, I went too. Cecil's working hours were sophisticated and taxing, which often required his staff to sleep overnight in the stage boxes. We were envied the security this underground theatre offered during the Blitz, until one night Sheila Borrett, who had been the BBC's first woman announcer, felt something wet on her face as she slept. The roof was not after all a safe concrete shield but black-painted glass, open in places to the sky. Outside it was raining.

Anyone working late at Broadcasting House on the other hand, spent the night in the Concert Hall. The seating had been removed and replaced with mattresses. As a symbol of chastity between the women's section on the right and the men's on the left, an uneven row of extremely permeable grey army blankets flapped from a rope strung down the centre aisle. I slept there occasionally after being sacked from the Criterion – 'too young, too inexperienced' – and it was more eventful than going to camp without Brown Owl.

Back in General Office I was beginning to feel like the last of the litter, the runt that nobody wanted, until a call came in from the Empire Service announcers who needed help with their fan mail.

They were all lively young men, spending the time while they waited to be called-up as wartime newsreaders on shortwave broadcasts to the dear, old-fashioned, colonies overseas. Franklyn Engelmann was there, and the Canadian actor, Robert Beatty, and Duncan Carse who went on after the war to become 'Dick Barton'. They didn't care about my shorthand and typing. I was eighteen and auburn haired and suited them just fine. This time I stayed and the torment of General Office was over.

The Service was expanding with the need to keep overseas territories in touch with London and soon we were moved from our makeshift office in the Restaurant Annexe of Broadcasting House, with its food smells and plasterboard partitions, to 200 Oxford Street, the old Peter Robinson building. Now there were dozens of us working twenty-four hours a day on the Overseas Service. My work became more clerical than secretarial, thank God, and even brought me glimpses of the studios below ground. One joyous day, May 24th, 1941, Noel Iliff asked me to read Thomas Nashe's poem 'Spring, the sweet Spring' in a programme he was producing, *Books and People* at 1500 GMT. The refrain 'Cuckoo, jug jug, pu we, to wittawoo' would sound silly, he said, in the deep voice of the presenter, the novelist Gerald Bullet. It sounded pretty silly in mine too, I thought. However, it didn't matter if only a handful of homesick Kenyan planters would hear me, I was on the wireless – at last.

4/CLIFF

Growing up in Cowes

My parents left their native Devonshire before the First World War. My father, suffering from tuberculosis, sought relief, as did so many others before and since, in the balmy air of Ventnor at the back of the Isle of Wight. The headstones in the cemeteries at Bonchurch and St Lawrence are a sad reminder that in those days the insidious disease took a heavy toll of young men and women. Very often it had been diagnosed too late and the chances of curing it in its advanced stages were slight.

> Martin Nicholas Riech of Georgetown, Demerara who while sojourning here in hope of receiving benefit to his health died on 27th July 1883 aged 40 . . . Alice Edith Compton Baker aged 18 . . . Paul Moyle Robins Beswetherick, Born Cornwall . . . aged 24 . . . Jenny Knight aged 24 . . . James Carnegy of Balnamoon, Forfarsburg, North Britain, 17 years and nine months . . .

When money ran out, the family moved north to Cowes where I was born. Arthur Clifford; 11th December 1919, the youngest of six children. The three girls were named after flowers, Violet, Ivy and Iris; the boys after kings, John, Harold and Arthur, later known as Cliff.

My father did not survive the move for very long. He died before I was two and I remember nothing about him. Our three up, three down terrace house, three rows back from the banks of the River Medina, was within sight, sound and smell of the shipyards and the gas works, and it was crowded when we were all at home. In order to get me out of the house and let my mother go to work and support the family, I was taken to school by my sister Molly and allowed to sit at her desk. But that is something else I do not remember. I do recall, however, my sister Ivy also dying of tuberculosis. She had a fire in her small bedroom, a pink knitted bed jacket and parchment pale cheeks. She looked serenely lovely. One evening, late, as I stood saying goodnight to her, she looked up and said 'Mum, the angels are coming for me'.

I did not understand what was happening. I went to the funeral because I asked to and I cried. Then I did understand.

When you are young and wrapped up in a small private world of sadness you have no thoughts for the suffering of those who are close to you. How did my mother cope with two deaths in as many years? She always seemed to me to manage her grief. Neighbours helped, but she was a very independent spirit. Her brothers in Devonshire and Wales offered to help, but she could not bring herself to accept any money. We did spend the occasional week with them but that was as much as she could bring herself to take.

Home was crowded with two older brothers and two sisters with boyfriends. I was sent morning, afternoon and evening to the United Methodist Church. At The Band of Hope Miss Warne guided my hand which was too young to sign The Pledge. The fact that I had not made my own mark saved my conscience from troubling me too much later in life when I indulged in strong drink.

I liked school and when we 'went up' from the Primary to the Senior School I came under the considerable influence of a headmaster and staff who, despite what must have been appalling overcrowding, managed to instil in us enthusiasm for our work and play. Cowes Senior School; Courage, Service, Self-control. Mr Guppy, the headmaster, had served in Gallipoli, was interested in the Oxford Group, played the organ in the Parish Church and took a more than fatherly interest in me. He encouraged me to take exams which I thought were beyond my reach. The science master E. S. Waller, captain of the Boys' Brigade company of which I was a member, Methodist lay preacher and strict disciplinarian, gave me extra lessons at his home twice a week. Miss Broome, our house mistress, the Mackenzie brothers, Mr Pennington, Mr Smith, Miss Neal, who was to become Mrs Smith, Miss Wadley and the rest were all willing to help all they could if you asked. I asked.

Soon after I had 'gone up', it was decided that now my sister Violet had married a farmer and they had a spare room, I should go and live with them for a time. Vi and her husband Joe were to bring a complete change in my life. At the time I did not realise it but the move was to provide my first taste of independence away from the family home. It was also to take me away from the streets, which in our part of the town were named after poets, such as Tennyson and Milton, and out to fields which were named after their acreage and position, 'five acres', 'top field' and the like. It was also to bring me close to a small collection of country-men, many of whom had not seen the streets of Cowes and had no wish to. The market in Newport on a Tuesday was about as far as any of them went and that journey they undertook very infrequently.

But what was I leaving behind? Although we lived close by the river, we were also within the kick of a football from Reads Field and from a small copse which lay between the cemetery and Marvin's Yard where the gentry kept their vast luxury yachts in the winter. Between the yard and the copse the little single-track railway line ran from Cowes and Mill Hill stations up to the 'capi-tal' of Newport.

Shamblers copse was full of secret places where our gang built hides and we played Tarzan. It was here that I became a juvenile de-linquent. The road to Newport climbed up a hill towards the cem-etery before it levelled out. The heavily-laden lorries found the going hard and slow. In the old days boys had caught hold of the tail-boards of horse-drawn wagons while passers-by shouted the warning 'whip behind, mister'. The carter would flick his whip over his shoulder to discourage or dislodge the hangers-on. Horses were later replaced by motor lorries which trundled up the hill to Newport, packed with fruit and vegetables for the market. 'We could jump on at the bottom,' Steve said, 'and pull off a box of fruit and have it in the hide-away before anyone could see us.'

Plans were laid. We even had a practice run to see if it would work. On the day it did. A long banana-box was the hit target. As the lumbering lorry got to the gate of the copse one heave and it was off.

At the hide we opened the box. It was full of green hands of bananas. They were uneatable. We could not even get the skins off them, so we decided to leave them for a few days to ripen. We buried them under hazel-nut branches and went home.

I was certain that the policeman would be round in the middle of the night. Similar thoughts must have gone through the minds of the other gang members. Next night we met at the hide and de-cided it would be safer to dispense with our loot. The streets were filled with in-need families, and so in the creeping evening light we wrapped the bananas in newspaper and left them on deserving doorsteps. After that we all felt better.

'I wonder,' said my mother 'why they did not leave any bananas for me or for Mrs Gawler or for Mrs Stephens. We could have done with them.'

Shamblers copse was to be left behind, so was the gang, football matches 'up the field', borrowing dinghies, mudlarks in the river, the fish and chip shop in Arctic Road and endless noisy games of 'kick-the-tin-releaso'. Ahead were early mornings, a bedroom to myself, delivering milk on the way to school, helping my sister in the dairy and discovering new smells and new skills such as coaxing milk from cows and finding hens' nests in the hedges.

Basketts Farm, Rew Street, was about a hundred acres around the main farmhouse, the yard, stables and the long barn whose roof is sagging to this day. There were horses, carts, cows, pigs, chickens and the ducks which were fattened each year for August week, when they would be on their way on to the tables of the Royal Yacht Squadron. 'You are a lucky duck,' my brother addressed a barrel-chested Aylesbury 'you're on your way to be eaten by the King.'

The farmhouse was red brick, four square, modern and, at first, without gas or electricity. The gas pipes arrived down the lane soon after I went there, to be followed by 'the electric' later in the year. We even had a street-lamp which was turned on by a bicycle lamp-lighter. Today, schoolchildren come and make sketches of it.

School homework was done at the top of the orchards by the lake, as we rather grandly called the big pond. I think that the lake caused my sister more trouble than anything else. When her first son Donald once went missing, we almost dragged it for his body, and were only stopped when Walter, the cowman, discovered him fast asleep on the top of the hay in the barn.

It seemed to me as a boy, that Walter was capable of doing just about everything. He could thatch, hedge and ditch, plough a furrow as straight as a die, cope with awkward horses by swearing at them, and milk a cow dry. When it came to summer-time and clocks were being put back and forward, he understood my bewilderment. ''Tis no good, they can turn the hands of the clock this way and that but it won't make much difference. God won't make the sun come up no sooner nor go down no later, whatever they do.' And when I asked 'what about the cows?' because at school they had been saying that it would upset the milking rhythms for them he replied 'never known a cow what can tell the time yet.'

Haymaking meant taking endless flasks of tea up the field – 'a nice drop of drink, Vi.' In summer, we would go over the top of the cliff and down into Thorness Bay or picnic on the cliff-tops looking across at the Beaulieu river and the RAF station at Calshot. Then would come the harvest and the visit from the threshing machine with its cracking drive-belts, spinning wheels and whipping dust into every pore, eye and nostril. The noise and the steam, the flying straw and bronzed wheat whistling into sacks, the men's trousers held up by braces and tied at the calf with binder twine. It was all as exciting to me as a roller-coaster ride would be to others. My sister and brother-in-law let me loose on their books. At home in Cowes we had a small selection of Zane Grey, the latest *Daily Herald* book offer, and the weekly 'Home Notes'. Not much more. At Basketts Farm there were the diaries of Scott of the Antarctic, tales of adventures, the odd encyclopaedia as well as the *Farmer and Stockbreeder* and books on animals and birds. These were formative times and I was greatly saddened when I had to go back into Cowes. Exams were looming on the horizon like black gathering clouds promising to dampen the days of the summer and it was decided that I should return home so that I could spend more time at school and on my homework.

The days when we sat for the Cambridge examinations were very hot. The invigilator was the Reverend C. E. Patterson and the venue the Holy Trinity Church Hall. There was not a clue to anything on the walls. No maps to help us scrape through in geography, no charts, nothing but pale blank walls and our minds equally blank with the terror at the prospect of failure.

Waiting for the results was relieved only by taking part in games of football and cricket. I was always a 'hearty' and games played a very large part in my life. I represented the house, school and county, wore my badges, and thought that I was a better performer than I was. It was only later when I came upon really talented players that I became aware of the great divide between the best and the rest. I did have a trial across at Southampton but I did not play well and so all thoughts of an international career at soccer faded.

At school I was doing pretty well. I was Head Boy and Captain of cricket, I threw the cricket ball further than anyone else in the school, failed miserably as a middle distance runner at which I rather fancied my chances and had a number of girlfriends. Which brings me to Hilda May. Hilda later changed her name to Gloria but that was after her marriage to, and divorce from, a friend of mine. As Gloria she went on to marry and divorce someone very rich from whom she got a record settlement when they parted. Many years later, after we met in a Reigate cinema, she and her sister came back to the little house Jean and I had just moved into and she talked endlessly about the swimming pool she was having installed, and the size of *her* house. I smiled at the memory of the young pert-nosed, heavily made-up Hilda with whom I was totally infatuated (as were half the boys in the school). We once went for a walk around the walls of the Ward Estate in Cowes. It rained, and she allowed me to put my arm around her waist, my fingers clinging to the hard rubber of her mac. Such romance and such innocence. She liked sweets. I could not afford even to give up the odd copper which I needed for my own sherbet dabs and liquorice laces so she took up with a boy whose father owned a shop and abandoned me.

Even without Hilda, there was so much to do. Twice a week Mr Waller gave me extra lessons at his home. His front room was transformed into a maths and science classroom every Tuesday and Thursday evening for an hour. There was no question of any payment for these lessons, although from time to time I did take along a dozen eggs from the farm, and some cream, or my sister's hand churned butter. I was lucky with my school teachers, which is probably why I liked school so much.

In those days I was also very much a 'joiner'. I was a member, for a short while, of the church Boys' Brigade, having been promoted – strictly on an age basis – from the Life Boys. I took part in Sunday School productions which had the themes of 'Buy British' and 'Stop the Re-armament'. I was a smiling fishmonger in the former, and John Bull in the latter. As John Bull I had to cut the cake of the national budget, giving little to the causes of education, housing, health, unemployment and so on, reserving for re-arming – the last slice – the largest chunk of all.

I was always doing something on the stage, but I was by no means stage-struck. It must be admitted that I did envy our local wireless 'star' Reggie Briggs. Reggie had lived at Tower House before he went off to London and became a page boy at the Savoy Hotel, where Henry Hall had heard him whistling at his work and then got him to whistle with his band. The whole town waited for his occasional broadcasts, the streets were empty. They said that his mother sat in front of her fretwork-fronted set with a glass of brandy in her hand in case Reggie dried up. He became quite famous, with pictures and articles about him in my mum's 'Home Notes'. But I did not aspire to that sort of performing. My voice was unable to achieve the notes I had in mind. I was turned down for the chorus of an operetta in which Hilda was to play the lead, as always. She was to be the Princess Ju-Ju and I was dying to chorus: 'Welcome to the Princess Ju-Ju, welcome from her subjects true, true. We'll bring her joy, without alloy . . .'

'I don't think so young Mitch,' Mr Guppy had said and that was that. I was never in a school play and took to the stage of the Sunday School because there the competition was not so strong.

I did stand with Doris, the Head Girl, and give a duet of thanks to the Reverend C. E. Patterson, not only for having come to Speech Day but also for having braved the rain at the School Sports Day at Westwood and stayed until the *very* end. Doris became my first two-way partner and she kept me in order because not only was I ambitious but I also got rather carried away with all the authority and responsibility. The school believed in letting the pupils run some of their own affairs which, in the thirties and in a council school, was avant-garde to say the least. The woodwork and handicrafts master Wally Capps once admitted that some of the teachers were even a bit scared of Doris and me. I only wish that I had known that at the time.

Even though the classes were hopelessly over-crowded and the building cramped, the staff more than made up for that drawback. They organised day trips across to Beaulieu and the New Forest by motor launch, as well as school journeys aboard liners to Gibraltar and North Africa. I went to Beaulieu, but had to withdraw from the liner voyage, even though we'd paid some instalments, because the money was needed elsewhere in the family. I never asked why. In spite of the lack of money, it was a satisfying and happy boyhood. All of us in the family had jobs of one kind or another. I supplemented the money that I made on the milk-round with waiting around Watchouse slipway when the dinghies came ashore from the boats out in Cowes Roads to pick up their provisions. 'Mind your boat, skip?' was the cry. We'd skull the little dinghies around and wait for the skippers to come back hoping for a few coppers in payment. We were never disappointed. Bearded Ben, who sat on the bench under the halfround corrugated iron roof of the shelter, would sourly observe 'My God they've got some appetites out there, and not one of 'em as done as much as a hand's turn on a line all week.' Ben, we thought, must know what he was talking about because he wore a hard, thick woollen jersey with the name of a yacht embroidered across the chest. He smoked Woodbines, drank mild and bitter at the Union and was always spitting. He was a hell of a man. 'He once ran straight up the mast of the *White Heather*, freed a shroudline, and fell off into the water, and they left him there because they were racing,' went the story. I never knew whether to believe it or not at first. Then I believed it, because I wanted to. I was that sort of a boy. Romantic.

Between the wars, Cowes was a fascinating place to grow up in. In winter, the narrow streets were just capable of taking the two-way traffic; the shops which displayed dozens of royal 'By Appointment' signs catered only for the people of the town; there was nothing much out in the Roads except the paddle steamers and occasionally the odd flying boat from Saunders-Roe. Up the river Medina the posh luxury yachts of the gentry wintered safely and warmly in the mud off Marvin's yard. Uffa Fox chased around the water in his latest dinghy, but the yacht clubs were shut tight-eyed against the weather. It was not a pretty sight now that I come to think of it. This town in which John Nash, architect and planner of Regent Street and Regent's Park was born, could have done with a touch of his elegant design. But Nash was born before this place of 'no account' became famous and fashionable. 'An inconvenient fishing village looking like a heap of superior dog kennels which had rolled down from the hill and brought up right on the edge of the water, altogether innocent of the attractions of a seaside resort; bathing machines were a rarity, nigger minstrels unknown, and hotel accommodation very limited' according to one chronicler of the time. When the Prince of Wales became Commodore of the Royal Yacht Squadron in 1882, the court followed the royals to the seaside and Cowes. Kings, emperors and princes flocked in for Cowes Week, turning 'Cowes Roads into two miles of floating hospitality'. As a result of this annual influx of gentility, trades-men of the town, chemists, photographers, grocers, provision merchants, ships chandlers and tailors were all able to grace the fronts of their stores with 'By Appointment' signs. They were still there in the 1930s when many of them had long since lost their thrones and their lives. But each year the Royal Yacht the *Victoria and Albert* would make its way gently from Portsmouth out into the Solent, so that the King could sail his great J-class *Britannia* and Queen Mary could do her rounds of the antique shops, admiring and expecting to be given the best pieces on view.

As boys we looked forward to August Week. The Parade was crowded; guns boomed out from the battery in front of the Squad-ron and flags ran up and down the mast and Mister Wagstaffe seemed to be in charge of it all; fleets of boats raced around the buoys, from the tiny Redwings to the huge magestic J-class yachts, *Endeavour, Shamrock, Valsheda, Westward, Astra* and *Britan-nia*. The week started with a twenty-one gun salute as the Royal Yacht and its escort arrived at the start of the week, and it ended with another great bang as the fireworks on Friday night signalled the end of the affair. The cry would go up 'better than last year' as another salvo of rockets were launched into the night sky. As boys we hoped that next year, we would be able to shout the same thing. We always did.

My brother always told me that King George V once patted me on the head and told me 'now you have seen me little boy, off you go and play'. I bet he didn't, but my brother said he did. My sister Violet was never home that week, because she was working in the sail-lofts of Ratsey and Lapthorn and spent most nights repairing the damage of the day to those unyielding canvas and cotton sails, which had to be ready for the next morning's races.

After Friday night's fireworks we went home, knowing that when we woke up in the morning, the Roads would be almost empty as if someone had pulled out the plug and they had all drained away. They would be off to the grouse moors of Scotland and we would be left with almost vacant streets and the last lingering smell of their cigars. The reefer jackets and white ducks would be put away in mothballs until next year.

The aircraft works, the shipyards of J. Samuel White's, the rope-walk and the boatyards would all be back to work and we would be back to school.

But for me, there was the uncomfortable prospect of the 'future' to be faced. Uncomfortable, because I did not like making up my mind about anything as uncertain as the future. Farming had no appeal because the long hours and weekend work would not allow me to play football and cricket. I toyed with the idea of using my science, maths and drawing talents(?) to get into a drawing office, and then after night school take some more exams. I even thought about going into the Methodist ministry, but the Reverend Mildon put me off that with his lecture upon the length of the training and the sacrifices such training entailed. It was ever only a distant prospect anyway. My mother had not even been able to afford the fares for me to attend the grammar school in Newport, so there was not a chance that any money could be found for me to go away to college. So how did I find myself sitting at a desk, remote from the dozen or so other desks, at a small schoolroom in Newport, taking an examination for entry into the Royal Air Force? I have not the remotest idea. There in front of me were a series of papers on science, maths and general knowledge, and within weeks it seemed I had an official letter advising me that I had 'satisfied the examination board' and would be accepted for training that summer. Scanning the enormous pass list I found my name surprisingly near the top. Carried along by my own enthusiasm and cocksuredness, I did not stop to consider what it was I was letting myself in for.

Here I was embarking upon a lifetime career about which I knew absolutely nothing. I did not know that I was set for at least three years in what the *London Illustrated News* had called 'The Academy of the Air'. Schools, workshops, flying, the chance to play any game that I chose, all appealed to a romantic-headed but remarkably foolhardy youth. I was, however, ambitious, and this, I had worked out, was a chance to get a great deal of what we now call 'further education' which would not cost my mother and family anything at all. In fact, I would even get paid whilst I was doing it. There seemed to be a certain logic in that. Little did I think that within a few years there would be a war.

I was almost sixteen years old when I accepted the King's Shilling.

5/CLIFF

The King's Shilling

There was nothing glamorous about Halton. For the first weeks it bore a remarkable resemblance to what I imagined Borstal to be like. The RAF drill and PT instructors set out to give us the 'short sharp shock treatment'. We were left in no doubt that we had joined a service which was highly disciplined, highly trained and whose motto meant what it said *Per Ardua ad Astra*. Through hardship to the stars.

Set in the soft Buckinghamshire hills, those harsh serried ranks of buildings were a ghastly eye-sore. The place was the size of a small town, complete with its own hospital, cinema, workshops, airfield, churches, shops, post office, power station and hundreds of acres of playing fields. And barrack squares: how I came to loathe the endless hours spent crushing the grey-black gravel; wheeling, advancing in review order, slow marching and quick marching. Behind their backs we sneered, as boys will, at the Flight Sergeants and Warrant Officers who strutted that narrow stage. We gave them nick-names, Warrant Officer Payne was 'Twinge' because he was too small to be a pain, Flight Sergeant Marshall was 'Slug' for equally obvious reasons, and Sergeant Pope was 'Holy Joe'. I am sure that they were all kinder to dumb animals than they were to us. There is no compassion on a drill square where blind obedience and unquestioning response is demanded.

'When I call "halt" I want you to bring the foot what's on the ground to the foot what's in the air and stay there stationary until I tell you to move.' 'Understand?' We all understood, imagining the

37

whole parade in a state of suspension an inch or two off the ground, both feet airborne.

We arrived, thinking we were going to learn about aircraft, engines, flying and such magical things, and here we were being trained like Grenadier Guardsmen. Our barrack rooms were burnished so brightly that even after lights-out they gleamed. In the moonlight the buckets shone like silver trophies, the floor took on the sheen of wet marble. In our wall lockers the kit layouts were geometrically precise, starched as stiff as cardboard blocks. If the inspecting officer had seen as much as a speck of dust or a smudged window-pane he would have confined the lot of us to our room for a week in case we spread the dirt disease to other rooms. The rooms smelled permanently of floor polish. We skated around with pieces of blankets attached to our shoes, so as not to miss a chance to put an extra gloss on the floor. The ablutions smelled so heavily of disinfectant that not only would it have killed every known germ, the stench would have knocked out all unknown germs as well.

'Pine-Coffin,' called Slug Marshall from a bathroom. 'This bath has not been scrubbed, smells of pee – that would give you all scarlet fever.' 'Clean it.' Pine-Coffin ordered up a fatigue squad to rid the bath of scarlet fever. We were as close to a representative cross section of British youth as you could get. The odd doctor's son, ex-public schoolboys, grammar schoolboys, and the son of a well-known cinema organist, shared the harsh horrors with boys from farms, mining villages and the back-streets of cities. Those of us with a burr to our voices were dubbed 'swede-bashers' but either the tone of our voices changed, or they got bored with calling us 'swedes', because after a month or so we were as accepted as any Taff or Jock or Mike. By then I had started to learn the facts of service life.

One of the senior entry boys *had* to get married to a girl in the village because she 'held him on'. All sorts of rumours circulated about her, none of which were true, I subsequently discovered, when I met the family some years later. They were a happy, handsome pair with a delightful boy. So much for the ugly 'Witch of Wendover'.

Lectures at the School of Tropical Medicine on 'personally transmittable diseases' sought to rid us of any further illusions we might have. 'If you think that *she* has been waiting all her young life for *you* to come and make love to her, think again you arrogant sods,' said the MO. 'She has probably just come back from Aldershot – and you know what soldiers are!'

We learned to describe the RAF ensign; something I can do to this day. 'On a field of azure blue three roundels are superimposed, red upon white, upon blue . . . in the dexter canton flies the flag of the union . . .'

We learned, too, how to escape from the confines of the camp. The high iron railings which surrounded it and kept us in were held in place by rivets top and bottom. Drill out the rivets, replace them with wing-nuts and hey presto! you could escape with the facility of a Houdini. Almost as soon as the Special Police – the snoops – had discovered and repaired several of these bolt-holes an adventurous pair found that the hot air ducts which honeycombed beneath the buildings came up outside the power station. They kept that to themselves and who can blame them. We were well schooled in the keeping of such secrets. It is no surprise that many of the escape plans in Stalags, Offlags and other German prison-of-war camps were organised by captured ex-Halton Brats.

After a year our pay rose from a shilling a day to one and six-pence (old money). Half of it was 'deferred' as savings, or to pay for any barrack damages that we might incur. Parcels arrived from home however, which helped make our existence more enjoyable. Roy James' mother in Ebbw Vale, sent him tins of soft buttery Welsh cakes, Raymond Tom Higgins had a monopoly on Lanca-shire toffee and both Rutherford and Russell were weekly recipi-ents of shortbread and Dundee cake from Scotland. Whatever we had we shared, or at least most of us did. Baker from Canterbury, however, locked up everything he got and never shared anything. He was in charge of the flight, and looked, he thought, like Clark Gable because he had black hair and a widow's peak. Baker forever talked about his 'lady-friend' and boasted of his conquests. When it came to 'Open Day' and the visit of 'the lady' his room fag spite-fully gave his trousers a double crease. We would fold our trousers, smooth the crease down and then lather the inside with shaving soap, so that after a night's sleep on them they would be as sharp and stiff as a knife. Giving Baker's a double irremovable crease was easy.

The three years I spent at the Buckinghamshire school probably had more effect upon me than I appreciated at the time. Again, some concerned schoolmasters left their mark; Professor Whit-taker, Bill Fallowfield who became the Secretary of the Rugby League, A. C. Kermode who wrote the standard work 'The Theory of Flight' among them.

The workshops also left their mark. My prowess at chiselling narrow grooves through mild steel blocks with a cross-cut chisel earned me an almost permanently bruised left thumb. But we did eventually learn the hows and whys of aircraft and engines and flying. Schools, workshops and airfield, took over from drill and fatigues and PT.

Nights were spent at the 'flicks' or listening to the gramophone.

We were not allowed to have wireless sets, lest we be corrupted by Radio Luxemburg and Radio Normandy. There were those who made tiny sets and hid them in tins and boxes with false bottoms, or else secreted them down the heating system. All good preparation for those P.O.W. camps.

At the end of three years we were 'ready to enter The Service', ready, too, for the great wide world waiting out there beyond the railings, Wendover Station, the beech-covered Chilterns, workshops, school and the aerodrome. We were eager to be off to face the future in our smart uniforms, now at least free of those badges which marked us as 'under training'. At last we would be on full pay and able to enjoy the Casanova-type of life the Brylcreem boys of the late thirties were supposed to be enjoying. We were about to bestow our favours upon a waiting Royal Air Force and upon the adoring maidens around the airfields of Andover, Catterick or Lossiemouth. Or so we thought.

Within weeks, we were actively involved in war exercises, Redland versus Blueland. Within months we were loading up sinister containers under the wings of our Fairey Battles, so that we could practise spraying poison gas over troops hiding on the North Yorkshire moors. That they contained nothing more than a mixture of aniseed did little to calm our real fears that when the war came we would be loading and spraying any one of a dozen types of lethal gas.

'Today's gas masks will be as useless as a wet handkerchief,' was the opinion of one staff officer who came to observe the 'coverage and penetration of such attacks from the air'.

We practised dispersal drill, flying from rough fields, and bombing and gunnery exercises were part of our daily routine. By the beginning of 1939 it was obvious that we would be at war some time soon, despite the shuttle diplomacy of Mr Chamberlain.

Back at Halton the Honours Board was about to lengthen with the hundreds of names of those awarded VC's, DSO's, DFC's, AFC's, DFM's and those Killed in Action.

When war came upon us I was in France, part of the Advanced Air Striking Force, a stirring title for a far from stirring force. We found the remnants and relics of the First World War all around our dispersed airfields at Berry-au-Bac. Bits of old shell cases and helmets, rusted wire and collapsed trenches. We took over where they left off twenty one years before. For eight months we were on inactive service. We flew a few leaflet raids, the odd border patrol which made certain not to intrude into enemy air space, and a little safe bombing and gunnery practice down in the Mediterranean. It was called the period of the 'Phoney War'.

Just before the shooting started, a football match was arranged in Paris between the AASF and the French Air Force. We reported to a small hotel near the stadium and found the Warrant Officer waiting. 'You are all confined to this hotel. No going out. We take a look at the stadium at 15.00 hours, light training, then supper then bed. Understand?' That old service instruction again. We understood. Everybody did when faced with a Warrant Officer. Came the night and after supper to a man we went down the fire escape and out into the streets of the sin-filled city of Paris. I ought to explain that so far in my life I had only breached my Band of Hope Pledge by having the occasional glass of shandy. Strong drink was not in me. That evening we sat in an *estaminet* and the drinks came strong and mixed. Starting at one end of the line of bottles we drank our way along; Cointreau, then Benedictine, Crème de menthe, brandy . . . it was the colour I liked. We were helped by the barmaid who, when we paid with a fifty-franc note, gave us the change plus our fifty-franc note back.

I was the first to go back to the hotel. Next morning I woke cradling a bottle of Negretti rum in my bed, but, surprisingly, I had no headache. There was also no sign of one of our players. Charlie the captain, a part-time professional with a West Country club and the centre-half, had not returned from the night's operations. The Warrant Officer demanded to know where he was. Out for a little training run. He would be back. He wasn't, and so a search party was despatched. We hailed a passing taxi which was driven by a man from Birmingham who had stayed on after 'the first lot'. After describing where we had been the night before, he took us direct to the local brothel out of which Charlie was falling. We put him in the taxi. He neither knew us nor where he was, nor where he had been. It was five minutes into the first half when he was felled. Our trainer came on and douched Charlie with the sponge. The black hair shook the water away, he felt his unshaven chin and asked. 'Which way are we kicking Mitch?' and 'what's the score?' 'We are one down and playing *that* way.' His rude reply shocked our trainer. His actions on the field of play shocked our French allies. He played a blinder. We won three-one and were promised medals to commemorate the event but we never got them.

After the war I met Charlie in Torquay. He was with his wife and he gave me a knowing wink and a conspiratorial smile. He had given up football and was driving a taxi. 'I like taxis,' he said.

After France it was Scotland. I rather think that they were getting me out of the way. Having been responsible, at least in part, for losing the Battle of France they did not want me losing the

Battle of Britain too. Any idea I had of being the heroic Biggles of the Second World War ended with an aircraft crash in a ditch. 'Sorry,' said the MO in that breezy way some of them have, 'you are no longer fit aircrew. Your eyesight is too bad. Astigmatism. Better get some glasses.'

As wars go, mine went along unremarkably after my recuperation down at Sidmouth. The closest I came to action was when I was home on leave, the night the Germans bombed hell out of Cowes. For the rest it was a round of stations, Group and Command Headquarters and the Air Ministry.

At Hixon, I shared a Nissen hut with Flying Officer Herbert Bowden, Lord Aylestone, boss of IBA-to-be, and with Flight Lieutenant William Glock, Sir William and Controller of Music BBC-to-be. At Gamston I helped Wing Commander Wooldridge knock down a wall of his quarters, so that we could get his grand piano in. 'Dim' Wooldridge married Margaretta Scott, the film star, composed music and was a highly decorated Mosquito pilot.

At Hornchurch I met a Sergeant WAAF who was a super cook and she looked a knock-out in her uniform. Unfortunately 'Blossom' went off and married an airman called Harry who sang with the Station Dance Band and did impressions of the Ink Spots. Today they live happily as Mr and Mrs Max Bygraves.

At the Air Ministry I met Flt Lt Primrose. We shared night duty together on one or two occasions and he introduced me to the art of the practical joker. He was the first person I ever met who actually 'did' the telephone trick. He would dial a number at random and when it was answered would say 'Ring London Wall two thousand tomorrow between ten and twelve and you will hear something to your advantage. London Wall two thousand, goodbye.' Next day he would ring London Wall 2000 and complain that he had been trying to get through all day etc. He had a not very popular uncle who was a director of whatever it was on London Wall 2000. Another time he decided to 'test the system for efficiency'. 'I bet they don't notice for a week,' he said. He moved all the in-trays up an office and all the out-trays down an office. A12g up to A12f, A12d to A12e and so on. I believe that it only took five days before they noticed. (The important in-trays, I should point out in his defence, were all under the lock of heavy security.)

Primrose also had connections. A close friend of mine returning from a long posting overseas, where he had been patrolling the Atlantic in flying boats, was sent way up to the north of Scotland and on the phone to me he had been moaning about his luck. Primrose fixed it. He sent off an urgent signal to Scotland. 'Flt Lt A. E.

Stephens to take 21 days embarkation leave immediately. Confirmation posting notice follows.' He had got the right code and Steve, now even more furious, came south on leave expecting yet another overseas posting. When he called to see us at the Air Ministry, Primrose cheerfully told him he looked as though he could do with three weeks off and then where did he fancy for his next posting? How about Cornwall? While Steve was enjoying his home leave his posting notice arrived. Cornwall it was. After the dangerous Atlantic and the far north it was a well-earned sinecure. Primrose had promised. Primrose had delivered. I don't know to this day how he arranged it nor, to my regret, what became of him after the war. He was the sort of man who could equally well have become a con-man or a captain of industry. Or both.

Air Ministry, Bomber Command Headquarters, Group Headquarters. I was for much of the time a long way from any sort of action, and closer to the staff officers with scrambled eggs on their hat peaks who treated Flight Lieutenants and Squadron Leaders like orderlies. 'If you are going to town, give my wife a lift to the Ministry. She has an appointment there. Then have a spot of lunch and bring her back', one of them instructed me as I was about to drive off in the staff car. I dropped her off, did what I had to do, counted the little money I had in my pocket and decided that it would have to be a very, very small spot of lunch. Her ladyship swept me away to a restaurant in Soho. It had heavy green curtains, white napkins, starched tablecloths and two menus. One menu was for show, the other menu was for regular customers, and she was clearly one of the latter. No snoek or vegetable cutlets for her, pheasant, salmon, pork? I said that I was not at all hungry and settled for a little Windsor soup. She daintily ate her way through the menu, she had wine, she had a brandy with her coffee. As she finished the maître came, 'I do hope that you enjoyed it.' 'I did,' she said, 'send the account to John, he is going to pay.' My stomach rumbled in rhythm with the Hillman all the way back.

For one nasty moment, I thought that I was going to be sent out to the Far East as soon as the war in Europe was over, but I managed to get myself on to an Air Disarmament Wing that was on its way to Denmark instead, and Denmark was a lovely place to be when the war was over. The larder of Europe was flowing with cream, butter, ham and strawberries, and with people happy to see us. From Denmark to Germany and to take a job for which I had no qualifications. Officer Commanding Royal Air Force Element the British Forces Network in Germany, Musikhalle, Hamburg.

How did I get into BFN? Well, I just drifted into the job. Squadron Leader Jimmy Urquhart who had been in charge of the RAF interests, was about to return to the BBC, where he had been an announcer. For the previous few months I had occasionally helped Don Gillett with his cricket commentaries on service games at Klein Flottbeck. I had been due to play in one of them but broke a finger in the nets the day before. Then Alan Clarke, a football commentator, was also on his way home, and so I had a go at the Scotland versus British Army of the Rhine football match at Bahrenfeld. A week later, at an Inter-Services rugby match, I met Air Marshal Bill Williams who, as a Wing-Commander, had been my CO on 12 Squadron in France. Within a week I was posted. I left my uncomfortable duties with an intensely boring Airfield Construction Wing and made my way to a house near the Lake in Hamburg. The Officers' Mess of BFN was a large comfortable house. I arrived in the early afternoon to find Jimmy Urquhart fast asleep in an armchair, a smouldering cigarette burning his fingers. I blew away the ash and eased the remainder of the cigarette from his hand. 'He is off tomorrow, back to the BBC. Hello I'm Barney Colehan.'

A Major with a wide smiling moustached face greeted me that day and took me to the office. Barney was head of Variety at that time and destined to produce Wilfred Pickles' *Have a Go* and television's *It's a Knockout* and *The Good Old Days* from the City Variety's, Leeds. Barney was a tremendous help to me in those early days. The staff were guardedly friendly. You sensed that each new face and voice posed a threat, and they were right. Little empires were being created in that baroque hall.

6/JEAN

A Forces Favourite

Autumn and Christmas passed after my poetic debut without so much as a card from Bulawayo to say how marvellous my cuckoo jug jugging had been. On February 21st the pewter sky was dropping rain in lumps as I arrived in Overseas Presentation to take over from the Duty Routine Clerk, Kitty O'Shea. The last thing the weather promised was a rainbow but Kitty was about to unveil a pot of gold. 'They want you to do an announcer's audition,' she said. After all those years of unsuccessful scheming, suddenly without warning, a load of ripe plums was falling into my lap. There was no time to prepare. No time for nerves. A quick lick of Tangee lipstick and I was off downstairs to the studio.

The War Office and BBC together had decided to start a world service of programmes for the Armed Forces. In the past a woman's voice among the Hibberds and Snagges had been as welcome as a moth in mohair but, since this was to be primarily light entertainment, it might not be too harmful to hand it over to an all-female team of presenters, instant girls-next-door, talking Vera Lynns. There were one or two ready-made woman announcers tucked away in the farthest corners of the Empire Service, where the higher pitch of their voices suited shortwave reception, but for the rest, it was a matter of finding likely candidates in a hurry. Sounding pleasant on the telephone, it was possible I might be one of them.

The first audition piece was peppered with pitfalls like an etiquette quiz in a woman's magazine. 'Cholmondeley' was there, to see if we knew it was pronounced 'Chumley', and 'Cockburn' –

45

'Co'burn', of course – and the sybillant Cirencester. Forty years ago, everyone who was anyone called it 'Sissester', though what you made of it if you lisped can only be imagined. After that came the cast list of *Carmen*. In the days before Marbella had become as common as Croydon, I didn't even recognise the names as Spanish. They could have been Esquimau for all I knew. And why were they typed on a machine so seedy it left squiggly tails beneath the letter 'c'? Clearly the whole thing was exceedingly foreign so I delivered it in ringing Ruritanian and hoped for the best. When I later discovered that I'd got it all wrong, my lapful of plums rotted before my eyes, good for nothing but a compost heap of missed opportunities. The next week passed in deep depression. Then it was March 2nd, my twentieth birthday. That morning the phone rang. (Still no bathroom, but now we had a telephone.) 'You've got the job,' said the Head of Overseas Presentation. 'Come and do your first shift tonight.'

It was brave, not to say reckless, of the BBC to trust me with their brand new General Forces Programme. I could have rocked its foundations before the roof was on. 'Sit in with Margaret Hubble before you take over,' I was told. In five terrifying hours Maggie showed me what to do ... turn the big black knob to open the microphone; talk sense with one half of your brain, while the other is reading the clock; never pause more than fifteen seconds or the enemy will jam your wavelength; play 'Lillibullero' before every News and remember in an emergency, 'A good announcer has at hand a stirring military band'.

I stuttered my way through the Service to North Africa which began at 5.30 and ended at half past ten. Maggie, golden-hearted Maggie, stayed with me all the time after she had completed her own long day's work. She is still the kind of person anyone would want to have with them on a life-raft. In the small hours she took me back to her flat in Crawford Street, cooked us rice with bacon and mushrooms, and put me to bed with enough hot milk and aspirins to send a Whirling Dervish to sleep.

My 'blooding' had not, it seemed, been a total fiasco and the North African bit of the GFP became my particular patch. As a wartime measure, news readers, the Head Boys of the announcing staff, had for the first time been allowed to be named. 'Here is the News from London and this is so-and-so reading it' reassured listeners that they were hearing the authentic voice of the BBC. Rank and file announcers followed suit. Pre-war remoteness had gone for good and the Corporation turned itself inside out to become a latterday Ziegfeld with a chorus line of vocal pin-ups on its hands. Betty Grable had nothing on Marjorie Anderson, Joan Griffiths,

Barbara McFadyean and the rest of us. We developed our own fol-
lowings and postcards were provided, printed with our photographs, for use in answering fan mail. It was heady stuff.

Forces Favourites was our showcase several times a day. With its
signature tune 'When You Wish upon a Star', these programmes of
requests from all the war zones were not even remote cousins of
Doris Arnold's dignified *These You Have Loved*. Black Brunswicks
of the Ink Spots were our bread-and-butter, along with the
Andrews Sisters, Mills Brothers, and of course, Vera and Bing.
Our listeners were quick to spot the personalities behind the
voices. Marjorie's fans were mainly officers bearing gifts of discreet perfume. Mine were NCOs and downwards who sent me
chairbacks sewn with camels and endless pairs of ginger nylons,
dense and indestructible as rubber, with unwearably tiny feet.

There wasn't a lot you could do with a request which simply
said 'Please play for me Anne Shelton singing "Lili Marlene".
Yours truly, Dennis Smith, Cpl', but if they included a colourful
nickname, to break the monotony we swooped on them like seagulls. Our sheltered up-bringing had not covered the mysteries of
Service slang. Day after day we used our lady-like accents on the
exotic words. They sounded as magical to us as the ones Tolkien
later invented for *Lord of the Rings*. It was some time before we discovered that the colour they brought to the programme was a rich,
Max Miller blue.

Tom Chalmers called us to his office and handed over a sealed
brown envelope with the warning – 'Read the contents privately'.
Inside was a letter from a submarine engineer. 'Dear Sir, me and
my mates can no longer bear to hear your refined young ladies
saying such *obscene* things over the air.' He enclosed a glossary
translating the strange and beautiful words into layman's
language. Most of the meanings were so perverted, so technical,
they were still incomprehensible. One particular word I had
always enjoyed saying had such disgusting implications it is seared
into my memory even now. I dread the day a dentist gives me gas,
in case I blurt it out, but I don't suppose he would understand it
either. On the offending list were two engaging entries – Desert
Lilies and Desert Roses. They had often suggested a welcome
fragrance when we played a request for 'the four Desert Lilies of
Company B' or 'the Desert Roses of 4 Squadron', but our Naval
adviser put paid to that. 'If you're taken short away from base,' he
explained 'you look for a Desert Lily or a Desert Rose. These are
oil drums sunk into the ground. The top rim is slit and bent over to
provide a kind of splashback.' This folded metal looked like the
petals of a flower. So all those precious records for DLs and DRs

had been wasted on stinking, rusty, front-line latrines.

Some of the requests had heart-warming stories behind them. The driver of an armoured car in the Western Desert wrote to tell me he'd been so excited to hear his name broadcast, his vehicle had swerved into the soft sand beside the road. The rest of the convoy had to go on without him. It was ambushed a few miles further on. 'I lost my stripes,' he told me 'for listening on duty to the General Forces Programme but you may have saved my life.' Then there was the young woman who wanted to get a message to her husband. His embarkation leave had ended only days before their first baby was due. It was strictly against the rules to pass messages from families in this country to their servicemen abroad, but Hazel and Roy had arranged a code. If the baby was a girl she would get me to play Mantovani's 'Pink Lady Waltz'. 'The Blue Danube' from Andrew Kostelanetz would mean he had a son. Roy's father phoned to say a 'Pink Lady' had arrived, so somewhere today there may be a middle-aged grandmother whose father heard about her birth on a troopship radio, going to war.

It sounds as though our days on the GFP were one long string of records in a bombproof studio. Not so. Most music was broadcast live by a 'repertory company' of musicians who were unfit for military service. The same faces and braces turned up in every orchestra . . . Grand Hotel and Strict Tempo, Sundays; Gipsy Strings and Someone's Quintet, Mondays. 'I'll play second fiddle for you if you'll play second fiddle for me.' The pity was, they rarely performed in the same place twice, so we trailed about London on buses and tubes at all hours of the day and night. Disregarding the blackout, everyone went to work in clothes which would be overdressed for a wedding today. I had a spare pair of white gloves in my handbag in case the first got dirty, a veil on my pill-box hat and a boutonnière on my collar. By half past three in the morning, when the BBC car took me to London Bridge to catch the newspaper train home, veil and buttonhole were drooping, and the cobbles, which paved the forecourt of the station, bit cruelly into my high-heeled feet. But, infallibly, there was a bright spark ahead. The ticket collector on Platform 4. He was a jolly pack-up-your-troubles kind of man with a huge stomach. The maroon pullover under his uniform jacket had been pulled over so many times it had sprung a gaping ladder on the right-hand side. Whenever I showed him my Third Class Season to Redhill he nudged me with his ticket-clipping arm and said 'Hello Daisy girl! Have you had a good night?' His assumption that I earned my living on the West End streets felt like a compliment at four in the morning, but I have always wondered how he explained that journey home to a tame town in Surrey. It was very tame and quiet at that time of day. There was an unforgettable peace about walking from Redhill to Reigate. I could hear the alarm clocks going off behind drawn curtains and knew that my blessed 'night's' sleep was about to begin.

Away from work I had an uneventful war. More sighs than screams. No bombs landed near enough for me to dive dramatically to the ground. No rape. No pillage. Colin and Father were in the Home Guard. Mother worked wonders with dried egg and snoek. When the Canadians moved into Surrey we were all besotted by their transatlantic voices. Few of us had met anyone before who sounded like a Hollywood film star. If you didn't look too closely you could imagine every one was a Gary Cooper. I was 'picked up' by Alfred from Ontario one Sunday evening on my way home from church. 'Bring him home' my parents told me 'so long as he's not a "Vingt-douze".' The reputation of these French Canadians made the Goths sound homely, but Alfred was a respectable member of the Army Medical Corps who quickly had the whole family in thrall. He had long legs, an open trusting smile and the first crew cut we had ever seen. Mother made him a pumpkin pie for Thanksgiving but, in wartime, without spices, it tasted like overcooked marrow. The holly wreath we hung on the door at Christmas because, Alfred said, they always did that back home, caused our neighbours to ask sadly who had died. He gave me a corsage like something Judy Garland would have worn and his single long-stemmed rose in cellophane would have done Joan Crawford proud.

He was a healthy young male at a time when all our local muscle was overseas and we missed him greatly when his unit prepared to leave in 1944. Nothing was said about their destination but we sensed that D-Day was approaching.

Alfred came through the war unscathed. In the years since then we have met him and his wife, Hester, several times. He has spent a Christmas with us and we have watched the Calgary Stampede with them. We write, he writes, and he counts himself, and will always be counted as, a member of the family.

In May 1944, Margaret Hubble and I were drafted back to Broadcasting House to begin work on the dummy runs of a new 'secret service'. We found ourselves in an uneasily mixed company of British, Canadian and American broadcasters who were to provide the Allied Expeditionary Forces Programme. It had been General Eisenhower's idea and the BBC gave it reluctant house room. For me the fourteen months it lasted were, to say the least, changeable: barometric pressure High when Major David Niven breezed in, uniform as bright as Berman's best, but the needle swung to Low whenever I was sent to Bedford to present Captain Glenn Miller's American Band of the AEF. He was a peculiarly distant man to his own musicians as well as the barely tolerated BBC announcer. Everything had to be rehearsed and ready before he made his entrance and no matter how you searched the gold-rimmed glasses and the eyes behind, there seemed to be nobody there. I was probably over-sensitive because the Canadian announcer, Charmian Sansom, got on well with everyone. She was the first person I ever saw blowing her nose on paper. We hadn't met Kleenex tissues before. Nor had we seen American Army uniforms at close quarters. The eyes, once set on those tight khaki buttocks, had the devil of a time looking anywhere else. The AEFP ended soon after VE Day with, I believe, an inner sigh of relief from all concerned. Like an over-long family Christmas, it had been stimulating to be together but we got on better when we were apart. That was when the Light Programme began.

With the war in Europe over, *Forces Favourites* was demobbed to become a family concern and at once there was a problem. Having encouraged informality in wartime, how could the BBC get the cork back in the bottle and restore its former decorum to a programme as frivolous as *Family Favourites*? When it began, forty years ago, they tried. They certainly tried.

Family Favourites Directive 27.11.45

We must be very strict with this programme or it will become unmanageable.

No anniversary requests.

Nothing resembling a message e.g. to play a tune 'with love from Joan' is wrong, so is 'because it reminds me of happy hours with the Amateur Operatic Society'.

No fiancées or girlfriends may be included.

Families only.

No names of schools or pubs may be mentioned because of indirect advertising.

No noisy advanced jazz, e.g. Stan Kenton, is allowed on Sundays.

Cut out the banter. This programme is not a vehicle for personality presentation.

The special Sunday edition was to link people at home with service personnel in occupied Germany and John Webster introduced it from London. He was the Richard Baker of the Light Programme whose speciality was serious music. *Two-Way Family Favourites* rarely reached higher than 'The Nun's Chorus' or '1812' so he was glad to hand the job over to me. No script. No censor. I loved it. We had millions of listeners and the sudden fame went to my head and my solar plexus. I became known as 'the girl with the laugh in her voice' or 'that bloody woman who never stops giggling'. The occupier of 33 Wydeville Manor Road, SE12 spoke for the latter: 'Your job is to introduce the artist not give comments on the weather and finish with a childish giggle. At times your remarks sound more like a child of fifteen than a woman of fifty.' I mentioned that letter on the air and received a carry-on-giggling message from one of Princess Margaret's chefs who said he always listened to *Two-Way* in the Royal Kitchen. It wasn't laughter alone which got up some people's noses. At a time when the popular newspapers and magazines wrote constantly about the *sincerity* we showed on *Family Favourites* – and I, for one, began to believe them – along came a gentleman from Bristol who said 'I must be frank, I don't like the programme or the sickly bathos you lay on in those condescending tones, but my wife would like you to play for her . . .' A bit cheeky, that. He sounded the sort of chap who'd picket Aintree for cruelty to horses with a Grand National betting slip in his pocket.

The records were, more often than not, boringly predictable but the people who chose them were fascinating. The widow in Plaistow, for instance, who had lost touch with her son for seven years. She thought he might be with the Army in Germany and the song 'On the Street Where You Live' sung by Vic Damone ('Victor Moan' she wrote) might bring him back. He was, and it did, with his wife and two children, to spend Christmas at Grandma's. Then there was a Mrs Evans who chose 'Llangollen Dreamer' to remind her son in the Welsh Guards of his birthplace. The Record Library had never heard of it but we eventually realised she wanted 'La golondrina' – Spanish for 'The Swallow'. That can't have done much to shorten the miles.

I was completely carried away by another card which said 'Please play the Danny Kaye record of "Triplets" for Edward and Jane in Sennelager. Tell them it comes from Lavinia who wishes she could be with them at this time of special celebration.' Such elegant names . . . what a lovely young couple Edward and Jane sound . . . how marvellous for them to have become the parents of three babies at once . . . I was out of control. We played the record and waited for warm thanks to pour in. What arrived was a cold shower. Lavinia, Edward and Jane were the triplets in question. Having broken her hip Lavinia could not travel with her brother and sister to stay with their great nephew in Germany. The visit was a celebration of the triplets *seventieth* birthday. I was less im-petuous after that and especially suspicious of a message which arrived in the course of a Sunday programme asking us to pass the news to Lance Corporal Michael McCollom in Detmold that his wife had just given birth to twins in Epsom Hospital. But it was true. I called in to see mother and babies on my way home, just to make sure.

With an average audience of twelve million, every record com-pany wanted its share of exposure for their latest product. Questions were asked in Parliament about bribery – 'Payola' it was called – but I must say nothing more substantial came my way than occasional lunches and a house filled with publisher's flowers whenever Christmas came round. My boss John McMillan, thought a New Record of the Week might be the solution but that only made the competition more frenzied and was soon replaced by a Most Requested Record instead. If we made a feature of the long list of names, mentioned briefly without messages, it would cut down the hundreds we had to disappoint every week, but 'Most Requested Record' was a tedious title. Driving to Town the next Sunday, at Banstead Crossroads it came to me in letters of fire, like Paul's vision on the road to Damascus. We would call it The Bumper Bundle. Now, when I hear the phrase in common usage – in Parliament, say, or on a literate discussion programme – I could hug myself with pride. Not exactly Dylan Thomas, but it's my gift to posterity!

The Musikhalle

Hamburg's Musikhalle was surrounded by a police station, jail, Wincklestrasse where the girls displayed themselves in small shop-windows, and a pathological laboratory conveniently close. Either end of Wincklestrasse was partially blocked by large boards declaring it to be 'Out of Bounds'.

There were no such boards when Lt Colonel Eric Maschwitz and Major John McMillan arrived at the front door of the Concert Hall and pinned to it an Army Form 80 which declared it to be 'Requisitioned for Army Broadcasting' and signed – or rather forged – 'By Order Bernard L. Montgomery'. They had been hoping to be able to take over the Hamburg Radio Station but had been beaten to the requisition order by the Psychological Warfare Group of the Foreign Office so they settled for Hamburg's best building instead. It was relatively undamaged by the bombing raids and the firestorm which had swept through the city. It was central, big enough for their purposes, and it was imposing. Apart from the main hall there were a number of recital and rehearsal rooms all of which could be turned into studios; the cloakrooms were made into offices and the splendidly ornate 'Brahmatorium', where the marble statue of Brahms would turn on its turntable to the press of a finger, became the library.

This was to be the home of the British Forces Network in Germany. The men who had come through France and Germany in their Field Broadcasting trucks now parked them around the Musikhalle and prepared to set up in the luxury of an almost-permanent home. At first they broadcast from newly soundproofed studios to only a few thousand receivers via long and medium-wave transmitters. Short-wave frequencies were soon added and it did not take long before BFN started to acquire a good audience and reputation not only among servicemen but also among the Germans, many of whom were hearing for the first time on their domestic radio sets the big band sounds, jazz, swing and American and British comedy shows. A lot of the output was recorded, some was relayed from the BBC but a growing number of programmes were being generated locally as there was no shortage of British servicemen or home-coming Germans wanting to be part of this broadcasting set-up.

The military bands and unit dance bands were filled with professional and semi-professional musicians, all of whom offered their services. There were staff orchestras made up either of British servicemen or returning Germans. Ray Martin, for example, formed his Melody from the Sky band from the 30 Corps Orchestra and some of the Hamburg Symphony musicians. There was the Concert Orchestra, the Theatre Orchestra and Die Weissen Raben in which the musicians were the same only the name was changed. They were conducted by Dr Milo Karacz, a medical man, who moved between the next door pathological laboratory and our studios with great facility.

Not only orchestras but also engineers were recruited from home-coming German troops. We even had an ex-Luftwaffe pilot among our drivers, one Baron von Reibnitz. BFN escaped the worst excesses of the non-fraternisation rules which laid down that there should be no social contact whatever with the German population; no shaking of hands, no visiting their homes, no smiling at their children, no sporting or cultural contacts and no chatting-up the frauleins. In the Musikhalle there was, of course, a very close and friendly working relationship struck between broadcasters and the relaxation of the 'non-frat' rules went almost un-noticed.

The Musikhalle was quickly assuming its post-war dual role of being the headquarters of the British Forces Network in Germany as well as main concert hall for the city. The Opera house, badly damaged in the air-raids, was being rebuilt, so it was to the Musikhalle that the orchestras, soloists and conductors came to perform for British and German audiences, as well as the radio audience in a series of Sunday Concerts.

The Hamburg Symphony, the Nord West Deutcherundfunk Orchestra, and the Hamburg State Opera Orchestra were regular performers. Later the Sadlers Wells Orchestra and the Glasgow Orpheus Choir came from Britain. Herbert von Karajan, Sergiu Celibidache, Eugen Jochum, Hans Schmidt-Isserstedt were among the conductors, and Eric Rohm, Richard Lewis, Lauritz Melchior, Erna Berger, Solomon, Isobel Baillie and Elizabeth Schumann were just some of the soloists.

When Furtwangler came to conduct the Berlin Philharmonic the queues for tickets started to gather three days before the concert. Furtwangler had recently been 'de-Nazified' and so he could take his place on a platform and what is more, he could expect to be transported from his hotel to the concert in a British car. Furtwangler expected a car in keeping with his status but sadly all we could offer was a very utility Volkswagen. So the great man stood on the top step of the entrance stamping his feet and refusing to move until we got him a bigger car. At last he was persuaded to move – more by the rain than by our protestations that Volkswagens were the only cars we had.

Days of reconciliation, rehabilitation and rebuilding, replaced those of retribution, reparations and recrimination. It was an uncomfortable time. Those of us who had been in Britain during the Blitz and had lost families and friends in the war found it hard to forget and forgive. Those of us who had been to any of the concentration camps found it next to impossible.

On a personal basis our relationship with the Germans we worked with was friendly enough, but there could be no disguising the fact that we blamed them for the war. You cannot, in a matter of a few months, or even years, forget the sense of disgust and outrage experienced at seeing those concentration camps. I for one found only small comfort in being part of that occupying force responsible for extracting some sanctions for the collective guilt of our former enemy. The War Crimes trials were still very fresh in our minds, so there was no easy way of forgetting, but BFN was to be responsible for attempting to bring both sides into contact and conversation again. Raymond Baxter undertook what I thought to be the thankless task of producing and presenting 'Operation Bridge-building'. I was among those who considered such a programme premature but it was, in its way, successful in exploring cultural cross-currents.

There had been and was, for a long time to come, a thriving black market in cigarettes, coffee, food and drink, in return for various luxuries and services. They could buy anything and one of our recitalists once asked to be paid in coal rather than cash – the soprano Margot Guillaume. I do not know whether or not she got coal or cash, but I do know that Lac Evans G. was in receipt of twenty-five cigarettes a week from everyone at BFN, so that he could have singing lessons from the renowned German baritone Theo Hermann. Lac Evans G. had been brought into BFN by

Trevor Harvey who had arranged for Hermann to hear Geraint. I have no doubt that the dark haired Welshman turned up to sing dressed, as he usually was, in shirt sleeves and his trousers held up by his tunic belt.

I treasure a tape of a closing announcement of a BFN programme at that time. 'You have been listening to *The Adventures of Robin Hood*, written by Margaret Potter and produced by Trevor Hill. The cast was as follows – Robin: Nigel Davenport; Little John: Cliff Michelmore; Guy de Guiseborn: Raymond Baxter; Maid Marian: Pat Selby; King Richard: Brian Matthew; Geraint Evans was Blondel the Wandering Minstrel; Will Scarlet: Bryan Forbes; and a Forester Roger Moore.' In those days anyone with any connections with the stage or music were co-opted into productions or into bands. Anyone who had even the remotest connections with the BBC were welcomed. So young Trevor Hill an ex-programme engineer turned his hand to production and Derek Jones to announcing. Trevor went on to become one of the best producers the BBC had in the North of England and Derek Jones went back to Bristol to specialise in wildlife programmes. It was a remarkable seedbed and forcing house for all sorts of talents. The attitude was, show me a good programme idea, that you can do it, and we will find you space in the schedule. There were satire shows such as *Parking Space*, pop shows such as *1600 Club* and *Music Shop*, which used records as well as local German and British performers, outside broadcasts of local events, and visiting Combined Services Entertainment performances. All that, together with the marvellous serious music output meant that it was a good station to listen to and, for anyone who was keen on broadcasting, it was *the* place to try and get into.

My arrival to take over the responsibility for the RAF staff, closely coincided with that of the arrival of a new civilian director, Alec Sutherland. Alec was a smallish, thin-faced be-spectacled, highly intelligent Scot, with enormous energy. It was from him that I learned about broadcasting. 'There are,' he said very early on, 'too many people here, just playing at broadcasting. Enjoying it is one thing, just playing at it is another.' Under Alec, standards rose as he became more demanding and more adventurous. It was he who encouraged the production of a major documentary on the Berlin Blockade by Trevor Hill.

For thirteen months, from June 24th, 1948, the Russians imposed a total ban on the movement of food into and out of Berlin. All road, rail and water links were cut and the only way to supply the city was from the air. Three corridors ran across East Germany into Berlin and it was down these that over a quarter of a million

wen and Joe Metcalfe on their wed-
ing day in Balham, 1922, with Annie
Nash, the bridesmaid

The tin bath at No. 34 'stuck on the wall
like a barnacle'

Seven years old with a new party frock and a new brother

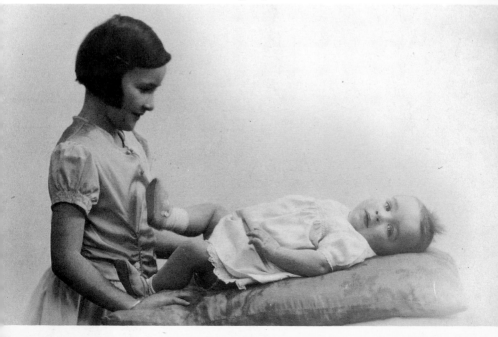

Cornwall 1933: Colin, Father, Uncle Tom, Mother and Jean, sulking with her doll 'Peggy'

Jean and Colin in 'the orchard' at No. 34

Reigate County School's 'Queen Victoria' with Jean Inglis as 'Prince Albert', 1938

Cliff with Mother. The youngest of six children – christened Arthur . . .

Cliff's father, a Special in the Devonshire Constabulary during the First World War

The first car on the farm – a bull-nosed Morris

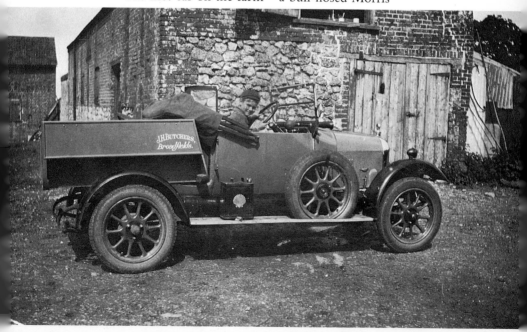

Cliff at thirteen in the school football team. Cliff is front left,
Headmaster S.J. Guppy is back left

Cliff as an RAF cadet

Part of Cliff's farm family: Vi, Joe, Pam and
Terry. The other one, Donald, took the
photograph

Grandpa Reed, Home
...ds Father and Tom, Canadian
...ldridge and Jean, Mother and
...dma Reed, Colin and evacuee
...Smith wearing borrowed tin

Marjorie Anderson   Jean Metcalfe   Joan Griffiths

THE BRITISH BROADCASTING CORPORATION, London, W. I

GENERAL OVERSEAS SERVICE

...of the cards the BBC provided
...nswering wartime fanmail

...orces Favourites, 1944: tea in the BBC
...anteen at 200 Oxford Street with General
...orces Programme listeners from the RAF,
...RNVR and Canadian Army

1948: the football commentator for British Forces Network in Hamburg

A civilian and Deputy Station Director BFN in Germany, 1949

The picture of Jean Cliff saw under the glass top of Trevor Hill's desk

Courting at the Café
Anglais, 1949

Isle of Wight, 1950: Cliff's niece
ela, sister Vi and brother-in-law Joe,
Eve Michelmore and her husband,
er Harold, and Cliff's sister Molly

Jean's first encounter
with Basketts farm and
its butter churn

The wedding. Yellow roses and a clove carnation, March 4th, 1950

'Half the town turned out to smile and stare'

Honeymoon breakfast at the Savoy in off-ration rayon from the Edmundo Ros Rumba Band

flights carried almost two and a half million tons of food, fuel and other supplies. At times the appalling weather almost shut down Templehof, Gatow and Tegel, but only for one period of three hours were the aircraft unable to land because of dense fog. For the rest of the time they landed almost blind on instruments. It was a dramatic story and one which BFN had to cover.

We had made recordings at various airfields around the zone; at the loading bays, in control rooms and cockpits of the aircraft. But then Sunderland Flying Boats started to land on the River Elbe and use it as a base. We managed to get our recording gear aboard one of the Sunderlands as it was being loaded with food. Then at night, we took off bound for the Berlin lakes, recording as we went, with only the light of the moon to show us the way along that invisible corridor. I spent three days in Berlin during the Blockade and was hustled out by John Stephenson, an RAF officer of somewhat superior rank to me. 'Out Michelmore, before you take root and consume too many rations.' There were a lot of us reporters, 'Getting in the way' was what he really meant, so we left.

When the Berlin Blockade was eventually lifted, I was sent to the Checkpoint where the barrier was to be raised and a token convoy allowed through. We went with the Outside Broadcasting truck to Helmstedt. I was to cover the raising of the blockade at one end of the autobahn, and Douglas Willis the BBC correspondent was to cover the Berlin end. 'Make it light-hearted,' ordered Sutherland, 'tell us what you see and no sombre reflections.' When I got to Helmstedt there was chaos. Every newspaper, magazine, radio station and even film company had decided to send a team to cover the event. The first convoy was an hour late forming up at the start because of the traffic jam and confusion. Then there were the usual 'on–off' reports, and flood of rumours always encountered at such times. As the deadline for the departure of that convoy drew closer, the chaos increased alarmingly. Cars were banging into one another; film crews in trucks lit flares and charged at the still-closed barriers with their cameras turning. Military Police tried desperately and unsuccessfully to keep some kind of order. On the Russian side of the barrier there was nothing to be seen. Peace may have been coming along the length of the autobahn between West and East Berlin and Helmstedt, but where I was pandemonium was breaking out.

There was shouting, as one more correspondent bounced off the front of someone's front bumper. An American ambulance which arrived late with sirens blaring, was found to have inside, not the sick but corps of newsmen and cameramen. It was shoved sideways into the ditch. In my headset I could hear the Light Programme announcer in London hand over to me in Helmstedt and I was off. As best I could, I described the extraordinary scene beneath me. How James Thurber would have enjoyed this. 'It is like a scene from *The Day the Bed Fell on Father*,' I heard myself saying.

Suddenly the Russian barrier was raised and the convoy moved through. I handed over to Douglas Willis in Berlin, at the other end of the autobahn.

Silence.

I tried again.

Silence again.

It had been arranged that I would hand over to Berlin on a time cue but our watches could not have been synchronised. The silence was awful and ominous, so I decided to fill it hoping that if they got hold of Willis, they would pull out my plug and put his in. At last this was what they did, but the BBC newsman was not pleased. It was all my fault he said. 'This man,' wrote Tom Chalmers, 'must never be let near a microphone again.' Alec Sutherland showed me the letter from the Light Programme boss. 'Don't worry. The trouble with Tom is that he is in London and we are out here. I will have a word with him.'

What had upset him particularly, I was to learn later, was the light-hearted Thurber remark. Tom Chalmers was not well acquainted with Thurber.

Other outside broadcasts posed their own particular problems. For example, when we decided to cover the Military Tattoos in Berlin and at Dusseldorf, we did not readily appreciate that whilst the military were precise at times when it suited them, when it didn't they could be as unreliable as any commuter train. So it was at Dusseldorf. Captain K. C. H. Mitchell Taylor, BFN's resident expert on military matters had arranged that we would start our broadcast at the time there was to be a noisy set-piece battle, which would be followed by massed bands accompanying a spectacular fireworks display. Dear Ken, however, had placed rather too much faith in the Army.

There is a limit, I soon learned, to what a commentator can say when confronted by two hundred men gently swinging Indian clubs to the rhythms of such inspiring music as 'Daisy, Daisy' and 'Down at the Old Bull and Bush' for ten minutes. As an outside broadcasting commentator I was learning the very hard way.

We also covered sports and were delighted when it was agreed that we could broadcast a live commentary on the German heavyweight championship between two ex-world-class fighters Walter

Neusel and Max Schmeling. Recordings were made at their training headquarters for our pre-fight broadcast and on the night of the
fight ringside seats were reserved for us. We were making this a big
production. Imagine my shocked surprise, when on getting to my
seat in the Tramshed, where the fight was held, to be asked for an
enormous on-the-spot fee by the promoter. 'If you don't pay, there
will be no fight. If you don't broadcast it, there will be no fight,' he
said. It was bare-faced, bare-fisted blackmail and the impatient
crowd had no idea of the ringside scrap between me and the promoter, as they yelled for the action to begin.

'All right', I conceded, 'there'll be no fight, because we can't pay
and that is that.' I picked up the microphone, my notes and stop-
watch and started to leave, following the furious promoter. But
out of the dressing-room Schmeling appeared, followed by
Neusel. The fight and broadcast began on time. We never did pay,
but we did get a look at two ageing boxers, prepared to slog it out
for ten rounds, for a few thousand marks. I for one did not blame
them.

It was like seeing 'two old men in bathchairs, trying to fight each
other' according to the local Hamburg newspaper next day, and
they just about had it right. I was pleased we had not paid.

Everybody at BFN at that time was expected to help everyone else.
Ken Mitchell-Taylor invented a quiz-master character 'Major
Clueless' for whom we all wrote questions. We all took part in Margaret Potter and Trevor Hills' plays, but introducing dance bands
was usually the exclusive preserve of Derek Jones and Jimmy
Kingsbury. Jazz was looked after by the librarian Alex, or as he
was later known, Alexis Korner. Presenting record programmes
was something we all had to do from the Station Director downwards.

In terms of record programmes, the most sought after was undoubtedly *Two-Way Family Favourites*, the Sunday lunchtime link
between the families at home and the forces abroad in Germany. It
was only when I read Doreen Taylor's book, *A Microphone and a
Frequency*, which covers forty years of Forces Broadcasting, that I
learned how the programme began in the first place. Scouring
BBC archives was no help to me, but her book tells the story.

> On 7th October 1945, one of the most famous and long-
> lasting programmes began. It was the first time *Family
> Favourites* was broadcast two-way between the BBC in
> London and BFN in Hamburg. The idea began when John

McMillan discovered a direct telephone circuit from
Hamburg to the exchange housed in a deep underground
railway tunnel at Goodge Street Station. After D-day, it had
been run by the Royal Corps of Signals for military traffic
between London and the Continent.

As always, McMillan had friends, and he asked his contacts
to put him through. 'Can you give me Langham 4468?' he
asked, and found himself talking to the BBC, and Tom
Chalmers, the Assistant Head of the new Light Programme.
In the weird atmosphere of finding themselves talking
between Germany and Britain once more, the idea of the
record programme, jointly presented, was born.

I have good reason to be grateful to Major McMillan for his discovery. It was to lead to a discovery of my own four years later.
Derek Jones the regular presenter, was quite suddenly taken into
hospital and we had no replacement for him on *Two-Way*. Alec
Sutherland told me to take over 'then we will see'. It had, until
then, been the rule that the presenter at the Hamburg end was
introduced by his rank and name. So it had been Sergeant Derek
Jones to whom Jean Metcalfe at the London end had talked. Now I
had to tell her that Derek was in hospital and I was taking his place.

'What do I call *you*?'

'Cliff . . . Cliff Michelmore.'

'Should I say Corporal or Sergeant?' She was trying to be tactful. As a Squadron Leader I should stick out like a foxglove among
buttercups. No officer had been allowed on the programme
before.

'I think that we had better dispense with rank,' I said.

How I got through that first *Two-Way* I shall never know. Afterwards, I remember walking down the front steps, getting into my
car and driving to the Officers' Country Club where I was due to
play tennis in the afternoon. I had been extremely nervous, but
somehow Jean had helped me along, for which I was grateful.
Now I had to face my colleagues. There had always been a great
deal of jealousy when it came to who did *Two-Way*. It was the Network's programme of the week, it was listened to by millions of
people in Britain. We knew that it could provide a helpful step
along the way for a freelance, trying to get into the ferociously
competitive broadcasting market.

In the past, a few of the Hamburg presenters had fallen foul of
both the BBC and the British Forces Broadcasting Service. A
record played on the programme could take off and become, if not
a bestseller, then a top-ten seller, and in those days, sheet music

sales as well as record sales could bring in huge rewards for publishers, performers and record companies. Song pluggers had
often come to Germany, intent on bending arms to get their tunes
included. They had come in various guises, some quite openly,
others as members of visiting bands, or as accompanists to singers.
We were warned to keep them at arms length. A strict watch was
kept on the records we chose to play each week. Tight rules were
laid down and had to be observed by both sides, which is why
when I had gone through the requests and decided on the records I
wanted to play, I would phone London and give them my lists. At
first I just phoned 'the office' in London. Later I must admit, I tried
to make the call when I knew Jean would be there.

From the very start, we were able to talk easily together. We
shared the same sense of humour and, we were to discover, we
were compatible in many other ways.

The getting-to-know-you process had all been done at a
distance. The bottle of Benedictine, the use of Alec Sutherland and
his wife as emissaries, the odd letter and the 'business' phone-calls
before each Sunday's programme, was as far as we had got.

Now I was about to have some leave.

I had been working and travelling hard in Germany. Back home
on the Isle of Wight my mother was rapidly dying of cancer. We
had taken her to Harley Street and Brompton Hospital but it was
too late. 'You must have some leave,' said the doctor, 'call it sick
leave if you like, or you will crack up.'

The Sunday before I was to go on leave, I mentioned to Jean that
it was possible that I would be in Broadcasting House seeing John
McMillan and perhaps I could call and see her. Nothing more than
that, because I had so far not fixed anything.

I left sooner than I had expected. An appointment had been
arranged for me at the BBC on the Wednesday. I hoped to be able
to make another appointment with Jean.

In the event, nothing had been arranged, I just turned up in her
studio, unannounced, after first visiting John McMillan and
briefly seeing Tom Chalmers.

'You must be Jean.'

'You must be Cliff.'

A Golden Cup of Coffee

It was only when I got back to Hamburg that I began to realise what a dramatic turn my life had taken in so very few days. There was a whole new future to be sorted out. My RAF service days were now behind me and soon so, too, would be my days at BFN. Ahead there was uncertainty but I relished the thought of being able to face up to that together with Jean.

Should I try to get a job on the staff of the BBC? I did not think that I was a BBC type and in any event two members of staff in one family might be more than they would contemplate.

If I were to become a freelance that would throw me into an overcrowded pool with a lot of well-known and established professionals such as Richard Dimbleby, Stewart Macpherson, Raymond Glendenning and hundreds more all fighting for survival. Self-perpetuation is the name of the game as a freelance and if it meant buying the Head of Sport pint after pint of beer in the George or the Feathers every lunchtime, then pints of beer he should have. Alec Sutherland counselled me against taking that route because, in his opinion, the life of a freelance seldom extended beyond two, or at the most three, years. A few last longer but not many.

There was also the question of what sort of work I was going after – writing, producing or performing? And where? Radio was already glancing sideways at the new upstart out at Alexandra Palace, television.

Whatever was decided we would do it together. *My* gratuity was to be *our* gratuity, and it was to become *our* home, and *our* future.

The following eight months were to be bridged by almost daily letters, weekly telephone calls and only a couple of meetings. Jean came to Hamburg for a few days and I was able to get a week or so at home but those were the only times that we met until Christmas 1949 when my BFN contract expired.

But there was always Sunday. As the *Radio Times* billing had it: 'From London the tunes you have asked us to play. From Germany the tunes that makes them think of you.' They published no names but everybody knew Jean Metcalfe's voice and the opening that preceded the signature tune, 'With a Song in My Heart'. 'In Britain it is twelve noon, in Germany it is one pm but at home and away it is time for *Two-Way Family Favourites*.' We tried to separate our own messages from those which were attached to the records which we played from Hamburg and London but naturally each tune took on significance. It was almost childish, but who cared?

Jean wrote in one letter of 'dreadfully cheap music, tinny and lashed with hollow sentiment, but to my enchanted ears, pro-found, written for and about *US*.' They were the sort of tunes I would not now take on a desert island but we found fun in them then. Our correspondents often caused some amusement. One Sunday morning I arrived at the studio to find a Top Priority signal from a military policeman which had been delivered by despatch rider. 'Please cancel request "Forever and Ever" for Sweetheart Rose. Please substitute "No Rose in All the World" for Sheila of...'

Already there were those who 'knew' that there was something between Jean and me. There were friends in the Musikhalle who really were in on the secret because secret it had to be. There was to be not even a hint of romance whilst I was still on the programme, the BBC had ordered. The press had already had a hint from people in BFN but I was still taken aback when confronted by a correspondent in Berlin who showed me the front page of the *Daily Mirror* with a picture of Jean beside the story. To keep our jobs we *had* to deny it, which with reluctance we did. It was irritat-ing that we were not allowed to tell them the truth.

By now we were laying plans. The idea of my living in London was abandoned and I was to live with Jean's parents in Reigate until we got a home of our own. It would give us time to look around. We aimed to announce our engagement as soon as I was off the programme and back home in England. Our letters betrayed our growing impatience with being apart at a time when we so much wanted to plan our future together. Doing that at a distance was not easy but then, we argued unconvincingly, noth-ing worth having comes easily. We knew that the going would be rough at times, but we were also filled with that wonderful optimism and dreaming that people about to face a life together share – or should share. Jean wrote 'I have all the right, *good* feelings about us. I want all the right, good things for us. The simple fundamental things that matter more than all the trimmings – a windowbox or a garden, a nearby tube station, or a car of our own, a flat in a backstreet or a house with blue shutters – what does it matter as long as we share the *real* things . . . the boy with your eyes, the girl with orange hair, the joy of creating something entirely of our own.'

When they finally arrived the children were the other way round – a boy with orange hair and a girl with my eyes. We never lived in a backstreet flat or a house with blue shutters. We didn't, as Jean had once visualised 'run a pub in Devon while the children rode and fished on the moors'. We were not to know that of all our aspirations the one which would be exactly realised was, as she put it in one of her last letters, 'us together, working hard side by side'.

The last record that we played on *our Two-Way Family Favourites* was 'I'll Be Seeing You'. My time at the British Forces Network in Germany had at last run out. The parting had been far too long delayed for my liking. Together with the new Station Director, Leslie Perowne, I went for one last look round. In Berlin we went into the Russian sector to go to the opera. Eric Kunz was in the *Magic Flute*. In the interval we drank undrinkable coffee and ate uneatable wurst served up by the HO, the Handel Organization. In Hamburg we toured the seedier parts of the city from the Reeperbahn to Wincklestrasse and then took to the more rural roads around Schleswig Holstein. I was not sad to leave it all behind.

Now in January 1950 what our friends and families had known for some time became public knowledge. We bought the ring and announced our engagement. Jean's father opened the champagne, she flashed the ring and I held her hand hard just to make certain that I did not lose her.

'It is true isn't it?' she had asked in a letter some months previously. Now it really was true and we enjoyed sharing our happiness. Telegrams, letters, telephone calls and flowers flooded in upon us. Well not so much 'us,' they were mainly addressed to Jean. As for me, well I quickly became 'Mr Metcalfe' to-be. There were those who envied me, and there were those who resented the fact that I had 'stolen' Jean away from them. From all sides I heard how lucky I was. They were right, I was a very lucky man.

Meanwhile my trunk containing all my clothes and bits and pieces had yet to arrive from Germany despite threatening calls and letters to the War Office. More to impress my wife-to-be than anything else I fired off a letter to our Member of Parliament, John Vaughan-Morgan, pointing out my problem. From my days in the Air Ministry I knew what effect a file containing a Ministerial Question had upon an office, so I was not surprised to get a letter from John Vaughan-Morgan telling me that 'The Minister has promised action on locating and delivering of your missing trunk. . . .' Next day an Army fifteen-hundredweight was outside No. 80 Deerings Road, Reigate. 'Squadron Leader Michelmore has had some trouble getting this back I believe. Sorry about that.'

It would be idle to pretend that being engaged to Jean did not help. It did. Not only did she have one of the loveliest voices on radio she was also one of the best-loved announcers.

In the meantime I was having some success in finding a job. Encouraging noises came from the Record Department, Outside Broadcasts, the Variety Department and from the West Region in Bristol. At least it looked as though I could get some work on radio. My first paid employment was given me by David Miller. A late-night dance band programme called *Design for Dancing* with Geraldo from the Piccadilly studio. Script by Cliff Michelmore with good bits by Jean Metcalfe (an old hand at this sort of thing!) Fee 8 guineas. The guinea fee was, I assume, to put broadcasters on a par with the other professions such as medicine and the law, both of whom were paid twenty-one shillings for a pound's worth of work. I did not complain. It was David Miller who also gave me the job as 'Britain's first radio square dance caller' on the National Barn Dance. Never having danced a do-se-do it was not exactly my scene but 8 guineas were 8 guineas and who complained? Not me! Phil Cardew and his Orchestra together with Cecil Ruault knew what it was all about which was more than I did. So I let them do most of the 'All join hands and down the middle, turn around to the tune of the fiddle' bit.

There was a lengthening uncertainty about the date of our wedding. There was always some excuse or reason why it could *not* be and no clear day when it *could be*. Finding indecision a bothersome thing, one evening I opened the diary and declared that we would get married on the nearest Saturday to the date on which I opened it.

'March the 4th. That's when.'

Protestations that it was only a couple of days away from her birthday, that it was only six weeks off, that they did not know if the church was free, or if Mr Nicholas would be on holiday or not, were all to no avail. The whole of the household was thrown into a fury of activity. Invitations, catering, church, flowers, clothes and cars were being arranged, and to add to the confusion we decided to have one reception in Reigate and then another at the Mandeville Hotel in London for BBC friends.

Alec Sutherland agreed to be my best man and I was to stay the night before with Jean's Aunt Norrie and Uncle Tom. Spare clothing coupons were 'found' for my new grey suit by my brother, Harold. He could 'find' anything from a side of un-rationed bacon to a precious un-available box of chocolates. Jean and I had bought an old worm-eaten, rusty long-case clock in a junk shop at Cowes and the family promised that they would bring it up with them from the island on the wedding day. Good as their word they wrapped 'George' up in a piece of sacking, tied it with binder twine and carted it across on the ferry to the train, changing at Guildford. Changing trains at Guildford wiped the wedding-party smiles from their faces and fellow passengers, thinking 'George' was a coffin, raised their hats in respect as they passed. The railway people claimed that loading and unloading him in and out of guardsvans had caused the late arrival of the Reigate train. Whatever the reason, I could not wait to greet them at the station for fear of being late at the ceremony myself. 'George' was hurriedly deposited in the left-luggage office and the Isle of Wight contingent had to run, in their glad-rags, all the way to the church. They arrived with only minutes to spare and, thanks to their long-suffering kindness, the clock still stands in the hall, refurbished now and always on time.

My wedding morning had started with tea in bed, a breakfast of Scotch eggs, freshly baked rolls and real coffee. Lovely Aunt Norrie was determined that I should join in the Metcalfe family from the very start and the Metcalfe's, as I was to discover, were fine trenchermen on festive occasions. Birthdays, Christmas, anniversaries were all celebrated in grand family tradition – excessively but lovingly.

By the time I was due in church Reigate High Street was jammed solid with people. 'That's Wilfred Pickles,' said a lady from the cakeshop spotting my best man Alec, 'and that's Sam Costa with the moustache.' It was in fact Captain K.C.H. Mitchell-Taylor from the British Forces Network, BFN and bar.

Jean arrived on the arm of her rightly proud Father. I turned and watched them come down the whole length of the aisle. She could not wait to join me soon enough. We became man and wife at twelve minutes past two. I looked at my watch!

Outside the whole town seemed as pleased as we were. The police stopped the traffic, Mr Whinney said that they had never done that for his taxi before, and we were on our way, husband

and wife and delighted to be so. I remember little of either reception except the policeman in the kitchen at Reigate and the smiling Mr Vann at the Mandeville Hotel. Because we needed the money so badly Jean was to interview Van Johnson on the stage of some London cinema the next night, at a première. As compensation we were to stay in the Savoy Hotel. At least our marriage was going to begin in style. The honeymoon was to be a few days spent at Alfriston in Sussex and the train was late getting us there as well.

We were, by now, like most newly-weds, exhausted by being nice to other people all the time. Now we were alone preparing to get our breath back and set out on our life together. Jean had managed the past six weeks with her usual external calm and concerned gentleness, helping her marvellous Mother and Aunt and placating me when I got impatient, which was quite often. I began to appreciate how right I had been all along. She was a remarkable girl I had met less than a year earlier. The girl for whom I had gone to get that golden cup of coffee at the Railway Fireman's boxing match. Well it was a golden cup of coffee as far as I was concerned.

9/JEAN

'Schubert's' Prediction

There is no difference between a factory floor and a BBC office where clairvoyance is concerned. Anyone professing second sight is immediately surrounded by a press of young female palms to be read. So it was with 'Schubert' in the 1940s. He was an Empire Service announcer who closely resembled the composer – tubby and balding, cherubic face behind wire-framed spectacles. His nickname was used so universally, I have forgotten the real one. It may have been merely an excuse for holding soft pink hands, but he made some unnervingly accurate pronouncements in the process. When it was my turn, he looked at my palm and regretted that it was not yet sufficiently lined to yield much information. However, he could say two things with certainty . . . I would marry on my twenty-seventh birthday, and never want for money. I was engaged at the time to an agreeable young man connected with our local church. He had a secure job to return to after war service and we hoped one day to afford a three-bedroomed house on a Davis estate. At the age of twenty-two I had no intention of waiting another five years to marry and we only aspired to being a little better off than our parents. Surely, this time 'Schubert' had got it wrong. His words had been forgotten by the time my enviable job came between us and we parted, but Mother wrote them down and tucked them away, with the souvenir sea-shells and broken beads, at the back of a dressing-table drawer.

Four years later, when that studio door opened and Cliff came into my life, it was as though something outside ourselves had shaken a kaleidoscope and handed it back with a completely different pattern inside. In no time at all our letters were full of plans for a life together. In July I baked him a cake and sent it to Hamburg, inside a tin, inside a calico binder. It was the time-honoured way of providing a suitor with your cookery credentials. Still hoarding the last crumbs in August, he wrote about its 'magnificence ... the almonds on top and fruit all through, without a single barren patch.' (I must have been relieved about that. You can never be sure of a cake until you cut it.) In the same letter he says that final divorce papers will soon be coming through, so have I already secretly eyed a ring? 'There is going to be no littleness on this occasion.' Oh poor innocent! What an invitation to plunder that was. Window-shopping in Regent Street on my way to Geraldo and his Orchestra in the Piccadilly Studio, I saw a pearl and diamond crossover displayed on dark blue velvet. The glow of pearl and glitter of diamond was stunning – and costly. When the time came, months later, to go together to buy 'our' ring, we consulted a jeweller friend of my Father at his elegant premises in Beauchamp Place behind Harrod's. Elegant and expensive, with a safe full of ducal plate and tiaras. 'Would you consider something old?' asked Mr Hawkes. 'You wouldn't have to pay tax on it and I've got a pretty ring an old lady brought in the other day.' It was a pearl and diamond crossover. 'Look inside and you'll see that the setting is as beautiful from the back as the front.' The diamond stood up in a circlet of platinum. The pearl had its own little calyx of gold. I don't remember Cliff wincing as he wrote the cheque but the words 'It's a good thing I've got my Air Force gratuity' come to mind.

Before any public display could take place we had to abide by the BBC's ruling that nothing official must be said until Cliff had left BFN and *Two-Way Family Favourites*. With his future career at stake we maintained a po-faced silence. Then one night I went to The People's Palace in Mile End Road to announce a Lester Ferguson concert. Inside the Stage Door a man came forward and introduced himself ... 'I'm just back from Hamburg and had to come and say how pleased we all are about you and Cliff.' Another BFN emissary? It certainly never occurred to me that he could be from the press. 'How did you know?' I asked and that was all he needed. Without another word a photographer appeared from behind a pile of scenery, flash and shutter going like a fairground. Naively I had thought that Michelmore and Metcalfe, were just two ordinary people waiting to become engaged. Now I heard myself shrilling Elizabeth Taylor phrases like 'just good friends' and 'no comment' while my mind raced in panic to Cliff's reaction when he saw in his morning paper that I'd let the cat out of the bag. With one phone call to Germany he calmed my hysteria and told me to contact the *Daily Mirror* Night Editor. As a result, only the initial run of provincial copies carried the story and Cliff's professional prospects escaped unharmed. That uncomfortable warning shot across the bows prepared us for press interest when we 'went public' in January. Maggie Hubble sent us freesias. Father opened champagne and Mother and I dithered about a date for the wedding.

By now I had been to the Isle of Wight to meet the Michelmore family. There were flocks of them all over Cowes and Ryde, and it took time to get Don, Pam, Terry, John, Garth, Michael, Jack, Harold, Molly and Violet allotted to the right parents and spouses. To a man they were welcoming, casual and relaxed. On the farm, in particular, Cliff's darling sister Vi behaved as though I was just another relative calling to collect some eggs. The wedding day would simply be ringed on the *Farmer's Weekly* calendar alongside an especially promising fat stock sale. But at home on the mainland the bride and her mother and aunt went into a ferment of ifs and buts and 'what about the Hartfield Metcalfe's?' Never a man to tolerate indecision, Cliff slapped his 1950 diary on the dining room table. 'Wherever it falls open, the nearest Saturday is the day's it's going to be or not at all.' The pages parted at the month of March. The nearest Saturday, printed at the top left hand corner was March 4th. So be it, we had only six weeks to prepare.

That sounds long enough to get the Lord Mayor's Show on the road but in early 1950 we still had rationing, a housing shortage – we would live with my parents until something turned up – and high on the list of problems was the matter of a church. Innocent party or not, Cliff's divorce might cause difficulties, and the Metcalfe's Congregational membership was longstanding and important to them. Registry Office weddings in those days seemed to be monopolised by men in untrustworthy suede shoes and film stars. We adopted expressions of nerveless integrity and went to put our case before the Minister at the Manse. As he opened the door, Rev. Nicholas said 'I can guess what you've come about. It's not uncommon. In the circumstances I should be sad to see you married elsewhere.' So the invitations went off to the printers and we turned to more diverting wedding details.

Colin and his old schoolfriends, 'Fishy' Smythe, Alan Bussey and Cliff Maybury, were to be the ushers. To save them expense we avoided morning dress and Cliff chose a suit of eloquent grey. In keeping with all this tasteful understatement I decided on a dress of ivory damask – cut up into patchwork many years ago – with slim sleeves, dozens of buttons, and the slightest suggestion of a train. The milliner in the town made a close fitting hat of the same material, wrapped with feathers round the face. To overcome shortages in the shops, Edmundo Ros and his band donated off-cuts from their new rumba costumes which turned into a bright rayon peignoir for the honeymoon. Minus maraccas, it was a passable imitation of my Norma Shearer dream. We had moved from Howard Road in 1947 to a bathroomed house in which it was possible, just, to hold the reception. Anyone who owed us a favour paid it back from their ration book. All the wedding flowers were to be white or yellow: lilac and tulips before the altar, and concealing the seedier corners of home. Outside London at the time, a fat cushion of carnations was the best bouquet most florists could produce, so we ordered a small crescent of yellow roses from Jacques Fleurs in the Strand, which the best man volunteered to collect on the day. Cliff had chosen Alec Sutherland for this job, and both of us were thrilled when he agreed.

March the 4th, 1950, was extraordinarily dulcet, warm enough for summer frocks without coats. Police held up the traffic for Father and me to drive across the square. As we sat in the back of Mr Whinney's old taxi our feeling of omnipotence turned its faded window blinds into Cleopatra's gold. At the church Mr Northover, the undertaker, had laid the red carpet he kept for special funerals all the way from kerb to altar. Half the town had turned out to spill off pavements and wave and smile and stare. I remember sun streaming through stained glass; the scent of Cliff's clove carnation, his reassuring smile and squeeze of the hand; the strangeness of office faces in fancy clothes and foreign surroundings; two policemen on the kitchen doorstep with four-inch slabs of wedding cake in their hands.

The postboy's bicycle had hardly left the house that day when he had to return with another bundle of telegrams. Almost a hundred, and far too many for even Alec's stalwart Scottish voice to read without flagging. We took them to London with us, to enjoy in the ankle-deep luxury of our honeymoon suite at the Savoy. Splashing out on the classiest bed-and-breakfast available compensated for my contract to interview Van Johnson at a film première the following evening. The days we planned to spend in the country, at Alfriston, had to wait. Work and money came first. We couldn't afford to *eat* at the Savoy but spent the £14 we paid for two nights in the suite, on trays of coffee and calls to friends on the first Horlicks-coloured telephone we'd ever seen.

Those telegrams bring a glow of pleasure still . . . the one Cliff sent me fifteen minutes before we met in church; 'Congratulations the best of health and luck to you both from All BBC Drivers, Weir Road, Balham'; 'All the happiness in the world = Geraldo';

'Good wishes for the future = Your eighty friends in the East-bourne Girls Choir'; 'Love and get crackin' = Billy Ternant and my boys'; 'Good luck always = The Staff BFN'; 'Sincere wishes for your happiness = Trevor Hill'; 'All the best = Steve Conway'; 'May your joint production of Family Favourites beat all records = Derek Jones'; 'Best possible good wishes for all future happiness = Norman Collins'; and so many, many more. Most touching are the ones from friends I made on wartime holidays in Devon – 'Postman Reg' Combe Martin, the Loverings, the Watkins, the Darches, the Pugsleys at 'The Dolphin' and 'All at Sea Glimpse'. The browning bits of paper, time- and date-stamped, bring back people and places better than any photo in an album ever could.

The only one we didn't enjoy reads 'May we now print a dis-claimer of your engagement? = Night Editor Daily Mirror'. On the other hand, it's satisfying to know that even a hard-bitten journalist can be as thin-skinned as the rest of us at times.

When we had finished reading them, at the bottom of the pile of telegrams, I found a crumpled piece of paper smelling of Coty face powder, and mothballs. On it, in Mother's handwriting, were the words: 'June 1945. "Schubert" said today that you will marry on your twenty-seventh birthday and never want for money.' Well, so far, we have not gone hungry. Thirty-six years of hard work have resulted in two houses with three bathrooms between them, which is certainly more affluence than we ever expected. And the day Cliff chose for our wedding – Saturday, March 4th, 1950 – was two days after my twenty-seventh birthday.

10/JEAN

Woman's Hour

We had our first row on honeymoon. Cliff stalking ahead through the Sussex lanes, while I dawdled behind in a sulk. We can't have been the first couple to wonder what madness had made us tie ourselves to this stranger. The lesson I learned has lasted thirty-six years. You can't win a fight with Cliff but, with cunning and kindness, it's surprising what can be achieved.

For months while we lived with my parents, their house looked like a jumble sale waiting for lift-off. The furniture accumulating for our future would have taken over entirely had we not spotted the removal van outside a small Georgian house on the other side of Reigate. Urgent indiscreet enquiries revealed that it was for rent, unfurnished. For £3.10s a week and no external repairs we knew as soon as we walked through the latticed porch and front door that we had found our first home.

The kitchen on the right was ordinary but ahead a spectacular staircase curved upwards beneath a high window. Another short flight led down to a glass-paned garden door below. To the left, through an archway, was a little front room, just right for suppers on trays, while behind it, looking on to the garden, was the drawing room. Its proportions, tall windows, corniced ceiling and marble mantle made it clear that this was no *lounge* or *sitting room*. This was unquestionably a *drawing room*. The equivalent space upstairs, the main bedroom, had huge windows too. Curtaining would be expensive but we could save on the two small bedrooms at the front. A bathroom tucked away under the roof was less appealing, but with so many glories we didn't care.

109A Bell Street was the main part of a larger house. The long garden at the back had been divided by a chain link fence, a disappointingly dull solution to the problem of shared land, but at least our bit was not too large for us to handle. There was a mulberry tree on our side. Within an hour we had signed the lease.

Cliff had written from Germany the year before, 'When the next few months have slipped away, there will be no more letters, just hurried notes left under the doorbell, by the milk bottles, stuck on the clock . . .' and his vision came true with a vengeance. I was free when he was working, and vice versa. This entry in my diary says it all. '15.9.52: C. in Peterborough for Battle of Britain Fly Past but back in London in time to eat supper together at Quality Inn. He went home. I returned to Light Continuity. Slept in office.' When just occasionally, we shared a day off it reads like a fortnight's holiday: '6.10.52: Milkman left extra in spite of shortage. Went shopping together. Bought pork (4 helpings – 4s.) and nylons in case they disappear again. There was a queue at the Invisible Menders last week. Home through Priory, all copper sun and dahlias. C. dusted and polished while I opened "Fayre" at South Park Church. Home to make cakes – coffee walnut and ginger meringues. C. planted bulbs – hyacinths in window box, daffs in border. Tea by fire. Then to Majestic to see A. Neagle (droopy dresses like nightgowns) and M. Wilding (toupé very patchy) in *Derby Day*. Finished red/white curtains for kitchen. To bed with two hot water bottles and Ertha Kitt on the record player. A lovely day.'

That reference to Cliff dusting and polishing is a reminder of how much he did to keep our heads domestically above water. All the washing, starching and ironing were mine – no washing machine or spin dryer then – and the cooking which, in its novelty, was more a pleasure than a pain, but Cliff was as houseproud as an advertisement for Mansion Polish and never minded turning his hand to window cleaning or carpet beating. At the same time he was travelling anywhere to do anything, even if it cost him £7 to get there for a fee of half as much. It must have been unnerving to be sometimes referred to, in all seriousness, as 'Mr Metcalfe'. I didn't like it either. It was gratifying years later to meet television viewers who recognised him, then turned to me with the enquiry 'Weren't you someone, Mrs Michelmore?'

I had never been ambitious. All the good things which came my way had been heaped upon me without being sought, and they included *Woman's Hour*. When Olive Shapley left the compère's job in August 1950, Mary Hill, the Deputy Editor, took over two days, while I was drafted in, as part of my announcing duties, on the other three. It was challenging to start work with Charlie Kunz,

74

say, at Maida Vale, then to Studio 4A, Broadcasting House, for *Woman's Hour* from 12.00 to 3.00. After that, back to Light Continuity for the rest of my shift, with perhaps a lecture in Walthamstow to top it all off in the evening.

When I joined *Woman's Hour* Gladys Young was the matriarch of radio drama and Arthur Marshall was still a young schoolmaster in the Shires who was occasionally let out to play on the wireless. The Light Programme was a polite, reliable service and *Woman's Hour's* function was to divert and inform tired housewives, in particular the younger ones whose children had been lulled to sleep by the closing music of *Listen with Mother*. The compère – no one had yet invented the term 'presenter' – was there primarily as a friendly voice to provide acceptable packaging and, in the process, cover the sounds of live speakers coming and going. Journalistic experience was not a requirement. My preparation for an off-the-cuff interview relied on a few perfunctory notes from the producer. I rarely studied press cuttings. Listening to well researched items nowadays I realise how casual, not to say superficial, my efforts must have been. First and foremost we aimed to please. We were not intentionally controversial.

The Editor during most of my years on the programme was Janet Quigley, a greatly loved, sympathetic lady with a low, calming voice. Although a disability caused her to limp when she walked, she always left the impression of a supremely graceful person. Her deputy, Joanna Scott-Moncrieff, was exceptionally tall and stooped to disguise it. This made her appear distant and reserved at first sight but once she became a friend her support and sincerity were constant and a smile gave her features a beauty to match Garbo's. Janet and Joanna made a memorable team. I'm glad I kept a diary through those years.

'27.2.52: Today met Madame Karsavina, rival of Pavlova, partner of Nijinski. Tiny. Wrinkled. Thin, straight and sharp as a needle. Carried peeling shopping bag of American cloth. At Gala Ballet before Queen Alexandra ("exquisite and miniature"). Russian Ambassador dozed and crashed from seat. Everyone startled but the Queen. Too deaf to hear.'

'6.10.52: Marvellous programme. Stephen Potter on "Wifemanship", Dobson and Young, Ambrose Heath, food expert, who complained about hotel coffee to waiter, who said "Really Sir? It was freshly made yesterday". Gladys Young, Guest Compère, gratifyingly dreary, like Lady Mayoress declaring funeral parlour open.'

'19.5.53: 'Eileen Joyce Guest of the Week. Beautiful woman. Once, in a hotel, was allowed to practise on piano they had provided for fellow artist Mark Hamburg. He told her. "Shut the window first in case they think it's me".'

'6.6.53: Vivian Ellis [composer of "Spread a Little Happiness" and "She's My Lovely"] asked my opinion on beads bought for sister's birthday, "because you are a snappy dresser". What a nice man!'

'13.6.53: Stuart Hibberd [Chief Announcer who was as famous as Wogan for his hushed announcement of the death of George V] looks more like a shrimp than ever since his retirement. His spats are displayed in Radio Coronation Exhibition. May be touched for 3d a time. S.H. says peevishly "Isn't 3d rather cheap?".'

'20.10.53: Interviewed Professor Lonsdale and wife Dame Kathleen, who won Nobel Prize for her crystallography. Asked what he most admired in her, he said "Her Mathematics".'

'23.2.54: Heard about silicones on WH today. Magical things which can be added to anything to repel finger marks and make cellophane peel away clean from sticky cakes. Sounds too good to be true.'

'24.3.54: Jack Hawkins was boy actor with Thorndyke – Casson Company guarded always by governess. Restless feet. Hair curly to the roots, so it's *not* permed!'

'4.5.54: Norman Wisdom bought first baggy 30s suit for job as assistant to struggling young conjuror – David Nixon.'

'12.5.54: Christopher Fry says since giving up smoking he can smell a lilac across the road, an animal, even a man on a bicycle.'

'29.12.54: Beatrice Lillie today. WH uniquely extravagant, gave her hideous bunch of chrysanths. Editor's explanation – "If you don't she asks 'Where are my flowers?'." Small, elderly, burned up with vitality and witty contempt. Wore one of her small "fez" hats; brown velvet with gilt beads and tassel. Mink coat over oatmeal dress bound with coffee coloured satin. Huge topaz ring and little square reading glasses. Embarking on Queen Mary at Southampton asked "When does this *place* get into New York?".'

'27.1.55: Blind edition today. Blind typist told of skirt zip breaking in office. Colleague said "Put on your mac while I

mend it"'! Later discovered the mac she was wearing was one
of the new transparent kind.'

'3.2.55: Interviewed B. Braden and B. Kelly. She proposed to
him – "I *told* him really". Seventeen when married. Most
attractive. Like a light going on wherever she goes.'

'14.4.55: Extraordinary woman, Barbara Woodhouse, talked
about taking her cows on holiday with her. In Argentina
tamed horses by breathing down her nose at them. Says that's
"horse" for "Good Morning".'

One evening in September 1955 I went after work to speak to a
women's organisation in Tooting. Questions afterwards included
one about Godfrey Winn, the writer who was a regular contributor to *Woman's Hour*. Was it true he knew all the best people and
was on first name terms with Lady Louis Mountbatten? They were
a lively audience and I let down my guard. It was true, all true. *And*
he had a mink lining to his overcoat.

The next time I met Godfrey in the studio his press cuttings
agency had sent him a report from the local paper – 'GODFREY
WEARS MINK' – and he was extremely upset. 'My readers are
humble folk who like to think I am one of them' he said, slinging
the fur-lined coat over his shoulders. He stormed out of the studio
with threats of litigation. I was unnerved. The coat certainly exis-
ted. Perhaps the lining was not mink but sable. Would that entitle
him to sue? I waited on tenterhooks for each post to arrive but
nothing happened.

A month later I was booked to record an interview with him at
his flat in Ebury St, 'Godfrey Winn at home' and all that. A bowl
planted with hyacinths came with me as a peace offering but there
was no need. He was as nice as pie. Gave me lunch in his dining
room hung with paintings by Sutherland, Epstein, Duncan Grant,
Paul Nash and Sickert. It was like eating in the Tate Gallery.

His man servant apologised for the sticks of picked-over chry-
santhemums in the vases so the promise of budding bulbs may
have helped after all. Godfrey was like that. Presents of Floris bath
oil one minute, threats of litigation the next.

'9.9.55: Interview Julian Bream. 22 now. First met him as a
schoolboy seven years ago. Still v. nice. Tonight playing first
ever Promenade Concert Guitar Concerto.'

'28.9.55: Sir Normal Birkett [later First Baron Birkett, Lord
Justice of Appeal] Guest of the Week. Gorgeous man. Over

lunch told of woman friend who mistakenly took another woman's umbrella on leaving train. Going home after Christmas shopping had bought several brollies for presents. Met same woman on return journey who said "*You've* had a good day I must say!".'

'29.9.55: *WH* interesting today, chiefly for unbroadcast talk over lunch table about spies Burgess and Maclean. Robert Reid says Burgess's American Desk at Foreign Office only glorified postman, but his knowledge of F.O. reactions to various approaches invaluable to Russians. BBC letters to Moscow unanswered until his defection but now replies received in impeccable F.O. English. All agreed he was charming, superficial, highly regarded as a guest. Invited for weekends by Churchill.'

'5.10.55: Rebecca West can only work in foolscap exercise books which she goes to Spain to buy, and on a *round* desk, so that she can move on when it gets cluttered.'

'5.3.56: Ideal Home preview. So much modernistic stuff made me feel I wanted *anything but* an ideal home. Give me fluff and warmth like the inside of old pocket any time. "House of the Future" perfectly frightful. Food treated with gamma rays keeps indefinitely. No guarantee of un-impaired flavour though. Heating under floors! Transparent walls! *Remote* control for TV! Even a machine which records telephone messages when you're out!! Can you imagine living with all that?'

'22.5.56: Covered Chelsea Flower Show for *Woman's Hour*. Flat shoes always know Latin names of plants.'

'26.5.56: Joyce Grenfell says Ernest Thesiger visiting Moscow with *Hamlet* borrowed pencil to write on lavatory wall "Burgess loves Maclean".'

'30.5.56: Ernest Thesiger, Guest of the Week. Says he didn't. Pity.'

'12.7.56: Asked Spike Milligan why he created "Goons". "If a nose itches you scratch it. You don't ask why does it itch".'

'1.7.56: Ruth Drew, top of *WH* popularity poll again. Has been looking after friend's canary. It died because they are Christian Scientists and wouldn't allow vet. Scurrilous rumour that, in spite of cooking hints, Ruth can't actually cook. Lunched at her flat and she warmed coffee cups before pouring. It can't be true, can it?'

I carried a great deal of tittle-tattle home from *Woman's Hour* lunches in the amiable, meandering fifties. Nowadays the programme is crisply professional from beginning to end. A mere handful of people put it together in a basement studio suite, editing tape, writing links, with only a sandwich to keep them going and no time to spare for rehearsal. In the era I remember we occupied a smaller studio, 4A, on the fourth floor, where the entire cast gathered for a complete run-through shortly before noon – two engineers, an overall producer, one or two secretaries, a compère and at least six or seven speakers with their personal producers. It was easy to separate speakers from staff. The speakers were the ones wearing hats.

Rehearsal over we crocodiled along to a windowless conference room for lunch. I always found this a wearing time, pouring out, handing round, with roguish humour from Macdonald Hastings in one ear and antique wisdom from Dr Maud Royden in the other. While *Listen with Mother* was on the air we led our speakers back to the studio via the lavatories, like a coach party preparing for a long journey. Naomi Jacob, stomping in mannish brogues, watch-chain over waistcoat, was once waved by mistake into the Gents. Minnie Pallister, our diarist, was invariably distracted over a bit of mislaid hand-luggage. She was a likeable but chaotic person who spent half her life broadcasting her experiences as a Women's Institute lecturer and the other half telling WIs about *us*. If Mabel Constanduros was on the programme, and she frequently was, it never ceased to surprise when this tiny, feminine person in pretty Queen Motherly clothes gave voice to her gruff and monstrous creation 'Grandma Biggins'. And then, of course, there was Cdr Ibbett whose series 'Spinning a Yarn' made him, late in life, the darling of our ladies. He was a dear man with courtly manners and a belief that he broadcast better on an empty stomach, so we all ate extra sandwiches when he was on the programme. Antonia Ridge was another regular who could do no wrong with our audience. A tall, angular woman, she wrote many of our best serials and read them herself. Her producer, Isa Benzie, always sat beside her with a glass of water into which she dipped her fingers from time to time and dabbed them on her temples while she spoke her strong and simple prose. That's one feature which hasn't changed, the serial, but in my day it was always live and the compère remained sitting opposite throughout. One dreadful day the reader, building nicely to the climax of the episode, turned her script and discovered that the last page was missing. She went into shock. I went into overdrive, brought the programme to a premature close and filled the time with minutes on end of the current signature tune, 'The Merry Wives of Windsor'. I wish now that I

79

had taken listeners into our confidence, explained what had happened and asked the poor actress to recount in her own words the contents of the absent script, but broadcasting wore 'corsets' in those days. We never referred to action behind the scenes.

Miraculously that only happened once in my experience. Slips of the tongue on the other hand were an everyday occurrence. Silly little things like 'new fresh papers' for 'fresh newspapers', 'thud and blunder' for 'blood and thunder'. There was nothing to be done then but laugh-it-off-and-upsidaisy. More difficult to explain away was the substitution of one word for another which had an entirely different meaning. I meant to say that the work of Henry James could be considered *esoteric* when the word *erotic* emerged instead. At a time when *Lady Chatterley's Lover* was on trial for obscenity this was hardly doing Mr James a favour. It was swiftly corrected of course but not before several librarians had suffered a moment's panic. They wrote to tell me so.

Times were chaste in the fifties. S. J. de Lotbinière, the seven foot tall Head of OBs, was in the habit of saying he would never employ someone who used foul language off-duty because they might resort to swearing 'under fire' on the air. My personal vocabulary has always been thin on cuss words which was fortunate one Tuesday when a particularly vague *Woman's Hour* producer ushered an unexpected woman into the studio to be interviewed. No one had told me who she was, why she was there or what we were supposed to discuss. It was like being asked to launch a ship without a bottle in your hand or a name in your head. I floundered near to tears while a scribbled note of explanation was pushed across the table. Mercifully memory does not recall the outcome except that the producer concerned transferred to calmer waters after that. *The Silver Lining* I think it was.

With modern talk-back facilities and the extensive use of pre-recording that sort of nightmare is not longer likely to occur. Even in my day recorded material had begun to take a larger share of *Woman's Hour*, not for reasons of safety but as a means of taking listeners out of the studio. I was sent with an unfathomable, so-called 'Midget' recorder to talk to stars in their homes, many of them off-shoots from my *Family Favourites* connections. The series was called 'House to House' and I loved it, visiting Vera Lynn in her Finchley 'palace' – she cooked us pork chops and mashed potatoes; Johnny Morris in Aldbourne where he lived in a little Queen Anne 'doll's house' with small scale furniture to match, loose-covered in striped pillow ticking and very smart too; Frankie Vaughan in Brent, where I tasted 'Mama's delectable cheesecake'; Jeanne de Casalis in Montague Square and Kenneth More in Palace

Gate. I went to Lewes to record Cdr Ibbett feeding a robin in his kitchen and to Brighton to talk to Gilbert Harding. All these celebrities were hospitable beyond the call of duty. They received only thanks and flowers in return, except for Winifred Atwell who had a present for her poodle instead. The authorised expenses chit is still in BBC Archives: '21.1.58: One diamante dog collar – 25s.'

This outside work extended my weekday role on *Woman's Hour* considerably while *Two-Way* continued to gobble up the best part of Sundays. No one can present a programme week after week without leaving a mark on it. After Cliff had left, BFN moved from Hamburg to Cologne and from there Dennis Scuse took over the German end of *Two-Way*. To my mind Dennis's finest legacy was his paraphrase of the movement from Beethoven's *Pastoral Symphony* which is known as Shepherd's Thanksgiving After the Storm. He called it 'Thank God it's stopped raining'.

When he in turn moved back to Britain, this exceptionally tall sophisticated man was replaced by five-foot-three Bill Crozier. Bill and I shared the programme for more years than any other team. He is a simple man in the best sense of the word, kind to a fault, sincere and emotional. Because we were both easily moved there were times in our partnership when a particularly touching message would give rise to gulping pauses in Britain and in Germany simultaneously. His trademark was the mythological knitting he purported to do while the London end was engaged in a half-hour link with Singapore or Cyprus. As we switched from Cologne and ultimately back again, Bill would be heard murmuring 'knit one, purl one, knit two together...' At least, I imagine his knitting was a myth. To this day he affects a coveted opera cloak which billows, ankle-length, like a half-opened umbrella. I suppose that cloak could possibly be the outcome of many years knitting on *Three-Way Family Favourites*.

The fifties were the most glamorous time of my professional life. They were also for both Cliff and me totally exhausting, catching trains before light and returning after midnight in fog and blizzard, Green Line coach and third-class carriage. But it was as though a steel wire was holding us together, supported on all sides by my indefatigable mother. The unexpected joy of coming home to find a meat pie left for supper and our leviathan boiler cleaned out and re-lit for hot baths, is something neither of us will ever forget. She should have accepted the awards and plaudits instead of sitting in a corner reticently proud.

An Explosion of Trivia

If you had to change direction in life and take up a totally new career I suppose that 1950 was about the best time to do it. Particularly if you were setting about working in television. I do not pretend that I saw the coming of the 'communications explosion' but there were some signs that television could soon become as important as radio.

In the first thirty years of my life I had seen such dramatic and rapid technological developments that many of them were taken for granted. The early days of wireless had meant tweaking a cat's whisker to pick up the faint scratchy sound of a far-off danceband. The thermionic valve brought us out of the old-fashioned days of wireless into radio, and within twenty years the cathode ray tube brought the first glimmerings of television. Although, to be honest, I had not even seen, as Jean had done, the television demonstrations at Radio-Olympia. 1948 saw the introduction of the transistor and suddenly a cornucopia of modern technology poured out new techniques and new equipment.

It would have taken an Arthur C. Clarke to know that within ten years the Russian Sputnik would be in orbit and five years after that we would be using the first communications satellite, Early Bird, as easily as dialling TIM. As for foreseeing man walking on the moon and talking back to the world below via television, you would, even then, have stood a good chance of being locked up.

In a very short time we were all to be struck by the force of that communications explosion. Television which in the late 40s could only be found in 3 per cent of the homes in the country would in a decade become a national obsession. Not everyone saw those days coming. Radio was still the dominant medium and there was no mistaking the disdain in which sound people held 'the new toy which will go down the drain with the bath water in a couple of years' as one newspaper critic saw it at the time.

Waiting for Jean one evening, I was having a drink in the BBC Club in Chandos Place. Frank Phillips, the doyen of newsreaders, was there and he asked me what I hoped to be doing. 'I would rather like to get into television,' I replied. 'That ought not to be too difficult, nobody much from here wants to go. But it won't last. Radio goes round corners, with television you have to stare it in the face all the time.'

There were, it is true, less than 130,000 combined radio and television licences taken out in 1949, and there were only a couple of transmitters to bring the still restricted programme to London and parts of the West Midlands. All broadcasting was then under the direct control of Broadcasting House, Portland Place, and the sound producers and performers did not, at that time, feel that they were 'a beleaguered garrison'. Those days were to come all too soon for some of them.

Television was not too much a matter of concern to the press either. It carried no news and was 'an expensive bit of trivia for the few who can afford it, or those who want to be one up on the Joneses and have an H-shaped antenna on the roof.' It was not a competition or a threat, merely a passing fad.

'We've got our telly,' joked Tommy Trinder. 'As soon as we put up the aerial, we realised how many friends we had all of a sudden. Never seen half of them before in our lives.'

Across the Atlantic, however, the new medium was taking hold, its great popularity sweeping it from coast to coast, causing Alistair Cooke to tell us that it was 'already as humble as a hot-dog'.

The BBC had ambitious but prudent plans to build new transmitters, acquire new studios and to expand the service, but the voice of the BBC establishment was always softened with caution when talking on television. 'Its full effects remain to be seen, but television is opening up a new prospect of enjoyment and interest for almost everybody', ran the Governors' report.

William Haley, the BBC's first post-war Director General, thought it was to be the 'natural extension of sound'. There was a great deal of talk about it being radiovision with 'shared shows' being simultaneously transmitted on radio and TV. Radio, went the argument, would continue to provide the staple balanced programmes for the home. The picture was an added extra.

Away from Broadcasting House there were other voices saying other things. They believed that television should be separate from sound and not tied to its apron and financial strings.

It was a conscious decision that I took when deciding not to put all my effort into one or the other, but to have a go at both. Jean was always rather suspicious of 'the box' but then she had always been a radio person. She had adored it as a child and was now one of its best practitioners, so I did not blame her. Nevertheless she raised no objection when I bought a set and had it installed in Deerings Road. Jean's Mother and her Aunt Norrie were at once addicted.

I bought it in time for Wimbledon because there in the *Radio Times* among the children's programmes was my very first ever billing – 4.15 pm, 15th July, Cliff Michelmore explains the rules and scoring of tennis and introduces the All-England Lawn Tennis Championships from Wimbledon.

We rehearsed so much that by the time I came to have the mud-thick make-up applied to face, hands and arms, I was quite enjoying it all. Michael Westmore was my confident and enthusiastic producer and he it was who encouraged me to become part of children's television. 'There is going to be a lot to do and there are not enough of us to do it all,' was his advice. Michael's undergraduate language was liberally spiced with 'old fruit' and 'old thing'. He was quick to praise and a joy to work with.

By the end of the year I had joined what Jean's Mother and Aunt called 'the little people'. I was becoming a television person and among those who were squashed into the confines of the soft grey nine-inch screen, which sat in the corner of the heavily-curtained, darkened room. The size and sharpness of the picture was one thing. There was also another problem. The picture would frequently be whited-out by a snowstorm when a passing unsuppressed motorbike engine showered the set with interference from its ignition system. Calling for legislation to counter this 'menace' the editor of the new 'TV Mirror' wrote: 'It [the legislation] must be extended to include motorists, and those who continue to offend must be given a lesson in a little thing called public spirit. The silencer became compulsory, to prevent the mass roar of car engines from making life hideous with noise; the suppressor will prevent one motorist from making a nuisance of himself to thousands of viewers.'

Legislation was not long in coming. The television net was spreading across whole new areas of the country and into the homes of whole new sections of the population. It was all part of the post-war social change. More and more families were acquiring a 'little car', a fridge, and a telly as their wealth increased. Audiences were growing at an extraordinary rate. One that was never envisaged a year or two before. The number of television licences rose from a third of a million in 1950 to four and a half million in 1955. Add to that the sizeable minority who cheated the BBC out of its income even then and you can see what was happening in those early 50s.

Television was no longer confined to those rich enough or those snobby enough to want to impress the neighbours. It took a firm and popular hold. Its detractors and critics were to continue to see its inherent and real dangers throughout the period of growth right up to the present day. It has always been thus. The Golden Age of Radio was passing.

We were about to live through, and I was to be at least a small part of, The Golden Age of Television, or that is what some called it. As far as rewards were concerned, some practitioners would find it much more golden than others. The industry began to attract many people who had worked in the theatre, or in films, and some, perhaps more significantly, in Fleet Street. In the 50s, television was in the process of discovering and developing its own form and standards. It was striking new attitudes and finding new faces and it was hugely enjoying the technical advances and new tricks which could be played with this medium. But compared with sound, it was still short of money and resources. At the time we were not very aware of being second generation pioneers – following on those who had made programmes in the confines of the two studios at Alexandra Palace on Muswell Hill to the north of London. We were made much more aware of the drive which came from Cecil McGivern. Cecil was the BBC Television Programme Controller but as far as we were concerned he was in charge of the service. McGivern saw everything through his thick-lensed glasses. He never seemed to miss a single shot in a show. In Asa Briggs's history of broadcasting, he is described as 'intense, dedicated, demanding and prickly. He was uninterested in getting on with people if he could get on with programmes and he was glued to the screen every night watching everything that happened.' He was rightly described by somebody else as 'the true architect of BBC television'.

The first studio to be opened in Lime Grove in May 1950 was Studio D, to be used for children's television. By September of that year the service for children was going to be doubled to an hour every afternoon. I had not really thought *what* I wanted to do, I just knew that I would like to be part of this new service and was prepared to take a chance on its survival and on mine. The hostility of some radio producers at Broadcasting House was such that they saw those who worked for both services as being almost traitors. Even Jean understood their point of view and wisely cautioned me not to abandon sound altogether. There was no chance that I would, because fees were low and work, in those early days, often hard to come by. There were still barren workless weeks and we needed all the work and fees we could get.

Gradually I got more and more work for outside broadcasts as a radio sports commentator covering football, cricket, speedway, tennis, air races, even the horseshoe-tossing world championships when they were held in Surrey. *Housewives' Choice* was a good money earner, as were the regular stints introducing Geraldo, Stanley Black and the Top Score Orchestra. But the record and dance band programmes had eventually to go, because television was becoming the important part of my life.

After my initial entry into a studio in July, I was beginning to spend more and more time at Lime Grove. With the expansion of the service, sudden small gaps would appear in the schedules, which quite often I would be called upon to fill. A quick dash down to the Science Museum to borrow a handful of their models (together with the explanatory cards) and there I had an instant ten minutes on such subjects as the development of the omnibus, the aeroplane or the paddle steamer. I also began to learn about directing and producing. Standing around in studios, watching from the back of the gallery, that was the way that everyone was picking up the production techniques. There was no television instructor appointed to BBC staff training until the middle of 1951, and no television training as such, until later that year. We were all trained 'on the job'.

My first solo TV production was at Alexandra Palace. I had been asked to put together some sports coaching programmes and Miss Lingstrom, Head of the Department and 'Mum' to everyone, suggested that we should start with something for the girls. 'For instance,' she had said, 'lacrosse.'

I had never even seen a game of lacrosse, let alone knew how to play it but, resourceful as I had by now learned to be, I dashed down to the Ancient House Bookshop in Reigate and bought myself a 'How to' paperback. There I found the address of the Lacrosse Union, and in no time I was watching my first lacrosse match. It was alarmingly fast and extremely mobile. Somehow I had to manage to contain it in the small box of a studio and shoot it on the cameras, which I thought must have been there since the 1930s. The single-lens cameras which moved across the floor on dollies fitted with bicycle wheels seemed as primitive as an early box camera does to today's photographers.

Working at Ally Pally, I came to admire the skills of those who had been responsible for the production of many large-scale dramas and opera. It must have been rather like producing Ben Hur in a broom cupboard, live!

As a producer I soon took over all the children's sports programmes on which we were fortunate to get such stars of the day as Stanley Matthews, Denis Compton and Godfrey Evans. Dan Maskell brought along two very young tennis players, Christine Truman and Bobby Wilson, and a whole host of others. At that time a TV annual described me a 'children's man of many parts. Stunt reporter, producer, director, commentator and talent spotter.' For the very life of me I cannot recall a single stunt on which I ever reported. I flew a glider with a camera aboard, I was attacked by the Special Effects department with 'pretend' bottles and guns and I drove the Golden Arrow engine, but more than that I do not remember. The 'talent-spotter' bit was perhaps one of the most enjoyable of my many jobs. Freda Lingstrom had wanted a monthly programme in which we showed children enjoying their hobbies, and displaying their talents. It was a very loose format, so that we could include a very wide range of children from all over the country, and it was to be called *All Your Own* and be introduced by Huw Wheldon.

Huw had come to the BBC as a publicity officer from the Arts Council after a distinguished war career. From the first it was clear that he wanted to be involved in programmes and did not want merely to publicise them. He came up with an idea for Children's Television to hold a nationwide knock-out conker's competition. We had thousands of entries. Huw handled the contestants in the studio with the enthusiasm of everybody's favourite cheerful, noisy uncle. He was a great success. Some adults thought his manner condescending. The children found him easy to talk to and deeply interested in what they were doing. He got the job as the interviewer on *All Your Own*.

I travelled the country, holding auditions, seeing children in their homes at their hobbies, and going to schools to hear well-recommended bands, plays and musicals. One Saturday afternoon in Manchester, my old ex-Hamburg friend Trevor Hill helped me out by lending me the pianist he was using in a children's radio programme, for my auditions. Dear Violet Carson, later of *Coronation Street*, came breezing in and, helpful as ever, accompanied all sorts of little acts from trumpet players to puppeteers. It was not surprising that many of those who first appeared on *All Your Own* later became famous. The most famous of all was Jacqueline du Prè, who charmed the cameramen out of their seats with her playing of the cello. We also had successes with another cellist Rohan de Saram, a group called the King Brothers, and the world champion ballroom dancers Anthony Hurley and Fay. 'Mum' Lingstrom thought the ballroom dancers 'vulgar'. The audience loved them, according to a BBC research report, but we did not have ballroom dancers again.

Quizzes, sports programmes, handicrafts, adventure stories and the fortnightly *Playbox* with Eamonn Andrews, took up a great deal of my time as a producer, but I was always looking for the chance to get on the other side of the cameras as well.

My break as a presenter came when the BBC decided to have two fortnightly magazine programmes on Saturday afternoon. One was to be *Whirligig* - all jolly fun and games – the other was to be rather more staid, in the manner of the *Children's Newspaper*, and called *Telescope*. Both were to have the ever-present resident puppet. No programme it seemed, could exist without one.

I did not introduce the first edition of *Telescope*, but a call from Cecil Madden had summoned me to the presence of the Programme Organiser and the Programme's Producer Jill Allgood. It would have helped if I had seen that first programme, but I had not. They had been told by Cecil McGivern to get me to take over as the presenter. It was my first ever magazine programme. *Telescope* never achieved the same level of success as did its fortnightly companion programme. Humphrey Lestocq and Hank and the Silver Steed puppet reigned supreme with the kids, and who could blame them. H.L. as he was known, had come across from radio, where he had played a comic RAF character, Flying Officer Kite. He brought the same zany-whacko attack to the show. Ours was much more worthy – dull even.

Valerie Hobson was in charge of our puppet 'Timothy Telescope', as well as being responsible for the 'How to' spot. How to make a flowerpot out of a 78rpm gramophone record. How to make dolls house cushions out of old silk handkerchiefs sort of thing. We had lovely little Elizabeth Cruft talking about breeds of puppies, parades of costumes from the collection of Doris Langley-Moore (most of which are now in the museum at Bath) and we attempted to interest children in chess. The radio critic of the *Daily Telegraph*, Leonard Marsland Gander, acted as the commentator/encourager each week, but had an unfortunate twitch that brought forth the wrath of Cecil McGivern. 'For God's sake,' he yelled from his office in the corridor, 'someone tell him to stop scratching his ass all the time.' It was on *Telescope* that I learned a valuable lesson. Those were the pre-Teleprompter days when everything had to be memorised. My memory has never been more retentive than a colander, so when called upon to give an example of a limerick, I heard myself saying 'There was an old cock on a stool, who laid all his eggs in a pool . . .' The right words continued to escape me, so I had to make a sudden, embarrassed dash from in front of the camera, grab the studio manager's script and dive back in vision again, and apologetically read out the limerick. Never again, I swore, would I be caught like that. Mind you, I have, but not very often.

Richard Dimbleby, I learned, noted down his prompts on little cards which he discreetly hid from the camera's gaze, but within his. I have been a card man ever since.

With children's television, I came dangerously close to joining the staff of the BBC as a producer and presenter. My mentor, Alec Sutherland, had told me that there was in existence a memo which said that no announcer was ever to be placed on a long-term contract. 'Their life span was no longer than five years,' it said. 'Viewers have no wish to see ageing juveniles.' He also warned me against being a freelance. He thought few of them ever went on for much more than five years. But attitudes were changing, so I resisted joining the staff. We thought that one member of the family bound, face and voice, to the Corporation was enough. Jean was permanent and pensionable. What more could we want? She had the steady income and I picked up 8 guineas here, 15 guineas there. We were in need of money, so I even rushed headlong around the West Country at weekends, covering all manner of sports for the handsome rewards of 3, or very occasionally as much as 4 guineas a time. I was counting on the fact that the experience was worth more to me than the money, although money was becoming increasingly important to Jean and me. We were looking for a house with furniture, carpets and such things of our own, and for that we were prepared to work all the hours we could. We did work all the hours we could as well. We came home absolutely exhausted night after night, day after day. It was to have an effect upon our hopes of raising a family which both of us so much wanted. The 'orange-headed girl and boy with brown eyes' were still very much in our future plans.

'The Coach Moves'

In the early hours of the morning on the 6th of February 1952 the King died in his sleep. No one was prepared for it. I was on a bus on my way to work when we heard a paperboy calling out the news from a Piccadilly pavement. In the office we learned that broadcasting was at a standstill except for news bulletins. We should not come to work until we were called. By the time I was on my way home at midday the shop windows in Oxford Street were dressed in black and purple and by evening the silence drove us early to bed. When programmes were resumed, nothing which could be considered 'light' was being broadcast until after the funeral, so instead of *Two-Way Family Favourites* I announced a Stanford Robinson concert of Elgar, Fauré and Franck. The Lying in State began on Tuesday, with a five-mile queue along the Embankment and back over the river. As my bus passed the shuffling thousands, the conductor said 'They can't all be sightseers. Would do old Stalin good to see what the people think of their King.' Cliff and I went on Tuesday, the 14th, catching the six o'clock 'workman's' train. Our place in the queue reached Lambeth Bridge by a quarter to eight and we were drinking cups of WVS tea in Westminster at nine. The long wait in the cold, the silence, shadows and whisper of feet in Westminster Hall, would have moved a stone to tears. Big Ben was striking ten as we came slowly away. Next day we returned for the funeral and found a place in Hyde Park, where the crowd was only two deep. I remember black trees, thin sunlight, dark greatcoats and relentlessly slow muffled drums. And then, quite suddenly, like a gap in the procession, a gun carriage pulled by sailors on foot. On it was the King's coffin. This was what we'd come to see and yet it took everyone by surprise. We quickly bowed our heads or turned away.

Within a year, broadcasting was preoccupied with the approaching Coronation. Television might be flexing its young muscles down the road in Shepherds Bush but in 1953 sound radio was the only way to provide live worldwide coverage of an occasion. More than twenty commentators would be needed but there was only one woman on the staff of Sound OBS, Audrey Russell, and she would be in Westminster Abbey with Howard Marshall. Brian Johnston was delegated to find four back-up girls to cover the minor human interest stories we were then allowed to call the Woman's Angle. He cajoled sixty of us to enter the auditions he'd arranged outside Buckingham Palace on five succeeding March mornings. A different band of candidates assembled at half-past ten each day to describe the scene and end their three-minute pieces with the spectacular passage of the Household Cavalry on their way to change the guard in Whitehall.

The recordings were to be anonymous, identified by numbers only. Brian had calculated that by standing on the corner and looking up Constitution Hill he could see the leading horses as they appeared round Hyde Park Corner. If he signalled at that moment it would give his contestants a couple of minutes in which to do a straight piece of scene-setting commentary before the soldiers and horses came by to supply a stirring climax to our contributions. It is surprising how much colourful talk can be squeezed into three minutes. Success depends almost entirely on a good ending which Brian felt sure the daily ritual would provide.

On Monday, Tuesday and Wednesday it worked like a charm. When it was my turn on Thursday, Brian gave us the signal to start by waving his handkerchief. It was unthinkable that the Household Cavalry should have been late leaving their barracks. Was it possible that they were delayed at Hyde Park Corner? Whatever the reason, instead of walking majestically down Constitution Hill they had to make up time and got an unaccustomed move on as they approached the Palace. We had no sooner got into our muted bits about the Victoria Memorial than, clatter, clatter, jingle, jingle, past at a trot came the Horse Guards and our Big Finish disappeared down the Mall towards Admiralty Arch.

Now what? There were minutes to fill and a hole in our homework where the Grand Finale should have been. Into the panic stricken pause which followed, a voice dropped the words '. . . the Queen unites us all . . . overseas visitors . . . native-born Londoners . . . young and old . . . and, symbolising this unity, in the crowd a scarlet-coated Chelsea Pensioner has lifted a little boy on to his shoulders to watch the Guards go by.' Purple patriotic stuff. Just what Brian wanted. But the voice was mine. The brain that should have accompanied it had run away in terror. There was no crowd to speak of. No overseas visitors. No little boy. Certainly no Chelsea Pensioner. I had as they say 'got out of the car and left the engine running'.

Having put the fiasco out of my mind and down to experience, Kenneth Adam telephoned a week or two later. 'How would you like to go to Buckingham Palace on Coronation Day?' he asked. I thought he might be offering me a ticket for a spectator's deck-chair on the roof. 'Oh yes please' I said. Then he explained that the BBC had been given permission to put a commentator inside the Palace on the day, close to the Queen's own private apartments. 'And' he went on, 'the panel of judges who listened to the audition recordings unanimously decided to send you because *you were the only one to spot the Chelsea Pensioner.*'

I felt such a cheat, a terrified cheat at that. There was no doubt the prize I had won brought its own built-in punishment for fabrication. The ensuing weeks of April and May were a nightmare of stage-fright – and guilt – which might well have sent Cliff back into the Air Force. But it didn't. Like Casabianca he stayed whence all but he had fled and tested me on the background information which flooded in from the Earl Marshall's office, the Pronunciation Unit and Room 608, Portland Place: 'A Duchess's train trails two yards on the ground, a Baroness's only one yard.' 'Correction to Note 46, The State Coach: for "bay horses" read "grey horses".' 'GULES – Heraldic term for "red" is pronounced GEWLZ (-g as in "get"; -ew as in "few").' Having thoroughly undermined the little hope I had of absorbing this wealth of required knowledge, a cryptic list of Dos and Don'ts arrived at the last minute:

1 Not Windsor Greys
2 It is the *King's* Troop RHA
3 Enthronement this time, not Enthronization
4 Bearskins, not Busbies for Guardsmen
5 Yeomen of the Guard, not Beefeaters
6 Australian slouch hats, not bush hats
7 The Act is the Crowning, not the Coronation
8 Don't say 'Can't see from here'
9 Don't talk over National Anthem
10 Court of St James's, not St James
11 Deanery of Westminster, not Diocese

12 Not State Trumpeters, but Trumpeters of Royal Military
School of Music

It was the list of contents of Coronation Day Hampers (BBC Issue)
which put the whole thing into perspective. 'Pack for One Person: 3
rounds Sandwiches a) Cream Cheese and Gherkin b) Ham and
Sweet Pickle c) Tongue; 2 Finger Rolls a) Creamed Chicken b)
Creamed Ham; 1 Meat Pie – Individual; 1 Buttered Bap; 1 Portion
Fruit Cake; 1 Hard Boiled Egg; 2 Tomatoes; 1 Apple; 1 Pear; 1
Banana; 1 Portion Gruyère or Demi Sel; 1 Bar Chocolate; 1
Penguin Biscuit; 2 Kia-Oras; 2 Straws; 1 Squill Salt; 2 Paper Ser-
viettes; 2 Paper Cups.'
    So the whole thing was really a highly organised party with mil-
lions of guests. I was only to be one of the waitresses. Just don't
drop your tray, that's all. I must admit it wobbled a bit when the
confidential description of the Queen's Coronation Dress arrived
marked 'Not for use until June 2nd. For Miss Metcalfe only'. 'Historic gown of white satin,' it read, '. . . the bodice, sleeves and
extreme hem are bordered with an embroidered band of golden
crystals, graduated diamonds and pearls', and I felt a tingle of excitement like a child at a pantomime.
    On Coronation Day all commentators had to be in their places
by 6 or 7 am according to its location. I don't know what the
imperturbable Wynford Vaughan Thomas did at five that morning but I got up from my bunk in a BBC outbuilding and put on
a face pack in the Ladies. Mrs Harmer who lived in Havelock
Road, Brighton had sent me a shamrock 'for luck on The Day' so I
tucked that into my bag and pinned the flower to my shoulder
which Cliff had given me the evening before. Then, with my new
hat and thin dress (no money to spare for a coat as well) I set out to
walk in pinching new shoes through the cold morning air to the
Palace. I showed my Special Pass to the policemen on the gate and,
bottom in, chest out, snooty as a peacock, swept across the forecourt while duffle-coated crowds watched in wonder through the
railings. Unfortunately, the Privy Purse Door was locked when I
got there and the wonder which had so warmed my back turned to
ridicule as I waited on the doorstep. A policeman remarked loudly
'I don't suppose they're up yet, Miss,' and everyone laughed but
me. The flunkey who eventually arrived to let me in was wearing
knee breeches and powdered hair like someone in *Der Rosenkava-
lier*. Not a wig. Real powder on real hair. There was breakfast provided in the Steward's Dining Room, then it was along to the Tape
Room from which I was to describe the Queen's departure for the
Abbey 'from her own front door'. Lionel Marson the newsreader,

93

was there as my number two, in morning dress and medals. And the engineer. And the threatening microphone. Below the window the State Coach was waiting with its patient horses. The Inner Courtyard was as quiet as a country Sunday. That was the unnerving part. Everything was ready for the party but would anyone turn up? Just as I felt I was lost in a vacuum, Prince Charles and Princess Anne, little children then, came noisily down the corridor and tumbled into the door opposite calling 'Mama, Mama!'. 'Mama' was the Queen and she was actually there, behind that door. There would after all be plenty to talk about. I was ready to have a go.

The seamstresses who had sewn her dress lined up to admire their workmanship as she passed. I remember smelling the lilies-of-the-valley she carried, the way she said 'Good Morning' to us all; Lionel Marson's medals clanking as he bent double in a deep bow and my own uncertain, unrehearsed curtsey. It was the first time I had 'bobbed' in earnest and the one bit of essential preparation I had overlooked.

What I said after Frank Gillard gave the cue 'We join Jean Metcalfe within Buckingham Palace' is a blank, with the exception of three all-important words, 'The Coach Moves.' The Royal Corps of Signals had twenty communications posts along the route to ensure that the whole procession, drawn up and waiting, two miles long, started off at precisely the same moment. Imagine the mayhem in Trafalgar Square if the ones in front stayed still when the men in the Mall began to march. So, in case technology failed, I was required to say 'The Coach Moves' to start the whole thing off. The trouble was, horses being horses and coaches being coaches, the blessed thing never stopped moving, even as it stood waiting to leave. That's why I can't remember the other words I plucked out of the air. In the event, of course, there was no mistaking the moment of departure. We all cried and warming messages of relief and congratulation came down the line. There was never again such a white point of terror. The rest of the day was relaxed and delightful, down to the end of my second piece, waiting for the balcony appearance at tea time. Then it was home in a train as empty as the feeling inside – 'it's all over and nobody cares'.

But they did care. It is difficult to appreciate nowadays the impact it was possible to make without pictures in 1953. Letters and telegrams came in for all of us involved, from every part of the world. Jean Barclay wrote from Queensland 'I thought you would like to know that we in Australia had good reception and your voice was particularly clear. The BBC certainly did a wonderful job.' The Twidles in Germany said 'Please accept from us all in

BOAR a very large thank you for Tuesday, June 2nd.' Marjorie Payne in Ontario was 'glued to the radio before 5 am (our time) . . . could almost *see* Princess Anne jumping up and down in delight at seeing her mother dressed so magnificently.' In Wellington, Marjorie Lawson said she listened to every word and 'loved it all. Half New Zealand felt it was in England.' Betty Allen in Otley Road, Leeds wrote 'You made one of your listeners weep (with pleasure!)', while B. M. Rae, bedridden in Edinburgh at the time, said 'I didn't need a TV set, I "saw" it all. Thank you for the most memorable day's listening I have had in my life.'

Ruth Drew, my dear old friend from *Woman's Hour*, took the trouble on holiday in Scotland to write kind comments, at the same time putting her finger right on the spot where nerves had been jumping for weeks beforehand. 'How thankful you must be that it's all over with no mistakes and you don't have to wake in a cold sweat at 5am thinking "If only I hadn't talked about Queen Victoria all the time instead of Queen Elizabeth".' Cliff understood about my terror, too, although he had more reason than most to resent it. In the note he gave me to read on Coronation morning he said '. . . it won't be long before we are together again with all tension snapped.' I agreed with him. Our nerves had been twanging of late, with my tantrums and his taut silences in response. But there was more to follow.

Royal occasions came thick and fast. There was a lot of it about. I was transferred to the Outside Broadcasts Department and loaned to Light Programme for *Family Favourites* and *Woman's Hour*, who incidentally, made me Guest of the Week on June 3rd 1953, because 'Queen Salote is otherwise engaged'. After that broadcast Mrs Dorothy Betts sent the nicest letter which was ever passed on to me by the programme's Editor: 'Hearing the Guest on Wednesday I decided I must tell you about our "Jean Metcalfe". She is a stuffed doll, 2ft tall, dressed in gaudy colours with a highly painted face. An uncle won her playing darts on the Pleasure Beach at Blackpool. My eldest girl, four years old, gave her the name because *Woman's Hour* follows closely on *Listen with Mother*. She is never just "Jean" but always gets her full title from all our family and the playmates who come to the door and ask for "Jean Metcalfe, she's the only one who fits in the push chair"!' In 1953, Mrs Betts said, her seams had all to be oversewn and she was generally the worse for wear but what a wonderful way to go – loved to death by children.

I was sent with Richard Dimbleby to cover the Coronation visit to Northern Ireland. After his years as a War Correspondent Richard had left the BBC to work as a freelance which included his television *tour de force* from Westminster Abbey in 1953. From then on anyone suggesting that it was unsuitable for so distinguished a broadcaster to take part in the radio parlour game *Twenty Questions* received the reply 'What am I supposed to do between Coronations? Starve?' It was a pleasure and a revelation to work in his team in Ulster. He always had time to give advice and ease my nerves with a joke. In spite of that I got one thing so wrong it was edited out of the evening programme of highlights of the Royal visit. In Londonerry the Queen wore a silk outfit in that brilliant shade which some see as kingfisher blue and others as sea green. I plumped for 'green for this emerald green island' and was almost taken off the air. Even then you didn't mention the colour green in Northern Ireland. Orange, yes. Green, no. Richard would never have made such a gaff.

If he was pompous as has been said, I never noticed it. When he and Dilys Dimbleby travelled a long way to one of our parties they brought a gift of new-laid eggs from their own hens and left us with a testimonial. To cover damaged plaster in the lavatory, Cliff had fixed a second toilet roll holder beside the first. On one we put smooth Bronco, on the other, soft matt tissue. Richard remarked that ours was the first house to offer him a choice of shiny paper for summer or the fluffy stuff for winter! It didn't sound pompous then – it doesn't now.

Coronation celebrations continued into 1954 and I was sent back to the Palace for the Queen and Duke of Edinburgh's return from their Commonwealth Tour. On this occasion OBs, bless their compassionate hearts, sent Cliff with me, in post suit and new bowler hat, to act as 'race reader' as it were. He spotted a Chipmunk plane flying overhead to welcome the Duke home, which made me sound very knowledgeable. This is what the diary records:

'May 14th: Today we went to the Palace for the first time together, to rehearse for tomorrow. Like anyone else's home when the family is away. Doors ajar. Dusters in corridors. Empty vases. Lights out in Great Hall, turning marbles in niches into Tussaud figures. One of the maids, Miss Ward, showed us her room. "I'm off tomorrow afternoon" she said, "Two of my friends are coming in to watch with me." Could see why. On top floor her window-seated window looked right down Mall, sun on standards, topped with unicorns and lions, and red and yellow tulip beds cut out like children's transfers on the grass. She collects glass animals and there they were surrounding signed photos of Kings and Queens. Staff love Princess Anne. "Never walks if she can run," says Miss W. "Never runs if she can dance. Always looks

forward to Thursday dancing lessons. She'll talk to anyone."
Bought two gardenias to wear tomorrow. 6d. each on a barrow.
Summer must be almost here.'

'May 15th: The sun shines. C. has his lemon gloves and bowler.
I have my gardenias. We are going to enjoy ourselves. At the
Palace by 12.30. Lunch provided – soup (unspecified), veal and
ham pie, stewed cherries and custard, demi sel cheese – but with
only four of us at huge table (C. and me, "Nogs" Newman and
another engineer) we had a job passing pickles. Controller
Supplies told us he received a Top Secret Admiralty message just
before Viscount Althorp left to join *Britannia* – "Five lettuces and
three pints of cream". Today lights are all on, doors shut and
shining, flowers everywhere. Orchids and roses, 2 great vases of
lilies from Royal Estates in Great Hall scenting the whole place,
and rhododendrons in the Bow Room where family greet the
Queen. Dozens of bouquets going into Queen's Suite including
small bunches people have handed in at back door all morning.
Behind pillars spotted small pedal car (Princess Anne's) and battery
driven model Austin (Prince Charles's). He's only been allowed
his recently because HM said he should go on pedalling until he
walked really well. It's been geared down to 5 mph but Controller
Supplies say it can still be pretty frightening, driven by small boy
and coming straight at you! At five every evening the Queen and
children come down into Great Hall and race cars among gilt pillars, rose carpets and baroque statuary. It's the only place where
they can do no harm! On arrival HM wore sovereign coloured silk
coat (some say "orchid pink", it depends how light falls) and the
children were in buttercup yellow. On the air, as I talked about
flowers, tears rose up. Could hardly speak. Embarrassing. When
they came down the corridor for their balcony appearance they
looked very brown and gave us a smile. C. and I ran down Privy
Purse stairs and out into forecourt to cheer with household (inside
railings) and crowd (outside). It's a great thing to have done and
wonderful above all to have done it together.'

The following Wednesday it was the City's turn to welcome the
Queen in the Mansion House. More gardenias for me and a morning suit for Dimbleby, although we were out of sight in the gallery
of the Egyptian Hall. Back to the diary:

'May 19th: Watched final preparations for banquet. Setting out
menus, thick as books, bound with red and white. Tables looked
better before the addition of gold loving cups. Flowers were red
carnations in banks of white iris, with taller vases of gladioli and
white delphiniums at corners. In front of Queen's place a vase of
pastel coloured orchids in case stronger colours clashed with her

dress. In fact she wore unbecoming outfit of sea green shot with black, matching hat with butterfly of feathers over right eye. Says much for her natural beauty that it still shone through. Queen Mother in apricot lace sounds like hell but looked devastating, with Catherine wheel of egret feathers in the same colour on her head. Princess Margaret wore oyster silk brocade, little cap like beech husk with a loop, like the stalk, on top. She looks more like Audrey Hepburn every time I see her. Felt sorry for the Queen. Everyone else on nice little crimson and gilt chairs but she had to have a great throne, so that no one could speak to her without leaning horizontally. Isolated. Menu: Avocado with shrimps. Scotch salmon. Norfolk asparagus. Spring chickens. Strawberry Melba and Maids of Honour. Two of the Royal Pages from the Palace served the Queen and the Duke but she ate very little. Took black coffee with 2 spoonsfuls of brown sugar. We had a look-out man posted below to signal when trumpeters were going to blow but warning and fanfare coincided just as I was in the middle of the Duchess of Gloucester's hat! It's a pity but already Royal occasions are beginning to lose their bloom.'

That was true. The rosy phrases were running out but I still had a few left for Princess Margaret's wedding – split my skirt climbing on to the top of OB van by Clarence House and never did return the safety pins an onlooker passed me – and the protracted arrival of Prince Andrew. When Television News returns to you in bulletin after bulletin, it takes a Godfrey Talbot to think of fresh ways of staying 'Still no news'. On the lines of my 'emerald green' boob in Londonderry, I said on the fourth occasion 'an air of expectancy hangs round the Palace'. Isn't it sad that you never remember the good bits of an extemporised commentary, only the things you will carry blushingly with you to your grave.

109a Bell Street

We had moved out of Jean's parents' house on the corner of Deerings Road to a small three-up three-down house on the main Brighton Road past which the Veteran Cars would run in November.

109a Bell Street was neither 'the flat in a backstreet or a home with blue shutters' Jean had written about only a year ago, but I was reminded of another letter she had written, 'What wonder there will be in getting off late buses and plunging *together* up our own steps and into our own front door. What joy to do those little things for you when you're tired, to be the first person to know the special things about you. . . .'

One of the 'special things' I had not told Jean about was my antipathy to gardening which almost amounted to allergy. Show me a garden in which I have planted a seed and I will show you a garden in which any form of cultivation suffers thence forward and the anarchy of wild weeds succeeds beyond their imagining. Which brings me to Ernie Bryant.

A long thin man with a weather-brown face and a slight stoop made his way through the open garage door and garden gate on to the grass patch which approximated to a lawn.

'Well Colonel,' he said, 'I hear you could do with a hand.' He had noticed my old RAF greatcoat in the garage. The epaulettes suggested 'Colonel' to him and so I remained until his dying day. Our Bell Street garden became the natural corollary to his full-time job with the Council Parks Department. Ernie was our unofficial rent rebate. If the Town Hall had yellow antirrhinums, we had yellow antirrhinums. Salvias by the Swimming Baths meant salvias at 109.

'They followed me home,' he used to say, looking sly and tapping the side of his nose. Once, just once, he arrived with a box of asters. 'These were given to me, all above board,' he announced. 'I brought them on the *front* of me bike.' Before long his wife Nellie came to give Jean a hand in the house and from then on, for almost the next thirty years, we were Bryant bright inside and out.

I mentioned Ernie walking through the garage just now. What I did not say was that the garage was empty. We did not own a car. 'Box 379' in the *Surrey Mirror*, our local paper, put that right. 'Riley Kestrel £150, or near offer.' We paid £125 in cash and it was ours.

Most people give their first car a name. This one was undoubtedly male, with a virile silver dynamo in front. We saw him as a well-bred old snob – seventeen owners who could all afford to wipe their feet on the cushions – and felt the name Digby would be appropriate. We were terribly proud to be in the door-slamming class at last. At his age he wasn't long for our world, of course. Webs of cracks spread across the windows, rushing asphalt could be seen through the gaps in the floor, and his troublesome cough restricted outings to a geriatric hundred miles round trip. When the time came to replace him with a humdrum, economical, tin box on wheels, the smaller car left ample space in the garage for a pram.

We were keen to start a family but here we were far from successful at first, with one mishap after another. We were heartened by wise friends who told us that it often happened but greatly saddened that it was happening to us. After the second miscarriage, which I had been told about before Jean was, we went away for a time to Scotland. Freda Lingstrom, the head of department of Children's Television, had told me to take as much time off as I wanted. I left a lot of work behind me and we went off north by car.

For breakfast at Matlock we had trout and in the Lake District it was pheasant for dinner. The Trossacks, the Highlands, Edinburgh, Inverness, Oban and the Ardnamurchan peninsula, the company of Jean's mother and father for part of the time all helped us not to forget our disappointment but to put it into perspective. We were in danger of feeling rather too sorry for ourselves.

Jean came back with a renewed determination to start a family. Our great friend and doctor, Ken Hughes, consulted John Beattie who had been his tutor at Bart's. John Beattie, as distinguished a gynaecologist and obstetric surgeon as you could wish, is a large warm friendly man and he lived on the edge of Reigate heath golf course on which Ken and I often played. We walked along the fairway of the second hole and were joined by John Beattie. 'So sorry to hear about Jean,' he said. 'Ken has been telling me all about it. I will drop in and see her if I may. We will get you a baby Clifford.'

Several years later when a small energetic adventurous young boy was crawling up through a rotten tree trunk on the heath, a voice from the garden called 'We didn't bring you into this world so that you could break your neck climbing dangerous trees young man.'

It was said with a smile but with purpose and seriousness. Guy never forgot, although it did nothing to curb his taste for the intrepid, adventurous and sometimes the foolhardy. Thank heavens. For years John Beattie would ask 'How is *our* boy?' and later 'How is *our* girl.'

14/JEAN

An Orange-Headed Boy
and a Girl with Brown Eyes

Unattractive things happen to me on television. My nose grows longer, my neck shorter and every surplus pound becomes a stone. I strut into the studios feeling fine but when a gargantuan Struwwelpeter takes over on the monitor, I fall apart with nerves. They say that people are shy because they think too much about themselves. I'm sure that's true. The fact that Esther is unselfconscious about her teeth, Claire about her weight and Libby about her nose is evidence that they think more about others than themselves. I wish I could emulate them but the peering camera reduces me to a metaphorical winkle on a pin and the first 'hate' letter from Mrs W. of Smethwick – 'who do you think you are, making an exhibition of yourself with your inane smile and hideous hands?' – is enough to send me back down my rabbit hole with the words 'Never again' tattooed on my heart. Cliff can stroll through a studio without appearing to care about his hands or feet or that wilful bit of hair showing behind an ear. 'Take me as I am' he seems to say, 'and if you don't like it, hard luck.' In my early married days people tried to get us to appear on TV as a couple, as well as individually. It would be nice to say that fear of spoiling his success deterred me, but I suspect it was more likely vanity, the prospect of tagging along behind, which put me off.

Nevertheless, a collecting box always follows a carnival and pressing invitations continued to come my way as a result of *Two-Way, Woman's Hour* and Outside Broadcasts. Billy Cotton Senior suggested I should introduce his *TV Band Show*. Dear old Bill, he worked hard to maintain his raucous public persona but, in private, he was generous and loyal. In one instance he paid the widow of a bandsman the salary her husband would have earned, for years after he died. Even so, my fondness for crusty Mr Cotton couldn't persuade me. Ronnie Waldman offered panel games and other programmes, so did Norman Collins, Howard Thomas and my one-time boss, Cecil Madden. They seemed to be dangling titbits to tempt me out of my radio cage, but I always felt, still do, that they had got it the wrong way round. Television is the cage and the number of technicians needed in sound, lighting, wardrobe and make-up, not to mention the director and all his cohorts far away and out of sight, are the bars between performer and viewer. It is an exceptional person who can squeeze through them. Sound radio on the other hand can function with no more fuss than a telephone link, speaker on one side, listener on the other, with only an engineer and possibly a producer in between. That is my idea of freedom.

It was ex-BFN man, Barney Colehan, who finally broke through. I'll bet he wished he hadn't. The programme was a live essay on the woollen mills at Saltaire in which I worried all the time about forgetting my words (the blissful teleprompter had yet to be invented) and failed to stop my interviewees turning their backs on the camera. Brian Johnston was on it too, and no more successful. At one point this normally bouncing, unworried man was seen sitting in a dark corner groaning to himself 'It's ghastly, ghastly. Most difficult thing I've ever done.' In the event, although neither of us could take much pride in our efforts, it was not disastrous enough to prevent further foolhardy Tele-people offering lollipops. *Saturday Night Out* was a series with Robert Beatty, and I was involved in one which dealt with troops and their families leaving for Germany from Harwich. It was sleeting, nose-pinching winter when Brian Cowgill and I travelled on the Troop Train from Liverpool Street Station. The intention was for the soldiers to get out at Harwich, form up on the platform and march off on the CO's command, while I followed, chatting amiably to wives and babies, as we walked behind them to the docks. All live, all in shot of course. The men lined up perfectly on the platform and we waited, cameras rolling, for them to move off. The CO's command never came. Cowgill snatched a military beret and, plunging thus disguised into the centre of the khaki column, roared 'By the left, quick march'. And they did. That doesn't sound a major problem, but it rattled me, I can tell you. Peter Dimmock's note from his snug headquarters office made no allowances. '13.12.55: you talked too much and you must remember in future not to introduce people before the camera can identify them.' Fat chance when you're knee deep in kitbags and longing to hand a stranger's baby back to its mother, soggy nappy and all. No, I was not a natural Tele-performer.

Juke Box Jury was more relaxing except when Raine Legge (later Lewisham, later Dartmouth, latest Spencer) took one look at my Brillo-pad coiffure and offered to lend me her hairdresser, and Katie Boyle suggested we could all benefit from a squirt of her 'Gold Spot' mouth spray. *Wednesday Magazine*, Television Centre's answer to *Woman's Hour*, brought in some extra money and Kenneth Adam, who had moved from Sound to be Controller of Programmes, wrote to the Editor 'I am delighted you are using J.M. She has more to offer TV than we have managed to get from her.' Kind words but his optimism was misplaced. Career Television and I parted company years ago without regret or recrimination. After all, Sound OBs at this time had opened a wide new prospect for me beyond that privileged keyhole glimpse of Buckingham Palace and life at Court.

Charles Max-Muller was the man in charge. Tall, distinguished, with a curious habit of pecking with his head like a rooster and jingling money in his pocket. Brian Johnston threatened to give him a set of rubber coins for his next birthday but he never did. Charles decided to send me in a team, headed by General Sir Brian Horrocks, to cover Army manoeuvers in Germany code-named 'Battle Royal'. My job was to provide a picture of military operations at dish-cloth level. In the process I got to know my first woman Army officer, who was to act as my own expert Personal Assistant. Her name was Major Sheila Puckle, boy-sized, boy-flat with glasses and projecting teeth. She was my lifebelt in Sennelager where speech was regimental jargon and etiquette like something through the looking-glass. One evening a Brigadier entered the Officers' Mess where we had gathered before dinner. All the chairs were taken. None of the men moved but, quick as a flash, little Major Puckle was on her feet crying 'Oh Sir, do have my seat', and the Brigadier accepted.

In 1955 they sent me to the Fire Service Headquarters in Lambeth to describe, in a programme called 'Escape from Fire', how it feels to be given a fireman's lift from a great height. Thirty years ago there were no natty little mobile packs for 'remote' broadcasting. We had sizeable handheld microphones and snaking heavy cables which didn't combine well with the essential requirement of a successful lift – shoulder-slung 'body' hanging inert and limp down the fireman's back. My diary entry on June 8th reads:

'I've never been so frightened in my life. Up the tower, looking down at little people below and hard, hard ground, heart thumping, I really thought "I can't get out over that window ledge". Smoke bombs on floor below asphyxiating, but thankfully obscuring everything, so I did. First rehearsal – halfway down ladder, slippery with rain, me clinging to mic. and beautifully slender (Oh dear!) young fireman Bailey, we were so tangled in the cable and I was falling off so much, had to swap over in mid-air and climb back *up*. Second rehearsal – no better. Had to climb *down*. Panic all round. Transmission, after secret rehearsal behind fire engine on the ground, success! Douglas Bailey went very fast – "When I go slowly you fidget." C. arrived to watch transmission. Very relieved. Glad he wasn't there earlier.'

All these activities, together with studio programmes, reviewing records, writing a newspaper column and frequently travelling as far afield as Luton to give a lecture after work made for an exacting lifestyle. Cliff was equally stretched. No wonder we were always tired. No wonder, with hindsight, these professional demands were met with private grief. Before we were even officially engaged we wrote in our letters about the children we would have one day. From Cliff in Hamburg, August 27th, 1949: 'If the children have your auburn hair I will be satisfied to the capacity of my heart. We will be so proud of them on the first trip home to let the family see the family . . .' When our first baby was conceived in 1952 we were overjoyed. It was a time when career wives had babies at their office desks. Mary Quant was said to have been back at work within days of her first-born's arrival. Dr Grantly Dick Read preached about the ability of African women to produce children like berries from a bush, picking the newborn infant up and walking on without a backward glance. I believed it all and carried on working, but, of course, no one can have everything without paying. Four months into the pregnancy I paid. Diary: May 16th, 1952: 'Hospital. Everyone started rushing around with hypodermics and gauze masks but somehow I knew it was useless. Every thought was of Clifford and how I wished he was here.' 'May 17th: We lost the baby early this morning. Sister phoned C. who rushed over to see me. Both he and I are reassured by our certainty that what matters most is that we are *together*. Our first big shock and small tragedy. We've come through, holding hands.' Don't worry, we were told. It's not unusual. With a first baby. At four months.

When the second child was on the way I took greater care and counted fewer chickens. Even then no one suggested leading a quieter life. That wasn't fashionable in 1956. As time went on it became a very public *Woman's Hour* pregnancy. 'Diary: January 30th, 1956: Heavy tramp of tiny garments begins to sound in office

– 5 pairs bootees, 3 matinee jackets (2 blue, 1 pink, so boys are leading at the moment) and an Edwardian medical book of singular horror and high colour. Page one "Disability of Infants – Hare lip"! Think beautiful thoughts?' March 22nd was the day before my maternity leave was due to begin. Mabel Constanduros and Janet Quigley both remarked on my look of well-being. 'Young and radiant' they said, 'the picture of healthy motherhood.' The next day I was rushed into hospital where a team of distinguished medical men tried unsuccessfully to keep me that way. Our own remarkable young doctor and closest friend, Ken Hughes, stayed with me most of the night only leaving to spend two miserable hours with Cliff breaking the news that the baby was already dead. Ken explained to him that it was important, for the sake of future pregnancies, that the birth, even a stillbirth, should go ahead as normal. He and Cliff had to spend the next twelve tormented hours keeping this secret from me. It must have been their longest day.

A nurse subsequently told me that the child was a boy – 'small flat ears, high cheekbones and dark wavy hair' – which should have made us even more desolate but somehow it didn't. We were consoled to know we had the ability to produce a handsome son or daughter and welcomed the medical advice that we should take a holiday, get our breath back, then start again as soon as possible. 'Diary May 26th, 1956: Among the multitude of flowers which came today was a little pot "from your girls in the florist's shop", a huge arrangement from C. "to look at" and another, just freesias and hyacinths, "to smell". Miss Lingstrom rang him to say "take a month off if you like" and *Woman's Hour* made a very touching announcement at the end of the programme. I begin, by evening, to feel better.' Of course, that 'better' feeling ebbed and flowed like a tide, but the loving, caring messages which flooded in kept us afloat when we might have been overwhelmed by introspective tears.

Dear, dear Jean
If sympathy can sustain anyone, you should be upheld by the biggest wave we have ever known. In Sheriff's tonight the staff were talking of you. Janet was in Yarner's at lunchtime and heard the waitresses feeling for you. I found the studio – the usual heterogeneous collection of 'worthy women' sitting in absolute silence. I hope so much love can uphold you in the courage Cliff said you were showing. He certainly is. Dear Jean, I prayed all yesterday afternoon and evening off and on (the phrase that kept coming to my mind was 'the peace of

God that passeth all undertanding'). Hoping that in trouble
you could catch a glimmer of it. May God bless you, and keep
your courage up. In love – and admiration,
Joanna S. M.

If ever I feel hesitant about writing to a friend who is grieving,
those letters written in 1956 remind me that nothing else can bring
such sustaining consolation.

Following the kindly medical advice we went on holiday to
Scotland where the size of the landscape put our problems into perspective. Six months later our third baby was on the way. This
time I behaved like a frail Victorian. Two months into the pregnancy I gave up work. Everyone on *Woman's Hour* patted me in
valediction like a retiring police horse and I lived life on a sofa with
such dedicated sloth it would have put Madame Recamier to
shame. No, that's going too far. I didn't lie about all day and every
day, but there were long spells of rest and the lightheaded enjoyment of simply being at home. Cliff took on more than his share of
the catering and my Mother did our shopping. We had been too
shaken by our previous experiences to be proudly independent
now. Towards the end of the waiting time our doctor friends pre-
scribed sedatives and a diuretic, an impractical combination when
you are struggling tranquillised to the lavatory at four in the morning. Like a drunk in charge of priceless china, I staggered once too
often and fell, valuables uppermost, fracturing a toe. Far from
fussed the doctors cheered. 'The baby's fine and if we leave that toe
just as it is without a splint you will have to stay right where you
are for the next three weeks. No hopping about.' And for me no
option.

At the end of August, no longer limping but walking on air,
Cliff drove me to Casterbridge Nursing Home. 'Diary August
26th, 1957: Lovely to arrive in warm starchy room and see cot
airing and nightgowns and nappies laid out *for use* at last.' August
27th: 'Ken said "You've got a son". I mumbled something about
having in that case to let him go off to New Zealand if he wanted
to! He was bathed by the fire and dressed just as though he'd been
here for ages. I *am* glad he's a boy. Now feel we've lost nothing but
time'. August 28th: 'He lies in his cot by my bed, our son, with
Titian coloured hair, sleeping, hands over his face like a small red
squirrel. He's a long baby. Hope he's going to be tall. Thank God,
we didn't really know how much we were missing last year.'

Choosing names for a child is the merriest of pastimes. We had
decided years before to stick to those which had a family connection and so avoid passing fancies which might cloy with fashion.

My father's name was Guy although he was always known as Joe. 'Guy Michelmore' we reckoned would make a goodlooking by-line when he was working for *The Times*. Cliff's mother's maiden name had been Alford so she could be perpetuated too with the initial 'A' in the middle. Thus Guy Alford Michelmore entered our world and we were the happiest of families. Well, almost the happiest. We had a child, a son, but, never satisfied, wouldn't it be perfect if we could achieve a daughter too?

There was almost too much joy to be contained when she was born two years later. A pretty little dark haired thing with slanting eyes and fine features. There was no mistaking that she was a girl as she lay asleep in the frilly cradle we had prepared for her at home. She was always going to be named Jenny. I loved Leigh Hunt's poem 'Jenny Kiss'd Me' and Cliff often called me Jenny when I was in his good books. My mother's name had been Gwen. Our greatest regret at this time was that she did not live to see her granddaughter but Jenny Gwen Michelmore carries her name and many of her loveliest qualities. So now, in 1959, our family was complete with a son and a daughter as unlike each other as their parents were when they met and, it seemed, as complementary. Guy – strong, balanced, witty and even-tempered. Jenny – resilient and determined, fiery sometimes, then so tenderly understanding and kind you wonder if this can possibly be the same person. There's a bit of both of us in both of them and a great deal that is uniquely their own.

Fans and Fenella

I hope I have conveyed how much the concern of listeners meant to Cliff and me when we lost our second baby. Among the letters we received was one in familiar blue handwriting from a woman who had sent me a cheque for £100 a few months earlier. That first communication had been lucid, but cramped on the page, from an address in Kilburn. The gift, said the donor, was 'in gratitude for pleasure derived from past broadcasts'. The cheque was of course returned the following day but it had been tempting. Our joint salaries came to little over £2,000 a year. I remember saying to Cliff 'it was like sitting on a gold mine without a pickaxe'. The tempter however was not to be so easily dissuaded. A replacement cheque arrived within a month. This time, with BBC approval, we donated it to charity, sent a receipt to the generous listener and that, we thought, was that. In May, after the announcement that we had lost the baby, a further letter arrived in the same small tight writing enclosing a cheque for £500 'for a recuperative holiday'. One hundred had been tempting. Five hundred was too much to begin to contemplate acceptance. There was no alternative but to seek out this teasing Good Fairy to explain and personally hand the money back. We looked up the name 'M. S. Sherlock, Miss' in the phone book alongside the correct address and set out.

The road was on the left before the railway bridge and there was the house on the right. A tall, gabled, stuccoed building, once handsome, but now decayed and divided into flats. A card by the bell indicated 'Sherlock' in the basement, below the front steps to the right. We both felt nervous as we went down and knocked but our apprehension turned to astonishment when a little old *man* opened the door. This must have shown on our faces because he immediately explained that the phone had been installed by his sister, long since dead, and he had never bothered to change the entry in the directory. He was cultured, gentlemanly, and clearly a recluse. The basement was empty except for six kitchen chairs and hundreds of mouldering copies of *The Financial Times*. He was, he said, in the process of moving but the odour and cobwebs were anything but temporary. He refused, adamantly, to take back his cheque so we finally left it on a dusty ledge and ran. It was a saddening, undignified encounter. We wished we could have done something to help but that would only have prolonged the wrangle, so we regarded the episode as closed.

Four months later, in October, a letter from solicitors in the Temple told me I had been named 'residuary legatee' in Mr Sherlock's will. So the frail old gentleman had died soon after we saw him, but there could hardly be much 'residue' from such poverty. For some reason I have now forgotten, I insisted on going alone to keep the appointment with his legal representatives. I don't think this had anything to do with hiding the amount from Cliff for we had always shared everything, good and bad. It was more a matter of needing to stand on my own feet occasionally, instead of expecting him to prop me up as he had done hitherto. As I climbed the twisting stairs to the lawyer's office I remember feeling strongly the strange presence of the little man we'd met in Kilburn. He was in my mind's eye in every detail, chuckling to see me so intrigued. In the Dickensian office, on the stroke of 10.45, two solicitors and a bank representative sat waiting in a row of leather chairs. They told me Mr Sherlock had taken his own life. He had not been insane and his only relatives were distant cousins with whom he had no contact. Since they were of substantial means they would not contest the will in which he left me three thousand pounds. To us in 1956 any sum of more than three figures was for saving, not spending. It did not, as they say, change our lives but we certainly felt, for the first time, supported by a cushion of security and that, I'm sure, is what our benefactor wanted. He's probably chuckling still to find himself so powerfully remembered.

It became clear in the weeks of press probing which followed that the mysterious Mr Sherlock was in every sense 'a fan', someone who had latched on to my voice as an extension of his lonely life. Radio is often said to free the imagination more than television. In my experience, the dottier the mind the greater the freedom. A lot of dotty people contributed to my mailbag in those days. One woman said I was responsible for all disasters in the world because I played 'heathen music' on Sundays and why didn't I bring down the wicked price of nylons while I was about it?

Then there was 'Fenella'. Her world was every woman's dream over the washing up. Most of us know it only exists in our minds and keep it there. She gave the fabricated gothic tale another dimension, almost reality, by writing it in a series of letters and sending them to me. The writing does not immediately suggest a 'Fenella', nor the paper, sometimes lined, torn off a pad, sometimes embellished with a fuzzy bunch of very mauve violets. The story they told has the grandeur of a Cartland novel.

9.3.53.   c/o 134 Rawling Road,
                                                              Gateshead 8,
                                                              Co. Durham.

My dear Miss Metcalfe,

I hope you don't mind my writing to you, but I felt I would like to send you my best wishes on your 3rd wedding anniversary which you celebrated on the same day as myself. . . . I came home to England in Oct. of last year to await the arrival of my first baby, who was expected about the end of April. However, on the 26th of Feb. I had been arranging some flowers in a large vase of the room and stepped back to admire them, forgetting about a large footstool just behind me. Down I went with a bang and that started things. My wee son was born two days later two months before time. He is such a scrap, hardly 6lb at birth but what lungs he has. My old nannie with whom I am staying while in England declares that his daddy in Singapore can hear him when he cries. . . . There are a lot of things we have in common. Not only the same wedding day but names also. Before I was married I was Fenella Metcalfe and now I am Mrs Torquil Clifford. See what I mean. In addition to that I have a small sister called Jean. She was born in Singapore and was only eighteen months old when my daddy and step-mummy and her were imprisoned by the Japs. Daddy in his own hospital compound. He is resident MO in a private hospital just on the outskirts of Singapore. My own Maman died when I was two, and I was brought up by Grandmère in Paris until I was eight, then I came to Northumberland to Gran and Gramp and my daddy's nanny took me in charge. In 1938 daddy married again and went to Singapore where he has been since. It wasn't until 1946 that I was allowed to go to him. By then I was 22 and had never seen my baby sister who was 6 years old. . . . In 1948 Romance with a capital R entered my life. A new arrival in the shape of Dr T. Clifford came from Scotland as assistant in the hospital. A braw Scot, and I fell in love just at sight. Well on March 4th 1950 we were married. . . . My husband is a Highland Scot and is very proud of his old name which has been in his family for 279 years. The eldest in every generation has been called Torquil. . . . You might expect that my scrap will rejoice in his daddy's name but Tor wants him called Bill for his dearest friend who was killed in the last war. They went to school together. His death was a sad blow to Tor. . . . I am longing to get back to him and to show him his son and now that he has arrived so promptly I will be on my way as soon as I am on my feet again. My nannie is going to sell up here and go back with me. She refuses to let me out of her sight now. I do not know how she will cope with my household. Can you imagine a Scotch nanny, a Chinese amah, a Chinese cook, 3 Malayan houseboys, an Indian gardener and his two assistants. To complete the household a Highland Boss Man and a half-English, half-French Mem. . . . Nannie is 69 but is quite unafraid of leaving her native land and going with me. Like me she has no one left in England now and feels she would like to spend the rest of her life bringing up her 3rd generation. She was a young girl when she took charge of my father and now she is so happy to be looking after my son. I hope, Miss Metcalfe, that your life is as happy as mine and that one day you will have the supreme joy of that day when your son is first laid in your arms. It is one of the most marvellous moments of your life. Now the only wish I have left is to be back with my darling Tor again. . . .

With belated good wishes for your future.

> I am,
> Yours sincerely,
> Fenella Clifford

P.S. I hope you will excuse the awful writing but I am still in bed.

In April 'Chapter Two' arrived from Fenella, still in Gateshead but now stricken with a mysterious and becoming paralysis of the legs.

'Nannie cabled for Tor and he flew here and was with me

112

within four days. . . . Now my baby is 9 weeks old and I am still tied to my bed. . . . my husband is captivated by his small son but wonders if I have produced him all on my own as he is all me, even the auburn curls. Only his eyes are blue and mine are green. Tor's gift to me to celebrate his arrival is a beautiful Indian necklace of seed pearls with hanging dew drops of aquamarines . . . . I have a most glamorous nightie of pale green lace [no Marks and Spencers nylon for Fenella you'll notice] which has had cod liver oil spilt on it. . . . I thought perhaps Miss Ruth Drew would have some advice to give. . . . Some weeks ago Tor was listening to a football commentary and asked Nanny who was giving it. That's Mister Clifford, Miss Jean's husband was her reply. Just as if you were both part of her family as Tor and I are . . . it won't be long before September and perhaps by then I shall be completely well again. If we go home by boat we shall be staying in London for a week or two. Would it be at all possible for you to make the acquaintance of my family. Perhaps you could come to our hotel for cocktails. I should so much like to show them to you.

Oh yes please, Fenella. Show me, show me! But it was not to be.

June 18th

My dear Jean,

After making a tentative arrangement to entertain you I have to apologise and tell you we shall not now be coming to London. We have had some rather shattering news about my father and my husband has already flown back to Singapore. He was most urgently needed at the hospital. . . . The shipping company has already removed my car and baby's pram so that is one worry less. As soon as we get settled here, nannie and I shall be flying from Newcastle airport to Paris. I have some property there left me by my Grandmère, the deeds of which I am having transferred to my son . . . we had Bill christened on June 6th at the little church adjoining 'The Manor' my old home. The Rector who christened him did the same for my daddy and me too. . . . Afterwards I laid the foundation stone for the new church hall which the villagers are erecting in memory of my grandparents. It is simply inscribed, 'In memory of Sir Colin Metcalfe. [Another coincidence. My brother's name is Colin.] . . . Squire of this parish and of Elfrida his dear wife.' It was rather a sad moment

113

for me as this was the first time I had been back to my old
home since my darlings died. 'The Manor' is now let on a
fifteen years lease and I hope by then we shall be able to take
up residence again. The Home Farm and cottages on the estate
had to be sold. I do wish you could see 'The Manor'. It's long,
low and rambling built round three sides of a courtyard and
covered with ivy. The East Wing is not very safe now and is
closed. It was built in 1541, and the strange thing about it is
that it was built for John Metcalfe who was married to Lady
Anne *Clifford*. . . . When looking through some magazines I
came across this picture of the West Wing. [A photograph of
an unnamed but majestic mansion was enclosed. And
referring to the Coronation broadcast Fenella says] I met
Princess Elizabeth when I was 'Presented' at a Presentation
garden party just after the war. . . . I am more than sorry we
have not been able to meet. However, it may yet be possible I
shall be coming to England again next year to open the Hall
for which I laid the foundation stone. . . .

Enclosed with this letter, as if by mistake, is a page of one Fenella
was sending to Torquil. It contains these memorable sentences
'What do you think Tor darling. Paul is now Major General. He
and Nicola are staying with Jean at 'Sparrow Point'. . . . I have
had the architect's report on 'The Manor House' and it seems
there is no hope of saving the East Wing. It will have to come
down. Another headache.'

But the East Wing's dry rot was not Fenella's only headache.
Worse was to come. One last letter arrived in August from
Gateshead, same paper, same pen, but this time in painstakingly
disguised script.

Dear Miss Metcalfe,

Will you forgive a grieving old body writing to you. You will
be sorry to hear that Dr Clifford and my dear Miss Fenella are
both dead. The doctor was killed at Singapore on July 23rd.
He and a young medical orderly were returning from Kuala
Lumpur after visiting a patient. One of the back tyres burst
and the car skidded and both were killed outright. Sir Robin
Metcalfe, his wife and daughter Jean flew here to bring the
news, and found my bairn in the throes of a heavy cold. She
collapsed on hearing the news, the illness turned to
pneumonia and she died on Aug. 10th. She was so utterly in
love with Master Torquil that I think she had no wish to go on
living without him. History has repeated itself. Thirty years

114

ago Master Robin then just twenty years old brought his baby daughter to me, her maman having died at her birth, and now I have my dear bairn's wee son to love and cherish.

The letter was signed 'Nannie Forrest (Mrs)' and ended with these words: 'Before she died Miss Fenella said ask Miss Metcalfe to think of me when I've gone.' [I did Fenella, I still do.]

Doris B. began as another Mills and Boon correspondent but sailed closer to the wind. She made personal contact. An unprepossessing girl who talked into your mouth instead of your eyes. This time I was seduced by greed. She had a car she would like to sell us cheap. We needed one badly so I smothered suspicions that we had another 'Fenella' here, albeit a downmarket one. But first, said Doris, let us go to the theatre together then we could meet her fiancé, Stephen. He was a brain surgeon. Of course. Doris, Cliff and I used the seats she had paid for but the fourth remained stubbornly empty. Stephen had been called to an urgent operation and never materialised. Our dreams of a cheap car failed to materialise also. We never met Doris again but she wrote some years later apologising for stringing us along and saying she was now 'well again' and back at her old job as a nursing assistant.

Would that all such encounters had positive endings. Whatever became of T. Nelson Fribbins for instance? Once met, never forgotten. His grease-stained trilby, plimsolls and impenetrable glasses remained in my mind long after he waylaid me outside Broadcasting House, but the only contact after that was through the post – a sequence of pasteboard weighing machine tickets with '10stone 9lb' on one side and 'Yours sincerely – T. Nelson Fribbins' on the other. And where is Gerald W. I wonder? The fuller the moon the dottier his letters became, but it was more disturbing when doorstep confrontations developed. One Sunday, in the weekend quiet of BH, I came upon him in an empty corridor, eyes wild and voice ranting that next time he would bring a breadknife with him. Thankfully there was no next time, perhaps because, after hospital treatment, he is now living at peace in some eminently sane suburb like Surbiton.

During the war a woman regularly arrived at Broadcasting House demanding to see Frank Phillips 'the father of her child'. One night she caught me as I was leaving the building and we stood outside on the pavement while she told me 'the wicked things Marjorie Anderson was saying about her on the wireless'. Knowing that disembodied voices tend to nourish persecution

115

mania I reasoned with her that Marjorie was too kind and sensitive a person to wish harm to anyone. None of this had any effect. If anything, she became more excited. Then Kath, one of our jolliest lavatory attendants, came to join us. She patted the woman's hand and said firmly 'Next time it happens dear just you turn your set off. That'll do the trick.' Away she went, the dotty one, never to return.

Olive Flack was rather fun. Eccentric but fun. After a long correspondence from Salisbury she came to London to meet me, an exceedingly thin woman with beady, birdy eyes peering between a good felt hat and a Burberry raincoat. 'Do take care of your teeth, dear,' she said. 'Somebody else's are not the same.' When I asked her whether she was Miss or Mrs she lowered her voice. 'I was married a long time ago, dear, but I had to leave Flack because he turned...' she paused then whispered 'v-e-g-e-t-a-r-i-a-n!'

Many letters in those days told tales of appalling hardship. One, from South Wales, concerned the struggles of a deserted mother with a desperately handicapped child. 'Although he is six he cannot stand' she wrote, 'he is incontinent and shuffles about the floor on his bottom. The whole house stinks. Have you any old woollens in which I can wrap him?' It sounded like something from *Nicholas Nickleby*. No one could ignore such horrifying destitution so I asked the local WRVS to see if any long-term help could be arranged. The writer, it emerged, had no child, no truant husband. She was in the rag and bone business. Stirling people, the WRVS. They helped me with Dinah R., too, in East London. Dinah's letter explained that a visitor was writing at her dictation because she was blind and crippled and lived alone. The account of her life was painful to read ... up before dawn to clean the front step so that no one should see her dragging herself along the ground; taking hours to prepare a meal; shunned by everyone in a wilderness of misery. I phoned her sometimes. Godfrey Winn, wrote an article about her glowing courage and miraculously spotless home. Together we asked the WRVS to intervene. It took several visits for them to discover that Dinah was neither blind nor crippled, simply undervalued and seeking attention. I didn't blame such able performers for trying their skills on gullible Godfrey and Jean but I did resent the holes they made in the already thin supply of goodwill available.

There wasn't much goodwill about when someone living near us in Reigate began spreading stories about the divorcing Michelmores. If we could have distanced ourselves sufficiently to study the anatomy of the rumour we might have been less distressed, but it was uncomfortable to find people we knew well believing what they heard, when we hadn't even been huffy over breakfast. Time had to pass before the bare bones began to emerge. The tale was that I had absconded with a handsome doctor who lived nearby. As it happened we had never met but scandalmongers are not deterred by details like that. People round about lapped up the story then spat it out in all directions, with embellishments. Once started there was no stopping its spread. The press began enquiries. They visited pubs and shops in the town, phoned local doctors and called at nearby houses where our neighbours' well meant 'no comment' or 'we do not enquire into other people's business' only fanned the flames.

Then a particularly keen reporter visited Dorothy Rolph. She was a twinkling, down-to-earth lady from Sunderland who helped me in the house and was more than a match for this kind of nonsense. Haven't you seen the Michelmores going into the house together? Have you asked them to their faces? she wanted to know. Dorothy had the good sense to tell us what was going on and only then did we discover what other friends had been too discreet to report. The rumour once begun had spread like burning bracken to London and beyond. Parents at the children's schools had heard it. Some had even passed the news abroad. I suppose we should have been flattered by such interest. The innocent doctor certainly wasn't. He later left the district but the woman who had planted the pernicious seed remained. She was, we understood, someone whose overtures to him had been rebuffed and this was her revenge.

Once we realised the scale of the 'infestation', Cliff and I felt we should talk to Guy and Jenny about it before their schoolfriends did. This was twelve or fourteen years ago. As we spoke, at our most sincere and grave, their shoulders heaved with stifled giggles, 'Who on earth would want to go off with either of *you*?' Now that hurt. That really did hurt. For a moment I had rather fancied myself as the imagined scarlet woman. It had been quite rejuvenating. But in the incredulous eyes of our children we could never be anything more torrid than balding Pa and spreading Ma. In an instant we were back to normal. The gossip continued to send out fresh shoots for another ten years. That's the trouble with rumour. You can't spot the source to spray it with weed-killer and the more you cut it down, the healthier it grows.

Perhaps it is the facelessness of a radio voice which adds credibility to such stories. Generally there is a lot to be said for being physically anonymous. At the height of *Two-Way Family Favourites'* popularity I was rarely recognised, except when I was trying to slope into one of the seedier bargain basements. It was always there, when my hair was unwinding in the rain, or my stockings were laddered, that the cry went up 'Oo, come over here Glad, Edna, Pauline. It's Jean Metcalfe. I recognised her voice.' Never in Fortnum & Mason's. I liked to buy an occasional pot of fishpaste there, rubbing shoulders with jars of caviare in mink coats. Disappointingly, no one ever batted an eyelid. But once, when I telephoned about something for a friend, the silky voice at the other end said 'May I say how nice it is to see you in the store, Madam?' 'Why didn't you say so at the time,' I asked and he replied 'Oh we're not allowed to do that in this establishment.' I still put on my best to go shopping at Fortnum's. You never know who may be watching.

Mind you, it doesn't pay to go around giving the public a thrill until you are sure they are your public and not someone else's. When Cliff and I were first married and I had dreadful trouble getting our tyrannical boiler to work, I was halfway through washing my hair when there was a ring at the door bell. A well-preserved gent stood on the doorstep, his face as pink and smooth as if it had just shed hot towels. In an organ-rich voice he told me his car had broken down and could he have some hot water for the radiator. With my hair still lacking its final rinse I said 'yes' through gritted teeth and he carried off three, no four, buckets of the precious stuff. By then the tap had run cold. With a final theatrical bow he said 'You have been so kind, madam, now I shall tell you. I am Raymond Newell and if you listen to your radio at six thirty tomorrow you will hear me singing in "Grand Hotel".' I was so maddened by the loss of hot water I screeched after him as he went away 'And if you listen on Sunday at twelve o'clock you'll hear *me!*'

Jeanne Heal, a famous television lady, wrote a newspaper column at the time and the story turned up there a few weeks later as having happened to her. Was it possible that Raymond Newell had struck lucky – or unlucky – twice running? Would he really have continued to drive with a leaky radiator? Or did he make a habit of pouring hot water down drains in order to drum up an audience? The suspicion persists that someone was short of column inches that week.

My life in radio brought me into contact with a bizzare but enthralling collection of people; some sadly insane; many vicious, inspired perhaps by envy – 'I hope all your brats die like this one', 'Why don't you get off the air. Can't your husband support you?' and so on; a few delightfully entertaining like Sgt Jesus Omati in Africa whose English was learnt from Shakespeare and a business correspondence manual – 'If thou dost love, pronounce it faithfully by an early reply', and, of course, 'Fenella of The Manor'. Among them all one jewel shines out undimmed by time. Her name is Biddy Bass.

Thirty years ago there was a group of housebound people who called themselves 'shut-ins'. Biddy was one of them. We were introduced at a hospice, St Columba's, in Swiss Cottage, where Biddy spent occasional holidays in the Matron's flat. Being an invalid she needed the constant care Miss Howlett could offer. I was to be the surprise guest at her birthday tea-party but I was the one who was surprised. Far from exacting pity, Bid was warm and outgoing, hungry for every bit of news, large or small, from the outside world. It is that intense interest in what you are saying which continues to make her the best listener I have ever known. If the Queen came calling I can imagine Her Majesty telling Biddy how her feet ache on receiving lines.

When Matron Howlett retired from St Columba's Biddy came to us for holidays. It was our equivalent of The Season with visitors flooding in from all sides to pour their secrets into her ear. Even Ernie used to squat beside her deckchair in 'his' garden and Nellie, duster idle in her hand, would stop and talk. We went on picnics, where she could smell heather and hear bees and Guy and Jenny together could bump her wheelchair over hummocks while I worried and Biddy just laughed. With Cliff's help we took her as far as Brighton to look at the sea for the first time since childhood. Biddy brought wonder back into our lives. Now she and I are too old for such adventures. Cliff sends her cards from all his travels and I go to Chesham at least once a year. That's where she lives with her tiny, indomitable sister, Doris, who always plays the understudy but is really the rock on which she rests.

Everyone should have a Biddy in their lives. Her independent spirit more than compensates for all the tricksters and pathos peddlers in the past. But then Biddy is saner than any of us.

Learning the trade

In these days when the entertainment business showers self-congratulation upon itself like confetti and radio and television awards are as common as garden gnomes, it is hard to imagine why in the early 50s the *Daily Mail* Radio and Television Awards were such sought-after accolades. These were not just voted upon and handed out by one's colleagues and friends. They were given according to the votes of a number of listener and viewer panels across the country and the winners were announced together with the runners-up in about a dozen different categories.

In 1953 our great friend Gilbert Harding won the Radio Personality award, Richard Dimbleby was second and Jean was third. 'They must be mad or desperately searching for variety but still it's exciting' she told her diary.

It was exciting on two counts. Jean was the first ever woman even to be mentioned in her category, and that when she was not even thought to be in the running. Jean was the 'unexpected newcomer to these lists and deservedly so' wrote one critic.

We waited for our invitations to the Ball: only one came and that was for Jean – on her own. Jean was furious and when she is angry it is best to keep your distance and hide the notepaper. She is inclined to fire off a really sharp stinging letter. Frank Covern got the full Metcalfe blast. 'I would not dream of going to any such event without being in the company of my husband. I wonder why it is that the men are invited together with their wives and I am expected to go unescorted by my husband.' I will spare you the rest of her broadside but we were both disappointed. Frank

Covern (and the *Daily Mail*) desperately tried to pretend that they had sent separate invitations, and that mine had got lost in the post. I never did believe them. Two days later a letter arrived inviting me to the dinner. When Gilbert Harding heard about it he joined in the row on our side. At the event we all very much enjoyed ourselves.

There was, for a time, a danger that I would become 'Mr Metcalfe', consort to the queen of radio. Whilst I delighted in sharing her successes, I was determined enough to want to be *me* and to make my way in broadcasting under my own name and by my own efforts. This could have been a problem but because Jean was so sensible and understanding it never was. We each needed our own identity.

The moment of Jean's crowning came in 1955 when she left Gilbert Harding and a field of distinguished broadcasters behind her and was voted 'The Personality of the Year'. Now she will not put this bit in her chapters, so I am going to. For both of us it was a splendidly happy time. Well almost.

My wife has a way of anticipating events and imbuing them with all the horrors imaginable. Even some horrors that are unimaginable. The days leading up to the awards ceremony and dinner were predictably tense. She is not good on the days before any event. It had happened when we became engaged. It was worse when we got married. But this was at least a professional occasion and she was a perfect professional. An uneasy air seemed to pervade the house; responses to ordinary, everyday simple questions evoked short, sharp responses; nerves became grazed rather than red raw, silences between us lengthened and the cool atmosphere dropped another degree or two to chilly.

It was the worrying about the hair, the dress, the shoes, the bits of jewellery, the show and what would they make her do, and what would she be expected to say.

Nights became sleeplessly shorter. The hours in the day were filled with shopping and beautifying, and there were her normal duties of a BBC announcer to be fitted in between whiles.

I appreciated her problems and tried to help by being there, on hand, fetching and carrying.

January 30th, the Scala Theatre. We were all there. Every member of the Metcalfe family now present to share the pride. The Master of Ceremonies, Franklin Engelmann, read out her list of achievements: Royal commentator, *Family Favourites, Woman's Hour* and so on. You could see why she was *The* Personality of the Year. A sketch in which she played the straight part to Arthur Askey went well. Then she carried off the tall silver microphone on the purple velvet lined case.

Telegrams of congratulations flooded in. Wilfred Greatorex dubbed her 'The First Lady of Radio', and the *Daily Mail* reported 'Gilbert Harding who has so often dominated one category or the other, relinquishes his title as Personality of the Year to Jean Metcalfe, with Freddie Grisewood, Raymond Glendenning, Wilfred Pickles and Eamonn Andrews in the running.'

Jean had looked absolutely stunning in her kingfisher blue satin dress with shoes dyed to match, 'to keep my courage up among the celebrated "Archers",' she said. There were diamanté earrings and bracelets all glittering. In the foyer afterwards, Jean was looking almost shy. There were orchids in celophane as well as the award to be carried home. We were all proud enough to burst.

In fact we very nearly achieved a family double with the awards that year, because my programme *All Your Own* was runner-up as the Most Enjoyable Programme on Children's Television, to the winning *Appleyards*.

We were often being asked to broadcast together, but it was becoming increasingly difficult to run two diaries as one. We were able to do the odd thing together but not often enough to become a double act. That was something that we were determined to avoid. We were separate people at work, which was just as well. The BBC preferred it that way. At least the hierarchy did, as we had already found out to our cost earlier.

Woman's Hour was running a series of talks by husbands and wives under the title 'How We Met'. I was invited to tell our story. I had already done a number of talks for them. The story of our first car and the tale of the mice we shared with our next door neighbours had gone down well so would I now tell the story of our meeting?

All the previous scripts had been joint efforts and so was this one. It must be said that we had our doubts about it but the script was written and *Woman's Hour* set the date for the broadcast. A few days before it was due to be heard the Controller of the Light Programme banned it. 'I feel that I ought to write you a note of explanation about taking out Cliff's script ... I have nothing against the script itself which I think is quite charming, but after consultation with DHB we both felt it would be quite wrong to bring out into the open on our wavelength the private life of a member of staff.'

The Home Broadcasts Committee at their meeting minuted 'Agreed that this series should not include romances of members of staff'. The newspapers were delighted to be able to bash the BBC for their 'stupidity', for being 'typically crabby'. The *Daily Mirror* weighed in with 'Once again the Bad Barons of the BBC have stepped in. Out of an orange-coloured sky – crash, wham – alacazam – radio hits love in the eye . . . and off comes the broadcast . . . for the BBC's 11,000 employees love must always be locked out. So cut those luncheon dates the rest of you, smother that smile. Back to the microphones you rabble! Spring is not for you.'

Jean had replied to the BBC with one of her letters. 'I would like you to know that it was only after a deal of persuasion that he undertook it . . . he had no wish to cash in on something which has had far more publicity than we would have chosen . . . we expressed the wish that it should be done anonymously and just as effectively.'

This was my wife protecting her husband. I was impressed because this was a side of her character which until then had been hidden from me. She could, when roused, be angry.

We did not work together very often although producers tried to get us to. I was number two to Jean when she covered the return of the Queen and Duke of Edinburgh from their Commonwealth tour and we did cross to the Channel Islands for a television programme with Nicholas Crocker but apart from that we were now steadily ploughing our own furrows. Jean's was somewhat straighter and steadier than mine. Her routine was pretty well set with regular programmes. Mine strayed all over the country, taking me anywhere there were a few guineas to be made.

Housewives' Choice on the radio paid well and was fairly undemanding, there were sports commentaries and other outside broadcasts coming along rather more frequently, and I still did a lot of programmes with the West Region of the BBC which had its headquarters in Bristol. In those days the region stretched from Land's End across to Brighton, up to Reading and again west to Gloucestershire. It was an enormous area to cover. It was a marvellous region to work in, because the people were, almost to a man, West Country people. They were rock-solid friends, who rather spurned the frenetic approach of the big name-making city slickers in television and radio. The pace was firm and measured but the quality of the programme was high.

Frank Gillard set the standard and his staff followed in his highly professional footsteps. Stuart Wyton, Laurie Mason, Michael Bowen, Nicholas Crocker and Peter Bale all helped me along in those days. Peter Bale and Nicholas Crocker started a new regional television 'opt-out' magazine programme. That is, they opted out of the London programme, and in its place put on their own, which came from the newly converted television studio in Bristol. *Westward Ho* was its title and wide was its brief. There was the inevitable shortage of money in the programme budget but no shortage of ideas or enthusiasm. I was to introduce it.

We did a series of small film reports for which Peter hired a little Bolex camera. It had no sound, so we made silent films on which we dubbed sound effects and commentary back in Bristol. It was all very primitive but it did let us take the television cameras out into the region, and we made a programme aimed specifically at local West Country people. The locals did not always approve of what we did. On one occasion the mayor of a Dorset town came to the studio, not in his capacity and office as a mayor, but as the Town Crier. Lowering the tone of the town yelled the local paper – a disgrace! Nonsense we replied, it goes to show what a marvellous town yours really is.

There were studio items along more predictable lines such as local cooks preparing local dishes. On one of these I was rightly reprimanded by Frank Gillard for not suppressing a giggle when a Wiltshire lady was describing making a pie with a pig's head. Her opening words were 'Now whatever you do don't forget to make sure you get your half of the brains. They sell these heads by halfs and some butchers will try and keep all their brains. Get your half. They are the tastiest bit of the whole head.' I do not know why I found it so amusing. At the time it was.

On another occasion we had brought into the studio an ancient machine which had recently been discovered in a house in Bath. The machine purported to turn out Latin hexameters at the pull of a lever. As the man demonstrated this literary computer it started to come apart at the joints but undeterred he kept pushing and pulling at its levers. Latin words dropped into window slots with a clank and a clutter. I was totally bemused by the whole affair.

In the studio that evening were two young men who had just been taken on by the BBC as general trainees. Two out of hundreds who had applied I was told. One of them came across the studio floor to take a closer look. 'But that is not an hexameter, it has only five instead of six feet.' Now as one who does not know a Latin hexameter from an iambic pentameter, I was quick to profess my ignorance. Just as well really, as the young BBC trainee was Alasdair Milne, Hons Mods Oxon '52 and now Director General of the BBC. The other was Patrick Dromgoole, Deputy Managing Director of HTV. Little did I know that Alasdair was to play a significant part in my future career with the BBC. Within the year he was at Lime Grove in the Television Talks Department and very soon we were to work together on *Highlight* and then *Tonight* on which he was a producer and then Editor. For ten years there was to be a firm thread to our friendship and working partnership.

You can never be too careful, you never know who it is you are meeting on the way up!

The West Region provided me with my first flavour of reporting on holidays, with their *Holiday Express* and they also gave me a great many other jobs as well. In those pre-motorway days the journey from Reigate to points west took time but it was time well spent. The learning curve was pretty steep. It just had to be.

Back in London apart from my regular children's television commitments, there came more sports reporting to be done. The odd interview spot on other people's programmes as well as an increasing number of radio programmes. The vast emptiness of my freelance diary began to fill up. There had been times when I would chase to the ends of the country for 5 or 6 guineas. Now in '54 and '55 I had to be a bit more choosey. I was beginning to be offered an enormously wide variety of work and the time was coming when I was going to have to make up my mind if I was going to continue to be a jack of all trades or if I was going to try to concentrate on one, or perhaps two.

Highlight

The BBC was building its new home at White City at the same time as a ferocious debate about the future of television was raging inside Parliament and across the country. The call had been made for a new competitive channel, commercial television. It was not to be operated and financed on the lines of the American system but would be essentially British in concept. It would have a system of licences and controls that would hopefully avoid the worst excesses of the American network.

Battle lines were drawn with the Labour Party and many Conservatives advocating its rejection. Lord Hailsham saw it like Caliban emerging from his 'slimy cavern'. Lord Esher though that it would be a 'planned premeditated orgy of vulgarity'. Hugh Gaitskell said 'It is utterly wrong that what we see in our homes should depend upon the desire of advertisers to make money.' Whilst Ness Edwards asked 'Do they really think that education, religion and subjects of social importance will be supported by beer, pools and pills?'

L. D. Gammans, however, the Assistant Postmaster General, took the opposite view, saying 'If we can trust people in this country to go on a jury, to give them freedom to buy a paper, or the right to vote and decide the destiny of this country, then I think they can be trusted to look at a little picture on their television screens.'

After a great deal of wrangling and lobbying, on July 30th 1954, the Royal Assent was given to the bill enabling the start of commercial television to begin within a year. The BBC also let it be

126

known that it, too, was going to expand its services by operating, in due time, a second channel of its own.

All this was encouraging for freelance people such as myself. The other changes that were in the wind had yet to be settled but one thing was certain: ITN were going to make their news and news reporting much more personal than anything as yet seen on the BBC. Christopher Chataway, a hero figure from the athletic track, was to be one of the 'personality' reporters, and Barbara Mandell and Lynne Reid Banks were named as two of the women reporters to be introduced.

For its part, BBC Television news was still in the hands of sound radio at Broadcasting House: a hold they were reluctant to relinquish. As for the projected 'news-in-vision service' there had been a great deal of dallying and dithering. For Fleet Street there seemed to be no threat from television as a source of news. The press agreed, in the main, with Lord Simon of Wythenshawe, Chairman of the Board of Governors, who as late at 1953 believed that 'A great majority of items are of such a nature that they cannot, either now or ever, be shown visually ... of those that could be shown on television the majority occur overseas, often in distant countries and it will be a long time before television films can be flown from all over the world to London on the day on which they happen. Television newsreels will, of course, continue to develop and be of the greatest interest and attraction but there is surely not the least possibility that they will ever replace news on sound.' John Snagge thought that the introduction of news readers would be a distraction only satisfying the curiosity of those who wanted to put a face to a name. 'I do not believe that any real value will be added to news and newsreel by showing the announcer in vision.'

Until March 29th, 1953 there had been no live television news bulletins. Then they were confined to headlines read after the end of the evening's programmes. Not exactly part of the fabric of television broadcasting. ITN was going to force a number of changes on the BBC, although the Corporation argues that they were in the process of changing without the uncomfortable boot of competition.

The BBC style had been stuffy, rigid, impersonal and scrupulously objective. News was news and all alone and ever more shall be so. No other department was allowed to encroach upon that sacred ground watched over by the mandarins at Broadcasting House. It was a closed shop.

Television talks were located at Lime Grove where I worked. 'Talks' was a departmental title hung over from sound radio some twenty years before. On television it had meant, until the advent of film, an illustrated talk. But now under Mary Adams, Leonard Miall and Grace Wyndham Goldie, Talks would become Current Affairs and form an important new block in the building of the BBC Television Service.

Across at ITN the new style reporters and newscasters were to emerge with a manner of questioning and interviewing that would raise many a Corporation eyebrow. At Lime Grove, Talks were starting new programmes which would also raise Broadcasting House eyebrows once they realised what was happening.

There was an influx of new producers and programme assistants. Some came on loan from other BBC departments, others direct from universities. They were nearly all young and ambitious to make this television service hum. Ludovic Kennedy, Chris Chataway, Robin Day and Reggie Bosanquet were not going to have it all their own way when they arrived on the screen at ITN, if Lime Grove had anything to do with it.

Panorama was being revamped and ordered to be a window on the world. Film cameras were being used much more effectively. Richard Dimbleby was to introduce it. More reporters were to be recruited. New sports programmes were started covering weekend fixtures and they needed reporters.

Lime Grove was where you had to be if you wanted to be part of this expanding and exciting service.

I was at Lime Grove most of the time, meeting other producers in canteens at lunchtime, or at the White Hart or British Prince in the early evenings. It proved to be a useful address to have.

At the end of 1955 Jean was to write 'This had been his golden year. . . .' But before the year even began, we had been approached by a number of agents, directors and producers to move across to the new 'commercial television'. The inducements were considerable compared with what we were being paid by the BBC. On offer were a cigarette commercial; a shoppers' magazine programme – which was one long commercial; would I become the head of a children's television department or join Associated Rediffusion as a 'jack of all trades'? The BBC had got wind of the approaches and soon we were being called to the upper floors of Broadcasting House to talk about 'the future'. Jean was against going commercial, so we settled for as good a deal as we could get with the BBC. Jean was to be promoted to grade A1 and moved across as an outside broadcast commentator, which would also allow her to do other programmes. I was put on a guarantee of £1,500 a year for my work on sound and in television. At least we could plan ahead with some sort of certainty, which was rare luxury for anyone who sets out in the world of the freelance where fortunes ebb and flow at alarming rates. One day your face will fit and the next you find you are out of favour for some reason of which you are not aware. It is rather like roller-skating on ice. Part of the time you go where you want to, the rest of the time you go wherever you end up. Frequently that can be on your backside without a cushion.

Jean's mother could not understand why they were going to pay us more money just for staying with the BBC. It was only when the work took me away so often did she realise that we were not being *given* the money. We had to earn it.

'Tonight I am alone, and so it will be until Sunday. Between now and then C. goes from Richmond to Glasgow to Liverpool to London to Plymouth, mostly on sleepers. He says "think of the 85 guineas". I say "I'd rather have 50 gns and 35 gns worth of you", the Diary records.

On September 22nd, 1955 Independent Television started broadcasting. On the same night a new BBC programme appeared on the early evening schedules. It was introduced by MacDonald Hastings with the words 'Let us first consider a slight case of murder'. Mac then interviewed the two script writers who had 'killed' Grace Archer in the evening's episode of *The Archers*. It was a publicity stunt timed to coincide with the ITA launch and it grabbed a lot of headlines.

'You feel badly about the death of Grace Archer. What do you think we feel? But why blame us. Do people blame Shakespeare for the death of Desdemona?' Ted Mason the scriptwriter asked MacDonald Hastings.

I did not see *Highlight* that night but rather wished I had next day. At either end of Lime Grove there was a pub. Turn left out of the door and at the Prince you would find children's producers and some people from drama. Turn right and at the Hart you would find the 'Young Turks' of the Talks Department, together with the sporty crowd.

'Did you see *Highlight* boy?' asked Donald Baverstock. I admitted that I had not. 'Take a look tonight, tell me what you think tomorrow.'

I did not see Donald for a day or so. The next time we met was in the backroom of a terraced house which he was using as an office. A row of houses had been taken over to relieve the crush for office space in the main studio blocks. It was becoming overcrowded. Caravans parked between buildings were also used as offices and every available cubby hole in the building was pressed into service as a film cutting room, editing suite, dubbing theatre or hospitality room.

The number of television licences in the country had by now reached four million and the transmitters covered a potential audience of thirty million. The television staff, which had only a few years before been numbered in handfuls, now topped the thousand mark and they all had to have somewhere to work. So not only did the BBC rent houses in Lime Grove but they also took over houses in neighbouring roads. One, used by us in children's programmes, turned out also to be the home of a well-known prostitute, which was a bit of a diversion when John Hunter-Blair was busy assembling *Blue Peter*.

Donald Baverstock's *Highlight* came out of a tiny backstairs studio which also doubled as a continuity suite. By the time you weaved your way around two cameras and a microphone boom there was just about enough room for three small chairs. The gallery outside could barely hold the vision mixer and director with one other onlooker jammed in the doorway and the sound control room was little bigger than a shoebox. That was where I was to learn my trade as an interviewer, or rather, that was where I was to re-learn my trade as an interviewer.

Donald and Grace Wyndham Goldie were fond of quoting the first-ever party political television broadcast by the Conservative party in which Leslie Mitchell, it was said, grilled the then Prime Minister Sir Anthony Eden. According to them, and again I did not see the broadcast, Leslie had to ask the PM 'Your opponents accuse you of being a war-monger. Is there one iota of truth in their allegations?'

As far as *Highlight* was concerned, that sort of questioning was only for the archives. There were questions to be asked and they would not be delivered by an interviewer on bended knees or tugging at his forelock. They were adamant about the requirements of their ten minute programme.

'We should be asking the questions the viewers would ask if they had thought of them. We must be asking the right questions and getting the answers.'

The production team was small but they had big ideas and an eye to the future. Donald Baverstock, Alasdair Milne, Cynthia Judah and Geoffrey Johnson Smith were all in the office when I was asked if I would 'do a week' to help them out. On the instructions of Cecil MacGivern they had to look for another interviewer. I already had quite a lot of work to do and it would mean that I would have to finish my afternoon productions and then get across to their offices to prepare for the interviews an hour or so later.

We tried it for a week.

Jean watched and reported:

'C. did *Highlight* well. Joined him and producer for a drink. Latter is v. pleased with him. More impressed than *I* am I think. . . . Want him to take fortnightly turns on it but he feels, and I agree, that it is too often. But experiment has obviously been worth while for prestige and practice. Also brought some property ham home.' (Diary) The ham I took home had been beautifully sliced by me. I am now, and have been ever since that night, rather good at slicing ham, and so I should be. When I went to the *Highlight* office the twelve minutes we had to fill that evening was it seemed, all accounted for. Edward Westrop, a financial journalist was to be interviewed about the state of the economy, the Welsh schoolmaster and author Gwyn Thomas was to be in the Cardiff studio to talk about a new production of *Under Milk Wood* and, finally, a young Scot who had just won the World Ham Slicing championship would top the whole thing off for a couple of minutes. In the event, the lines between London and Cardiff somehow failed to make the connection and Edward Westrop trying to beat the rush hour had come by an underground train which had broken down at Notting Hill Gate. So all we were left with was our ham slicing champion.

I reckoned we deserved to have some of the ham after having talked about the damned stuff for twelve long minutes. A justifiable perk.

Against my imperfect judgement (and Jean's agreement) I did take on the job of interviewing on *Highlight* for a fortnight at a time. Geoffrey Johnson Smith alternated with me. The interviews and studio items would cover 'anything that will interest us and, by definition, the viewer. If it pleases or disturbs us, then it will please or disturb the viewer,' Baverstock told me. They did just that.

Those who ran the programme were an intellectually tough little bunch. They were the hardest task masters that I had ever worked with. If they felt that you had let them down, their criticisms were as devastatingly sharp as they were precise. Their praise was given much less often and was less fulsome when it did come.

At one point Jean reflected. 'C. is not happy with *Highlight* tonight, because of a panicky producer.'

There were quite a lot of nights like that, when after a day in the studio producing *Playbox, All Your Own, Children's Sport* or *Real Adventure* with Adrian Seligman, I would then have to change gear quickly and start swotting for *Highlight*. There were also sound broadcasts to be done as well, so even though I was still in my mid-thirties, I would often arrive home feeling as though I had been through the mangle. Poor Jean had to put up with a lot.

Independence Day said the Diary.

'C. asserted his independence too, saying frightfully rude things to innocent motorists along Bell Street, because he had waited minutes to get out. I nearly got out at Reigate Station. Quite unnerved me. This brought to the surface long suspected feeling that a tranquil mind is sought. Face is getting drawn with wear and tear. I must control myself,' she wrote. 'C. I regret to say is too far gone. Anyway, an unlined face looks silly on *Highlight*. . . . Very good *Highlight* tonight incidentally, with a piece on the Queen in galebound Oban, and an American who bought up the entire stocks of two antique shops because "they like chandeliers in Texas".' Other days brought the famous.

'C. talked to Andre Maurois tonight, and would have paid them to do it. Suez situation seems to be settling a little into indecisive inactivity.'

'C. interviewed Louis Armstrong tonight for the whole of the programme and loved him. At Command Performance he turned to the Royal Box and said "Rex this is for you . . . sir". His mother was a prostitute and he was sent as a juvenile delinquent to a children's home. Now here he is, the best paid musician in the world they say. Uses hands all the time to demonstrate with or without trumpet. He says if his lips crack (he wipes them all the time with witch hazel) they'll have to come and hear me *sing*! Clearly a sincere man who loves every moment of his music. (He has been telling me all the questions he did not ask).'

Among the questions I did not ask on the air was one I had put to him when we were in the taxi on our way to Shepherds Bush.

'You travel all over the world, you never stop working and playing the horn. How do you keep so fit and well?' Which he was.

'Every mornin' I get into the bathroom and I sit on that seat and I play that just like a horn. Regular, regular, regular.'

His wife had smiled in agreement at that graphic description of the Armstrong morning ablutions. I liked Louis Armstrong, but there were those for whom 'liking' was not the word.

Krishna Menon was such a man. He was the Minister Without Portfolio in the Indian Government and on his way from the United Nations in New York back to India. Grace Wyndham Goldie who knew him, had persuaded him to appear on *Highlight*. I wish she had not.

Krishna Menon was the leader of the Indian delegation to the United Nations and he had greatly upset the Secretary-General of the UN and the Americans by his intervention in the discussions upon the problems of the Far East. In particular Menon had been having talks with Chou En-Lai about Formosa and the Chinese

Nationalists' possible evacuation of the off-shore islands. There was also a Summit meeting in the offing. Menon had been to talk with Harold Macmillan and the meeting had clearly not gone well. Krishna Menon's dark face looked even darker as he sat downstairs in the hospitality room. His bony fingers gripped the top of his walking cane and his steely eyes shot out devastating looks like lazer beams at anyone who dared even approach him with talk.

The interview had been very carefully pre-planned. The detailed questioning had been worked out by Alasdair Milne, with help from Grace Wyndham Goldie, and other members of the team. I had very little time to contribute or even to read all the background briefing, press cuttings and so on. That was a mistake.

On the air his grip tightened on his cane and his eyes blackened. Each question was dismissed with a standard short, sharp rebuke. 'That question is not cast in the mould of my thinking.'

Each delicate, calculated probe was blunted and I was totally crushed. Chou En-Lai, the Russians and India, Formosa and the United Nations, Indian relations with Britain, all failed to elicit any response from the Indian statesman.

I had learned a number of valuable lessons. You cannot go into any interview *over* prepared. Under prepared yes, but never over prepared. Another thing I was learning was that a guest can be gentle, mild and pleasant right up to the moment the red light in the studio goes on, and then he can turn. With disturbing suddenness he can become vicious, explosive, and unmanageable. You must be prepared for anything to happen. One day it will.

All this, however, was giving me valuable experience as I got to interview a variety of people from Spike Milligan to Gian Carlo Mennoti, the Italian composer, and cover anything from the field of politics, sport, the arts or international affairs. A new kind of television journalism was at long, long last beginning to develop at Lime Grove and the sound of alarm signals were heard in the corridors of Broadcasting House. The old-fashioned deferential conservative BBC style was out. Questions were now put in much more colloquial language and with a respectful firmness.

The whole tone of television interviewing was changing. Interviewers were now looking for answers of some substance and were not prepared to accept anodyne evasions. That was particularly true when it came to politicians and members of the establishment who, until then, had almost demanded to be treated with kowtowing deference, even with gentility. In the past they had expected to get away with banal generalisations and to use television as a platform for putting forward their programme and policies unchallenged.

Broadcasting House was expressing concern that *Highlight* was already encroaching upon the sacred ground of news. What we were able to present as comment was, they argued, all too often making news itself. The other concern they had was the style of the interviewing techniques being developed and practiced by us. The complaints ranged from the accusation that we were unneccessarily rude, to those who said that we were acting, all too often, as prosecuting counsel in a television kangaroo court.

'We do not "grill",' Baverstock told a journalist. 'We ask sensible, relevant questions and look for sensible relevant answers. We *do* examine subjects and motives but we do not set out to be other than polite in carrying out that examination.'

At Independent Television News the interviewing style was attracting even more criticism than ours was. Their brash, abrasive, edge upset a number of interviewees but their bulletins attracted large audiences who soon came to appreciate the new look news programmes. This new look was eventually to spread across channels to the BBC. The anonymous news reader was to be replaced.

Remember there had been no regular Television News Bulletin on the BBC until late in 1955. Now the time had come when, despite John Snagge's belief that no 'real value will be added to newsreel by showing the announcer in picture', news readers would have recognisable names, faces and voices. It was the dawning of the day of the 'personality' news readers, newscasters and interviewers.

In America they were, according to Sig Mickelson, Vice President of CBS, 'firmly wedded to building the broadcast around the personality', in a much modified form that was now happening in Britain. That was the background to the beginning of what came to be called 'The Golden Age of Television'.

We have, by now, all heard the saying that what was gold in 1955 could be the dross of 1985. In 1955 we had no idea that we were embarking upon anything new, other than producing some programmes to fill the increasing number of hours that the demand for television was creating. Not only was I doing my fortnightly stint on *Highlight*, I was also taken on as a reporter on the new sports programme called *Saturday Sport*, and on *Panorama*. That took me travelling even more. My first *Panorama* story was among the gold diggers of North Wales, where we attempted to uncover the hoards of gold we suspected lay hidden in chests of drawers. We never did, but we did get into the mine workings at Dolgellau. We went to Liverpool Docks and reported that in the rebuilding programme about to be implemented, a famous Liverpool institution would be lost. The Punch and Judy man would lose his pitch. Liverpudlians rallied to the call. Rob Wilton, Ted Ray and Arthur Askey all cried 'shame', but the Punch and Judy man had to move on. So I had a strike rate of two failures and no successes in my first two stories. There were more serious moments for me on *Panorama*. The Suez crisis had us abandoning everything we had planned in order to interview ministers, members of parliament, churchmen and anyone it seemed who had anything relevant to say about Suez. I talked with a number of pilots who had been responsible for guiding the ships through the canal. They were convinced that there were no other pilots who could take their places. There were, of course, but at the time we did not know that.

Then at the same time came the Hungarian Revolution. Richard Dimbleby was sent off to Austria to report on the plight of the refugees who were getting out of their country. I was called upon almost to fill the Dimbleby chair in the *Panorama* studio. At that time *Panorama* was the BBC's flagship and Richard was seen to be the man at the helm. Rock steady, reliable, totally in command and ready at a moment's notice to cover any national or international event or incident. He was the BBC's first reporter, its most experienced and trusted, and one who had been in the front line throughout the war. He had flown on bombing missions to Germany and he had been in battles on land and at sea. Now he was 'the voice of the nation' according to *The Times*. So his was not a comfortable seat in which to sit.

Diary: November 20th. 'Tried to get Vienna and only did so for ten worthwhile minutes. An ancient lady from Wallingford was declared to be the oldest person living in Britain; she is 108. She still goes to church, reads the *Daily Telegraph* because it is cheaper than *The Times*, but it does have "all those deaths" in it.'

'R.D. not pleased that C. filled his chair on *Panorama*.'

There are other entries in Jean's diary which reminded me of otherwise long forgotten programmes.

'C. had to rehearse the Bolshoi Ballet commentary. Very funny – my earth-voiced husband doing ballet introduction.'

'We all watched Bolshoi on television. C.'s commentary on the introduction was good. So earthy you could not possibly mistake *him* for one of *them*. Ulanova was wonderful.'

One entry I do remember well was an encounter at Victoria Station. 'Story of the day belongs to C. but he's bedded down too far to tell it. He missed the 7.49 (which I was on) and having drink in Golden Arrow bar was interrupted by small voices. Round pink heads of hair saying "Scu me are you Clifflemore?" Satisfied, they returned again with a screw of sticky paper containing sweets. "Have a fweet Clifflemore". *That* is recognition to warm even jaded cockles of hearts.' So it was. Recognition was becoming a bit of a problem, and not only for me.

'C. caused accident today. He was standing at gate watching the traffic go by when one car-load turned to stare and ran into something coming the other way. Lucky they did not hit *him*. Good thing they do not hate *Highlight* or story might be different.'

There were, of course, times when it paid to be recognised such as the time we went to Paris and as we boarded the Golden Arrow we were shown into a private saloon all of our own by the conductor. But generally coming to terms with being a piece of public property was I must admit a bit difficult. It does take some getting used to. After all, few of us are born to it, are we?

Everyone lays claim to have been on the receiving end of those self-deprecating stories. The lift boy who eyes you and because he has not seen you on the screen for a couple of days says, 'Didn't you used to be Cliff Michelmore?' That never happened to me. At St Ives the other one really did. 'Don't I recognise you from somewhere?' 'I don't think so,' I reply in feigning modesty. After a suitable pause the questioner comes back. 'Ah thee's the butcher in Blackburn.'

My most face-slapping moment came on a train going to Bournemouth. A jewelled lady: 'I first of all thought that you were that nice Mr Dimbleby. Now I see you are that nasty Mr Michelmore.'

From the start, I found it very difficult to take criticism or personal attacks wisely or well. I learned painfully and slowly that if you have an ego that is easily bruised or colossal vanity, then being in the front of camera is an uncomfortable place. That screen may protect you from the verbal brickbats that viewers throw at you in the privacy of their own homes, when they disagree with what you are saying or doing, but once you emerge from a television studio and appear in public, then you are fair game as everyone's Aunt Sally. Gilbert Harding once reminded me 'Nobody asked us to go on radio or television. We did it because we wanted to, and we must be prepared to take the consequences of our own actions. You chose it – accept it.'

There are those, albeit very few, who can live with the transient fame of the entertainment business and remain polite, even when asked for an autograph in mid-spoonful at dinner. My wife is far better at it than I am but then I have always put my apparent (occasional) surliness down to my innate shyness!

It was no good, however, hiding behind a screen of shyness when it came to being a commentator at football matches. Crowds loved to see us struggling up vertical ladders to the tops of grand-stands from which we usually did our television commentaries. By 1956 I was beginning to take on more and more television commentaries and less and less for sound. We did it all on film with the commentator telling the cameraman when to roll and then doing his commentary simultaneously. At the end of the first half of the match the film would be rushed by despatch riders to laboratories for processing, then on to the cutting rooms for editing. As the match finished, we would belt to the waiting aircraft or car and leg it hot-foot to the studio. Within a few hours the films would be all cut and ready for the late evening round up. Kenneth Wolsten-holme was the number one commentator and got the pick of the matches, but I remember covering some memorable matches such as Bournemouth's little FA Cup run against Spurs and Manchester United, and the first game young Denis Law ever played in the League for Huddersfield. Those were enjoyable weekend jobs, but they did take me away from home a great deal, which I did not like. By the end of 1956 things were happening which would change the pattern of life for us both.

December 20th. 'C. very elated because huge new proramme – a Baverstock/Milne Enterprise is mooted and they want C. to intro-duce it. Forty-five minues every night. This really has been his golden year.'

With the new programme, so far unnamed, it was proposed to fill the gap in the programme schedules between six and seven o'clock in the evenings. That had long been known for the 'Toddlers Truce' – a period which was deliberately kept void of programmes, so that parents could put the toddlers to bed. Com-mercial television could no longer afford to have that much poss-ible remunerative revenue earning time unfilled. In February 1957 they were going to fill it and the BBC would be forced to follow suit, with among other things an extended version of *Highlight*. It would be called *Tonight*.

Tonight

1957 began expectantly. Jean could look forward to having a baby again and it was confirmed that it was due sometime in late August. 'No salt eh? 1,200 calories eh? Is it worth it eh?' We were both delighted. This time every care was to be taken in spite of Jean's joke in the diary.

Jean kept on saying that she wanted something simple, a musical instrument on which she could make a noise. For 30 shillings I bought her a mandoline because the tutor that went with it claimed that the beginner 'may soon attain a proficiency gratifying to himself and pleasurable to his friends'. She said that she was delighted but I cannot recall ever hearing Jean put plectrum to strings. Dust has gathered these past thirty years on the battered case and all those spare Black Diamond and Cathedral G strings wound on silver plated steel. She did learn to play Scrabble and cribbage; she did leave the BBC for her maternity leave very early and she was cosseted by us all. I rather enjoyed having her home. 'Had breakfast brought to me in bed. Eggs. At this rate we shall have a bouncing Rhode Island Red', she wrote.

Jean's 'First day of freedom. First day in purdah,' was on February 11th. That was a week before the first night of *Tonight*.

The 'huge new programme' which had been mooted in the late days of '56 had been accepted on a trial basis. It was to run for forty-five minutes five nights a week. A number of titles had been suggested, Roundabout After Work, Watch, Witness and Outlook among them. They settled for *Tonight*: Look Around with Cliff Michelmore.

Grace Wyndham Goldie, Donald Baverstock and Alasdair Milne had been investigating the problems and possibilities of filling the Toddler's Truce period and had come to some definite conclusions. Not least that it could be done. Grace Wyndham Goldie wrote 'Any such project would have to be related to our assessment of what the audience would be likely to be doing between 6pm and 7pm. We made enquiries. They would be coming and going: women getting meals for teenagers who were going out and preparing suppers for husbands who were coming in; men in the North would be having their tea; commuters in the South would be arriving home. There is no likelihood of an audience which would be ready to view steadily for half an hour at a time. What seemed necessary was a continuous programme held together by a permanent staff of compères, reporters and interviewers, but consisting of separate items so that any viewer who happened to be around could dip into it knowing that something different would soon follow and that he had lost nothing by not being able to watch from the beginning.' It was then to be a cross-departmental programme with an outside broadcast, and a light entertainment producer as well as its own senior film editor. It would, first of all, have to find a studio of its own. There was no room at the existing studios which were under strain and in danger of bursting at the seams, and the new studio centre at White City was a long way from being able to provide any space. A studio was discovered in a small Kensington cul-de-sac, St Mary Abbott's Place. It had been used for training, now it was put back into working order and it was to be the home of *Tonight* for the three months of its trial.

Back in the terraced houses of Lime Grove which were the offices of *Highlight*, Baverstock and Milne were getting programme ideas, recruiting staff and looking for people to become regular contributors. The vogue word at that time was 'style'. This was a new programme, a totally new concept for British television and in order for the venture to succeed there had to be a new team assembled to work under the *Highlight* editors. Little did any of us think that the programme would run for eight years and clock up 1,800 editions. It was the first regular nightly topical magazine programme. From out of its inventiveness, experience and ideas were to come, *That Was the Week That Was* and *Whicker's World* among many other well-known series. It was to bring into people's homes for the first time the familiar faces of Fyffe Robertson, Trevor Philpot, Alan Whicker, Macdonald Hastings, John Morgan, Polly Elwes, Derek Hart, and many more; it was to give the freedom of its film cameras to new directors of the calibre of

Jack Gold, Michael Tuchner, Kevin Billington and John Schlesinger. It was also to become part of the early evening television ritual in many homes across the country. A BBC watcher observed 'If *Panorama* had to become the voice of authority *Tonight* was rapidly to become the voice of the people.'

There is no doubt that *Tonight* was fortunate in being the right programme in the right place at the opportune time. Bernard Levin, a prominent and regular contributor summed it up. 'It's journalism nowadays is very common but in those days it was not common. It was inquisitive and thrusting, its interviews were edged without being bullying and the whole thing summed up what people really wanted. It was popular because that was the way people were feeling. Viewers wanted *Tonight* and wanted it that way because it was helping to shape the mood and attitude of the country, and the mood and attitude of the country helped shape *Tonight*. I always think that if it had started five years earlier it would have had no effect because the country was not thinking that way. If it had started five years later it would not have been arresting and original. It got the timing absolutely right because it got the mood of the country absolutely right.'

The concept of the programme was that it should be on the side of the audience. It would look at people and events as ordinary people looked at them, and take the attitude and ask the questions that ordinary people would ask. At no time were we to ask a question that was out of sympathy with the viewing public or give the impression that we were superior. All these years later it seems strange that we had to be so conscious of the patronising attitude which had been so prevalent in many BBC programmes.

As Bernard Levin has said the mood and attitude of the country was changing. The Suez débâcle of three months before had left Sir Anthony Eden a physical wreck and he resigned, leaving the way clear for Harold Macmillan to become Prime Minister. Hugh Gaitskell led the Labour Party, the sixties had not yet started to sway let alone swing, and package holidays and jet travel were by no means part of everyday life.

Nevertheless by those late 1950s television journalism and camera crews were travelling abroad much more and *Tonight* was to add to their numbers. It was also getting somewhat easier to persuade people to take part in programmes. We had often found it difficult to get guests to come into the *Highlight* studio but now television was growing up and out, and its widespread popular appeal meant there were few who would now pass up the chance of their views being heard and their faces seen by millions. In our very early days, for example, the audience was measured at two and a quarter million. Within months the audience figures reached five million and then they rose to a peak of just over seven million viewers after we moved to a slightly later time.

Tonight was always an experiment. It had less than three months in which to prove that it could work. Some ideas were proposed, tried and thrown out in a matter of days. Others lasted a little longer. The review of the day's papers and the conjuror did not stay with us very long. Nor did a young man brought in from the Cambridge Footlights. Jonathan Miller performed a short series of sketches in which he threw himself all round the studio floor acting out his observations on such diverse topics of the day as shopping in Charing Cross Road and the death of Nelson. It was Nelson who did for Jonathan. Every man, woman and boy who had ever stood to attention at the raising and lowering of the white ensign bayed for his blood after that Nelson sketch. So he left us. The topical calypso was a much more permanent fixture at the start of each programme. This was a cunning device which allowed the programme to comment upon the happenings of the day in a way in which the BBC was certainly not allowed to. Many of the calypsos were written by Bernard Levin and sung by Cy Grant, Rory MacEwan or Noel Harrison. Some were quite sharp in tone and content but nobody complained so we just kept them going.

Our first night was on February 18th, 1957. The tiny studio at St Mary Abbott's Place was crowded. Upstairs was the room in which we talked to the interviewees. Downstairs a sliding hatch opened on to a minute kitchen which was the canteen. Outside the studio window a small courtyard allowed us a bit of elbow-room occasionally.

We transmitted live the draw for the next round of the FA Cup direct from Lancaster Gate. We had got in the Bournemouth manager, Freddie Cox, because they had disposed of the mighty Tottenham Hotspurs in the previous round. To everyone's delight they drew Manchester United. To everyone's sadness it was not a glorious encounter when the match was played.

The initial response was mixed. 'This was television at its best – alive vital, immediate – and just what *Tonight* must brim with to be a success. Unfortunately it did not brim last night. Geoffrey Johnson Smith interviewed the Dame of Sark. A young actor, Derek Hart, talked to Ed Murrow the famous American broadcaster. Too much time was devoted to the controversial statue of Aphrodite at Richmond, about which 10,000,000 viewers couldn't care tuppence.' The *Daily Express* did go on to say that it had 'possibilities'.

The *Daily Telegraph* said that 'It had variety, some spice and reasonable pace but lacked compelling interest and gaiety.' Gay had a different meaning in those days.

The *Tribune* ticked me off. 'The whole extraordinary *mélange* is conducted by Cliff Michelmore, who sits about on a desk making bad jokes and smiling hopefully at his viewers. When they are not producing items which any intelligent toddler would reject with scorn, they hit upon some first-class ideas.' In general the view was that we could and must do better.

Cecil McGivern was prepared to reserve judgement, at least to us. But we were made aware of his views which were not very complimentary. Our friends in *Panorama* were pleased at the cool reception we were given in those opening days. There never was any love lost, won or exchanged between *Tonight* and *Panorama*.

We were always in trouble. Even such a non-controversial interview as the one we had with Lady Baden-Powell reached up to Board of Governors level. We had shown an old piece of film of BP doing some physical jerks which was considered by the movement to be in bad taste. As for the questions we asked about Scouting behind the Iron Curtain, they were beyond the pale. We avoided Scouts, Cubs and Girl Guides for some time.

There was no avoiding the long tread of touring filmstars on their publicity rounds of the studios. We had more than our fair share of them. Geoffrey Johnson Smith, handsome, sandy hair, bright fresh-faced always seemed to get the sex goddesses to interview. Brigitte Bardot was beautifully outrageous and flirty with Geoffrey when he interviewed her. After which the Controller Programmes Tel., Kenneth Adam sent a note saying 'The sexiness of this item sent my eyebrows up'. The raised eyebrow was part of the attitude of the programme; irreverence, enterprise, enjoyment, liveliness and importance were some of the other ingredients of the series which brought me into direct contact with the famous and infamous, the celebrated and the notorious. It was an exhilarating experience but also an exhausting one.

What C. P. Tel. made of another of Geoffrey's encounters is not recorded but those of us who were there all have our own memories of Jayne Mansfield. She was taken into our one tiny dressing room – she emerged wearing a leopardskin affair which looked as though she had been poured into it. It hugged every bit of her body tightly down to her ankles. She shuffled across the studio floor and stood leaning against a piece of scenery. She declined the offer of a chair with a lift of the eyebrow. Then a stool was tried, at which point Miss Mansfield politely informed us that 'This dress ain't for sittin', this dress ain't for walking, all this dress is for is leanin'.'

And lean she did. Geoffrey gently blushed throughout the interview but with his peachy complexion and in black and white it did not notice. Anyway he was *the* gentleman of the team and carried the interview off with considerably more aplomb than I could have done. Geoffrey did get his own back by cunningly taking the ladies aside all on his own and never introducing us to any of them. A politician in the forming.

I had less than enjoyed my own half an hour of discomfort not long before. Eartha Kitt, that slinkiest, sexiest of singers had accepted an invitation to appear. She arrived late, surrounded by a number of hard-faced, hard-eyed 'minders'. Miss Kitt wore a spinach green dress and coat trimmed with ocelot, my wife remembers. I remember her wearing a steady lowering frown all the time. I tried to get her into conversation before the interview but not one word did I get out of her in that hospitality room. Came the time to get into the studio and the procession moved along silent corridors. Silently. She sat opposite to me with a couple of minutes to go. Still no word but the steady frown persisted. I was not apprehensive, I was terrified that I had another Krishna Menon situation on my hands. I put the first question, 'Would she really settle down if she ever found an old-fashioned millionaire who could give her yachts, oil wells and all the things she sang about?'

The light went red on her camera, and it was as though it had lit her blue touch-paper. The star of Broadway and Hollywood fizzed, sparkled and shone for ten lovely glorious minutes. It was one hell of a performance. 'Miss Kitt thank you,' I said in both gratitude and relief. A final slow smile from those moody eyes, a lengthening of the upper lip and a slight pout from the lower. As the camera light went out so did her firework display. Out in the corridor she became once more immersed in her own silence. Her managers were delighted and told her so. She just sat gently smouldering in her corner.

Many months later, away from the studio, we were to exchange words. 'Hullooooo . . .' she said. But that was all. Just Hullo, nothing more.

When I am told how wonderful it must be to meet all those fascinating and famous stars I remember Miss Eartha Kitt – and some others like her. But our life was not all film stars and glamour. Increasingly politicians were becoming more willing to be interviewed. Some of them would be making news as they did. For example one evening we opened, not with our calypso, but with this:

CM: We open our programme somewhat differently, with

the big news of the day. The Chancellor's resignation* last
night and that of his junior ministers has provided a political
bombshell almost without parallel in recent years. Lord
Hailsham is the Chairman of the Conservative Party and he
has just arrived. I believe the Prime Minister leaving for his
Commonwealth tour said at London Airport that these were
'little local difficulties'. Is this how you see them?

Lord Hailsham: Well I'm not going on a world tour you know,
but of course the great thing about the Prime Minister is his
absolute unflappability and that's what makes him so good to
have as a leader and a colleague.

[Lord Hailsham had just sent telegrams to the Tory
constituencies as a result of the Chancellor of the Exchequer's
resignation.]

CM: In this telegram you used the words 'grave news'. Were
you disappointed when the Prime Minister described them as
'little local difficulties'.

Lord Hailsham: Perhaps I was being a little pompous. I never
should be. I won't again.

CM: Do you regret what you said then?

Lord Hailsham: No, I don't regret things of that kind. There's
nothing immoral about being pompous.

Nobody had heard of 'Unflappable Mac' until then and it
quickly passed into the language.

Some of my friends were now thinking that I was in danger of
getting pompous and a bit above myself. If there had been any
danger that my pomposity would get out of hand, all they had to
do was to come to the post-mortem meeting after each night's programme. It was a free-for-all. Everyone charged in with why they
thought this or that was wrong, why a studio item was not up to
standard or an interview failed. They were ruthless in their
ferocity. No one was spared the tongue-lashing and it was useless
pleading a previous engagement that evening. 'Listen boy,' would
come the cry and you had to.

One evening Tony Hancock came in to see *Tonight* go on the air
and sat in the control gallery. Tony lived not far from us. I met him
quite often and he asked me if he could see how it worked. He was
shocked and amazed at the character-shredding self-criticism that

* Mr Thornycroft as Chancellor had put forward an economic plan which the
Prime Minister had rejected so he and some colleagues resigned.

144

went on afterwards in the BBC Club, but he thought it was a marvellous thing to do. 'We ought to do that after our programmes. All we do is tell each other how good we are.'

Our producers kept the contributors firmly in their place. *Tonight* was not going to become a celebrity showcase, editors decided. But it was not only their corrective criticisms that we had to contend with. The press cuttings started to mount:

> He's six feet tall but no Duke of Edinburgh. He has fair hair behind that apparently ebbing browline. But he wears spectacles and is no Viking.

> ... his smile reminds me of a benevolent hippopotamus from some half-recalled children's comic ...

> Plump, almost bucolic, in appearance with nothing in the way of glamour.

> He is no quivering Presley or capering Hughie Green, but avuncular, pink-faced, middle-brow with a middle-class accent and occasional schoolboy squeak in his voice.

> Slightly Bunteresque in appearance.

Burly, paunchy, robust, pale, plump, benign, were all common descriptions alongside 'a comfortable owl of a man', 'John Bull of the small screen' and I cannot forbear to mention 'the face that dogs, children and maiden aunts trust on sight'. More and worse were to come, so I was left in no doubt that I was *not* the glamour boy of the programme. Jean was not worried. She was too busy at home waiting. With a week to go before the baby was due she broke her toe and was confined to bed.

More Leading Men Than Elizabeth Taylor

I cry a lot, always at weddings, seldom at funerals. A nativity play is my Wailing Wall. *Jim'll Fix It, This is Your Life*, nothing is too trivial or sentimental to start eyes, nose and mascara running in unison. I blame this on Grandfather Reed whose paisley handkerchief was always sopping by the end of the King's Christmas broadcast and his toast to 'Absent Friends' croaked with swallowed sobs. I cried when Cliff and I moved into our Georgian doll's house, remembering all the years as a sheltered daughter which would never come again. I cried when we moved out. For a man whose patience is easily tried, Cliff has always surprised me with his forbearance over my public dissolves. That day in September 1958 he understood completely why I sobbed in the cellar that the moving men on the floor above were carrying away seven years of our lives. He too would miss the mulberry tree, the curving staircase, even the ugly fence which separated our half of the garden from our neighbours, Ursula and Peter. Ah now, the neighbours. That was it. We had shared so much with them, diets and clothes and the loss of children. When we graduated from waiting list to ownership, they had the first proud ice from our first proud refrigerator. They gave us apples. We gave them Ernie's cucumbers. The mice which commuted beneath our common wall feasted in both our kitchens. Anyone would think from the drama I made of it that we were going to move to Alaska but our new home was only a mile away on the other side of Reigate.

After Guy was born I stayed on the staff of the BBC just long enough to collect my maternity pay. Even so, they were painful months of instinctive animal longing and as soon as possible, I left to become a freelance part-time broadcaster. This was the time when Gilbert Harding was television's first supernova. His outbursts on *What's My Line* brought him colossal fame and notoriety. More often than not it was pretentiousness which angered him. He couldn't abide anyone pretending to be something they were not, whether challenger, panellist or chairman, and subjected the offender to tirades of abuse. Asthma and alcohol shortened his temper but when he had recovered there were generous, equally public, apologies. After that his self-destructive demon would lie low for a while until the next display. Gilbert was the topic of endless conversation and conjecture. To us who are old enough to remember him he still is.

There seemed to be two people living in the same skin; the famous Harding, irascible, wittily sarcastic, leading a disreputable life on the seamier side of London; the other, commuting to his home in Brighton where he lived in stylish but comfortable domesticity. The cross-patch personality he wore like protective clothing could melt in tears when a careless remark struck a sensitive memory or when he was unexpectedly touched by someone else's happiness. Not long ago I went to speak to Ebbisham Townswomen's Guild. I do this sort of thing in return for a donation to the Telephones for the Blind Fund of which Cliff and I are joint Presidents. Proposing the vote of thanks a member said 'I am old enough to remember the day in 1950 when Gilbert Harding was our speaker. He rushed into the hall very excited, flushed with pleasure, and announced to everyone there "I must tell you – Jean and Cliff are engaged!"' I had not realised before quite how hungry he was to share the small joys and sorrows of other people's lives.

We always knew he loved children. 'They are the only people who receive presents from me' he used to say. And when he was inundated with charity invitations, his way of dealing with them was to set a date, hire a Rolls, then whizz round opening as many as ten fêtes in a day. He was immensely celebrated but when we telephoned one Christmas he was about to sit and watch *High Noon* on television – alone.

In the single channel fifties when one cross word from Gilbert made newspaper headlines, Cliff's daily appearances on *Highlight*, and later *Tonight*, brought immediate fame and spiralling demands. Fan-mail requires a secretary who needs an office, which calls for larger premises, which means more staff, who eat more food, which involves more shopping, which demands a second car

. . . and so the ripples spread. It would be idle to deny the pleasures of such an expansive lifestyle but, once on the roundabout, there's no getting off until the ride is over. You can't cut down in the media. It's an all or nothing world. Cliff was working fit to bust, while part of me yearned to stay at home discovering whether I was actually capable of looking after him and Guy single-handed, but my wobbly confidence told me to stick with the job at which I had proved a success. Besides, in 1960 Cliff's BBC salary was tiny by today's standards. We needed my earnings from *Two-Way*, Outside Broadcasts and occasional bits of television. It was time to employ living-in help.

First, Maureen came to look after Guy when I was away, until past sorrows caught up with her in the form of a breakdown. When she went into hospital Patty arrived to take over. Pat Mann disliked the term 'nanny' as much as we did. She was a nursery nurse, recently qualified at the local day nursery, brisk and young with inexhaustible energy, just what Guy's ageing parents needed. Patty, my widowed father who had come to live with us, Guy, and the possibility of a second child made it necessary to move on.

The new house was unquestionably a mongrel, part 16th century with ebony hard black beams, part wandering Victorian extensions. It gave us bedrooms to spare and a spreading garden only a stone's throw from Ernie and Nellie Bryant's home. Overnight we had a sizeable house and the staff to go with it. We felt like landed gentry. Until the 'staff' were on holiday, that is. 'Landed' we remained. 'Gentry' we were not. Nothing sharpens the performance as much as talented understudies waiting in the wings. In Ernie's absence Cliff mowed into the twilight. While Nellie was away I found that a quick rub of polish on a table was enough to suggest by its smell alone that dusting and sweeping had also been done. I am, I confess, a slut at heart, the unmade bed beneath an immaculate counterpane. But when Pat was off duty there were no short cuts. Inexperienced and twice her age, I tried to keep up with her schedule.

Eleven o'clock: should have put baby in pram by now.

Eleven fifteen: still soaking bottles in Milton.

Eleven thirty: at last, baby in pram, under cat net, on lawn. I've tried to immobilise hands and feet in tightly wrapped blanket like Pat does.

Eleven forty-five: washing nappies, I spy through window, rocking pram, waving fist, kicking foot and flailing blanket.

Twelve o'clock: pram stops rocking.

Twelve five: crawl on hands and knees to check that a) he's asleep and b) still breathing. Rise slowly to peep over hood and his eyes, wide awake, meet mine. I retreat. He screams. And off we go again. Thank heaven he can't talk yet or he would tell Pat what a fumble-fisted mother I am.

It wasn't long before he could, of course. Talk, I mean. With one finger pointing skywards like a tombstone angel, Guy said 'Sh! Air-bee' as a plane flew over and we knew we had a fourteen-month-old genius for a son. The illusion lasted until Jenny arrived when he was two. With her the first years were a doddle. She slept like a kitten and ate like a horse. I was undoubtedly less paranoid the second time round about resting in prams, and scrubbing bibs before Patty returned. Nevertheless brother and sister were dab hands at playing us off against each other. 'Pat lets us' they told me when they fancied biscuits at bedtime. She was less easily swayed. 'Whatever you do with your mother is no concern of mine,' she'd say. 'While I'm in charge you'll do things my way.' Now that they are adults, Guy and Jenny admit they knew precisely what they were doing when they cried in the night. If Patty responded it was a case of 'Damn and blast! She won't stand any nonsense. Might as well go to sleep,' but if I answered the call they knew it was fun-and-games time . . .

Inevitably, Pat and I twinged with jealousy over each other's successes. I envied her outdoor skills with campfires and tree climbing. My strengths lay in story-telling and make-believe. But through it all Pat and I were, and remain, fiercely fond friends. The hours of child-talk we were able to share kept me sane when Cliff was away. His absences gave our rare days together as a family red-letter importance. I remember them with the sharpness of black and white snapshots; walking to the baker's on Good Friday morning to buy hot cross buns steaming from the ovens; hunting in the garden for chocolate eggs on Easter Day; going to church on toboggans one Sunday when there was too much snow to get to Broadcasting House; skating on Fourwents pond by the light of car headlamps; Cliff and Guy face down on Austrian bobsleighs, Jenny and me on a safer slower sledge behind; cooking breakfast on the beach and supper on the downs; searching for hamsters at midnight and Scottish deer at dawn; flying kites and chasing seagulls, rowing boats and feeding ducks. Every parent's memory bank must be full of such things but that was just the point. They were occasions when we could do ordinary family things, made extraordinary because we couldn't share them all the time. To this day the sight of a young mother and father with a pramful of children, all of them clean and well fed, all bright and smiling, fills me with awed admiration. They manage that production day after day with little help and less money. We had plenty of both and still made mistakes. If I hadn't given in and put toys away, their flats would be tidier today. If we had been less willing to replace lost treasures – watches, pens, radios, records – they might not be quite so casual about expensive possessions now. A little more order in their personal correspondence would not come amiss. I picked up too much of that when they were young. Too often we took the easy way out. Everyone must be as happy as possible as often as possible. There was always something sweet to follow bitter medicine. Nevertheless, their innate strengths – honesty, wit, zest for life, loyalty to friends, self respect and moral courage survived our mistakes undamaged in spite of having one huge extra hurdle to overcome, Father's Famous Face and the Great British Public.

I don't know how long it was before the children realised that going out with Father meant being on parade but, for Cliff and me, the simmering threat of constant recognition boiled right over one summer in St Ives. Jenny was eighteen months old and Guy was three and a half. To lay the ghost once and for all, we stayed in the hotel where I had spent those homesick childhood holidays.

Everyone made us welcome. The man who rented us a tent on Porthminster beach threw in a spectacular blue and white striped awning as well. Every morning we set up camp on the sands with the usual paraphernalia of buckets and spades, rubber rings and sandy sandwiches. Every morning our 'island in the sun' was invaded by autograph hunters as eager to tackle the '*Tonight* Man' as if he was opening a charity bazaar. As an experiment one day we sent Pat and the children on ahead to the beach, while we watched from the hotel balcony above. They put up the awning and, as if a starting gun had fired, a column of sightseers began to amble from one end of the shore to the other, passing and re-passing the canvas shelter with its ostentatious accessory. From then on we kept the sunblind rolled up and Cliff out of sight at the back of the tent.

A Kodak Brownie delivered the *coup de grâce*. If she gave them half a crown, would Guy and Jenny allow its owner to take their photo 'because they were Cliff Michelmore's children'? Ingenuously we had always hoped that they would be allowed to grow up, to make their own mistakes and successes, without being spot-lit because their father happened to earn his living on television. The lady with the camera brought us to our senses and pointed to the pitfalls ahead.

On balance, we decided not to repeat the St Ives experiment. Perhaps next year we could rent somewhere by the sea? Cliff said he knew the very place. There was a village on the Isle of Wight where so many people let their houses to the nobility in the summer, they would be unlikely to notice a mere television personality. The name of this haven was Bembridge. Towards the end of July the following year, I was stocking up in the village grocer's, having put down roots in our rented house just up the road from the Lifeboat Station, when the owner said kindly but loudly 'Oh, Mrs Michelmore, we can't have *you* standing in the queue. I will send the boy round with your goods later.' Cliff was not at all put out by this unsought segregation. He simply said 'Hold your horses. Wait and see.' August 1st. Cowes Week. In the grocer's again, but now the white 'cardies' have given way to reefer jackets. I am fighting my way to the bacon counter when the owner bustles up again with a gesture towards a woman in faded Jaeger. 'Have you put up her Grace's order yet?' he asks an assistant, elbowing me out of the way. With a sigh of relief I realise I am back where I belong, with the hoi-poloi, and that is where we have been on family holidays ever since, in Bembridge.

Everyone in television recognises that 'public ownership' is the toll you have to pay, but to expect a man to settle his dues when he is scruffily out with his children is like asking Placido Domingo to give you a song while he's sitting in his bath. I am fairly ambivalent about the problem, since few know or care what I look like, or remember my name, but I did mind very much that we had to pack our bags and run from a visit to North Devon because of the persistent prodding, tugging and jostling Cliff received from the crowds in Barnstaple Market. On the other hand I admit I was put out when Senior Engineer Mr Bottle, swept a party of visitors into Light Continuity with the words 'of course you all know this famous lady – Miss Joan Gilbert.' No one could be blamed for saying at this point 'With some people, you just can't win!'

In spite of their father's fame, I suspect that the children's biggest burden was the intensity of their parents love. We would willingly have died for them. Any time. Although what's left of our lives is now somewhat threadbare, the offer still stands. Such a concentrated beam of caring beating on the backs of their necks all the time must have made them terrified of failure, of letting us down. I think we sensed this and that was why we were so proud of their achievements which owed nothing to either of us.

Cliff had never learnt to swim for instance, because of boyhood cramp, and I was no Esther Williams, so when Guy and Jenny became extremely good swimmers early in their lives we were intolerably proud. They both developed musical talents which thrilled us even more. A mouth-organ in a Christmas stocking turned Guy into a budding Larry Adler at the age of eight. He played 'Jerusalem the Golden', at a Junior School Concert and strong men wept. So did I. A clarinet helped him to learn to read music and at last the grand piano we had bought as a fetching piece of furniture came into its own. Jenny began to sing like a bird when she was very young. Cliff's mother and mine had both had pretty voices but our own cupboards were totally bare in that department. All through her schooldays the beautiful singing went on and on. Her first Winner's Certificate at a Music Festival brought tears of pride flooding once more and her 'Pié Jesu' in Fauré's *Requiem* was almost more poignant than we could bear.

Guy was a multi-talented butterfly as a little boy, settling on music one day, fluttering tentatively towards poetry the next. By the end of the week he'd be showing all the signs of a career at the Bar. More often than not he thought he'd like to be a policeman so a local Inspector arranged a visit to the 'Nick', complete with fingerprints, for a seventh birthday treat. No ambitions lasted long. It was very unsettling. All we could do was spread a wide selection of flowers before him and leave him to decide which nectar tasted best.

Jenny's future career was easier to detect. Her life peaked with dancing lessons, school plays and 'The Black and White Minstrels' on television. Instead of a mouth-organ there was a tinselled tu-tu in her Christmas stocking. When she had been excused from the table, leaving Pat and Guy, my father and I lingering over second cups of tea, a voice would command from behind the kitchen door 'Make Ta-raa!'. With a sigh and a mouthful of cake crumbs we would manage a make-do fanfare. Then, while we hummed our way through 'Waltz of the Flowers', this lump of mauve net and chubby limbs would thump and spin round the kitchen like a demented ball of wool with knitting needles for arms and legs. 'She'll grow out of it' we thought. 'All little girls behave like this.' One day a friend asked her what name she would use if ever she went on the stage and I overheard our nine-year-old answering gravely that ' "Jenny Oliver" would be nice but I think I'll keep the name Michelmore at the beginning to give me a start'. She was not to know then that nothing could be more hindering but it made us realise that such calculated determination deserved to be taken seriously.

Once the children were both at school, Pat felt her work was done and left to visit relatives in New Zealand. Eventually she had

J.M., the outside broadcast commentator on a Civil Defence exercise in 1955

...viewing Jack Hawkins
...oman's Hour
...rch, 1954

...riefing the commentary team ...r 'Battle Royal' manoeuvres, ...ermany, 1954: General Sir ...rian Horrocks, Jean, Robert ...eid, Brian Johnston and Henry ...iddell

'I've never been so frightened in my life.' The fireman's lift that went wrong
on Escape from Fire, 1955

The first *Tonight* studio, St Mary Abbotts Place, with Ned Sherrin one of its first directors

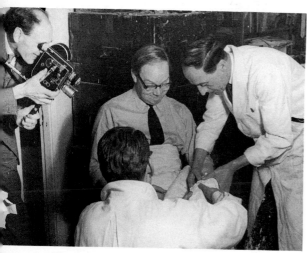

...eraman Slim Hewitt films ...f being 'cast' for Madame ...sauds

An Isle of Wight newspaper comments on Cliff's Tussauds figure, 1959

Waiting for Guy and reading Alan Burgess

Waiting for Jenny. Guy and Cliff on Cowes Esplanade, summer, 1959

The Michelmores and a beagle called 'Lady'

With Michelmore, an interview series included Sir Matt Busby

Prince Charles' first television interview. With Cliff is Brian Connell

Cliff by David Bailey, 1968

The photograph that Karsh took in 1963

'A suitable way to grow old', Jean remembers Grandfather's tearful Christmas toast to Absent Friends

Golf at Gleneagles with Bruce Forsyth, Alan Shepard, the astronaut, and Burt Lancaster

The best of times, then and now. *En famille* in Inverness and Nottingham

her own home and family a short distance away from us in Reigate, so we still see and love her.

Talking about her two fine sons she once confessed 'It's easier to discipline someone else's children than your own', which made me feel good, and I added that sometimes a husband was simpler to handle than his offspring. That really was my opinion, until the night Cliff crashed his head on a low doorway in the kitchen. It had been a taxing day with Guy and Jenny, so the last thing I wanted at that moment was 'another great baby moaning about a little bump on the head'. 'If it's that bad,' I snapped 'go and lie down on the sofa.' He did, and went early to bed. He wasn't looking his usual robust self next morning when he left for the office but I felt, as you do when you make complaining children go to school, he'd be better when he was working.

Around tea-time, a phone call from the BBC told me 'There's nothing to worry about but Cliff is not very well. Could you ask his doctor to get in touch.' Now my conscience went into overdrive. Worse was to come. After words with the BBC medical man, Ken Hughes told me that Cliff had collapsed with delayed concussion. I felt as though I had sent an ailing pet on its own to the vet's to be put down. Ken would go himself to Lime Grove to bring Cliff home. Later that evening Dr Hughes and my white-faced husband returned, followed in another car by the programme's worried Editor and Deputy Editor, Donald Baverstock and Alasdair Milne. Not far behind was a caravan of reporters. While I settled Cliff into bed – clean sheets by now of course and flowers fit for a wedding – the *Daily Mirror* and *Daily Express* were at the door. Ken was firmer than I could have been. 'You can't see him,' he said 'He's not here.' It had been a close shave in every respect. Cliff's concussion proved to be quite severe. He couldn't remember where he'd left his car or the time or day of the week. I never again pooh-poohed his ailments and that treacherous doorway has gone forever.

They were stirring times when Cliff was presenting *Tonight* and continued to be so when it was replaced by the extended late night programme *24 Hours*. Cliff's times of work were now anti-social in the extreme, leaving for the office around midday and returning in the small hours. Life was difficult with young children to be taken to school every morning, while their father was still in bed, and all of us were asleep when he got home at 1am to spend the equivalent of an unwinding evening alone with a book downstairs. As a result of an interview on the programme, Cliff received a death threat which, in the authorities' opinion, was serious enough to warrant police protection. It must have been a chilling experience for the potential victim but he kept his feelings from us and went to work as usual, as though nothing was wrong. We at home had no idea that, when we put out lights and locked doors at night, plain clothes men were taking up position behind trees in the garden and outside in the road. Had he known, Guy would have been able to watch his beloved police in action. Had I known, I should have been paranoid with fear. One afternoon Jenny and I were walking back from school when we noticed the beat police-man in front of us speaking into his personal radio. We tried to catch him up to hear what exciting message he might be relaying, but as soon as we did, he stopped talking and went on down the road past the house. When I told Cliff about it he at last explained what had been going on. The constable was reporting that 'Mrs Michelmore and daughter have now returned'. We had been watched for days every step of the way without the slightest awareness. It was an uncanny feeling. I need not add that the worrying episode ended without incident and from then on we wholeheartedly shared Guy's admiration for the way the Force operates in times of trouble. If, in later years, he had decided to join them as a full-time career we would have backed him to the hilt.

Those anti-social hours on the late night programme brought the Michelmores to a turning point. To survive it was necessary to become separate units with the children and me on one side and Cliff by himself on the other. He was free at weekends but Guy's schooling now included Saturdays and I worked every Sunday. It seemed as though the four of us would never coincide. Our lives were relentlessly dividing, whereas we had always seen ourselves as inter-dependent, sharing, each member relying on the rest for support. Although it would be a leap in the dark and our finances might suffer, Cliff decided that family unity must come first and left *24 Hours*. I began to withdraw from *Two-Way Family Favourites*.

Anna Instone, the Head of Gramophone Department was un-expectedly understanding about the dilemma, suggesting that instead of leaving altogether as I had anticipated, it should be poss-ible to share the job with another presenter, six months on, six months off. By a curious irony the Variety Club chose this moment to make me their Radio Personality of the Year 1963. The Awards Luncheon would be a good time to announce the change.

I bought a Mary Quant navy crêpe coat dress and a new white hat for the occasion. As I arrived at the Dorchester on March 20th, 1964, it was slightly disconcerting to be greeted by the commiss-ionaire as 'Miss Vera Lynn'. I daresay I minded less than Vera would have done if she had known. I didn't eat much because the

154

prospect of making a speech before a host of recognisable celebrities played havoc with my stomach. Harold Wilson was handing out the Silver Hearts that year but he worried me less than the audience which was largely composed of professional comedians. Although he was working and unable to attend, Cliff had given me a good line to use. 'On *Two-Way*' I said, as he had primed 'I've had more leading men than Elizabeth Taylor. But I only married one of them.' He was right. They liked that.

I went on to announce that I was going to leave the programme for six months of the year. 'If that is the case,' said Mr Wilson as he gave me the award 'this is a time of national crisis.' He would, as was the custom at such times, take the grave step of moving the adjournment of the House at 10 o'clock that night.

Judith Chalmers was to present *Two-Way* during the summer months and I would take care of the winter for a few more years. But things were changing. Instead of occasional live links with Forces Broadcasting round the world, moves were afoot to include regular recorded contributions of civilian requests from Canada, Australia and New Zealand. The spontaneous Forces element was slipping away and my interest with it.

For us at home in 1964 the first Sunday I did not go to the studio was the beginning of a normal life again for all of us, with weekend roasts instead of pre-cooked stews and Father's commanding voice at children's parties. The Michelmores were together once more.

If You Think You've Got Problems

Before I forget: some thoughts on bringing up children.

Every child is jealous of the new baby. Some hide it better than others, that's all. They are the ones to watch. Guy began to stutter after Jenny was born and who could blame him, with this child, cherubic enough to spout water from a Roman fountain, mopping up every stranger's attention? Taking no notice and praying hard, he reverted to an articulate talking machine after six months and has not faltered since.

When someone says how polite and charming our usually boorish children are in her house, we should think ourselves lucky things are not the other way round.

There is a bit of bitch or bully in every girl or boy. Parties for boys end at the age of six, unless mud-wrestling can be arranged in the front room.

Timing is not a child's strong point. Sex questions arise when you are dishing up. Bridesmaids' milk teeth fall out on the morning of the wedding. Carsick children throw up when you are miles from home without a bowl. When this happens, ignore tidy houses which have their eyes shut. Knock at the scruffiest semi in the road with tricycles where the garden used to be. We did that once in Horndean and our Good Samaritans, surrounded by their bounding children, produced towels, soap and water in a matter of minutes, not to mention a drink containing glucose 'to settle the little one's stomach'. I am grateful to them still.

Brother and sister are rarely perfect at the same time. One goes up as the other goes down. Make the most of the relatively peaceful overlap.

If your taste in clothes/friends/music is the same as your children's, something is wrong somewhere.

You can be certain the moment you feel at ease with a teenage daughter's boyfriend, they are on the point of splitting up.

When at last they know where they're going and are everything you always hoped they'd be, rest assured your children are about to wave you goodbye and belong to somebody else.

We got one thing right on our uncertain progress through parenthood. No matter how outlandish they seem at the time, treating children's opinions with respect helps them stick to their guns later on. Railing against unhealthy trends gets you nowhere if they haven't already learnt what's right for them and have the stamina to swim against the tide. We were relieved when our two began to show signs of this kind of confidence. Now there was a liferaft in their luggage. That, and the cheering words of two good friends got us through many a sticky patch; Guy's reluctance to go to school for example, and Jenny's moody spells. Alasdair Milne's endearing wife Sheila said 'When he's eight or nine you will think you have the nicest son in the world', and the genial journalist Robert Cannell remarked 'My daughter is fourteen now and believe me, they get better and better'. We were lucky. They were right. At the end of a foul day – and we had plenty of them when father and son were tangling, or mother and daughter played 'bitch to bitch' – hang on to the thought that there will be others so perfect from morning to night that you won't want the day to go down with the sun. Those are the memories which should be tucked away, like 'mad money' in your corsets, to be retrieved later when the going gets rough.

I wish my personal memory bank contained more significant memories, because I find increasingly nowadays that the big things are forgotten while the small are remembered. There are clearer recollections of the bad than the good. The night Cliff received his BAFTA award as Television Personality of 1958 has faded into an undefined haze of happiness, whereas the Award Evening in 1963 returns as if it was yesterday. Everyone involved in Current Affairs broadcasting left, shocked and silent, to return to work before the dinner because the news had come through of President Kennedy's assassination. Cliff's first historic satellite transmission is less clear in my mind than the day we heard he was going into Madame Tassaud's. I never thought I should share a bed, let alone a toothbrush, with a man whose wax effigy was expected to draw the crowds. The professional Gilbert Harding is less alive to me now than the one we knew as a friend. During his spells of ill-health he would ask his driver to stop at our door so that we could take the children out to sit with him in the car. He gave Guy a furry toy which the shop assistant told him loftily was a hare not a rabbit. He mistook the date of Jenny's christening (a week late to the day) and shared instead a warmed over weekend joint in the kitchen. We were very fond of Gilbert.

It seems such a pity I cannot remember what Karsh of Ottawa looked like when he came to take my photo in 1963. I only know that the man who was called 'the greatest photographer in the world' ate none of the florentines I'd made for tea, Svengali-ed his sitter into total unselfconsciousness and needed somewhere without daylight in which to reload his camera. The only place we could find without a window was the linen cupboard, so I held a blanket over the door while Karsh changed films among discarded bolsters and sheets.

Godfrey Winn, came to do a piece for a magazine which I remember less for the printed outcome than the cube-shaped maroon-coloured box he brought with him. All through the interview that box sent me messages that it contained something very tasteful, very Asprey, for his hostess. But it lied. A photographer arrived to take pictures and Godfrey lifted the lid to reveal . . . his toupé! Do I remember Cliff's 'Our World' Television hook-up with the adorable Beatles *et al*? I do not. But ask me what he said to Dame Edith Sitwell on *Highlight* and I can tell you precisely. When he enquired about the hostile reception *Façade* received at its first performance she said 'Have you ever addressed an audience of mental defectives?' and he answered 'That is not a question to ask *me* Dame Edith!'

Most of *Juke Box Jury* has faded from my mind, too, apart from the fog-bound edition we did from Manchester. We waited at the airport to fly home after the programme but fog persisted, so we were bussed to Liverpool instead. Late at night, planes still grounded, it looked as though we should have to sleep there until morning. My one superstition has always been that if you prepare for the worst it will never happen. I bought from a kiosk the cheapest essential for an overnight stay – a toothbrush. Instantly the fog lifted and the plane took off. The 'toothbrush syndrome' has been a family talisman ever since. You see what I mean? These memories are more pinafore than party frock.

The family, I daresay, provides the reason for my amnesia about outside events from now on. They were of consuming interest as the gap between generations closed. We made short trips abroad in the Easter school holidays: to Paris where Guy's first escargots *and* calvados cost him a visit to Sacré Coeur; to Athens where Jenny and I missed the Acropolis for similar reasons; to the Algarve where we collected pink shells from the beaches and picnicked under pines in the Monchique mountains; and to Normandy where we saw mistletoe growing like knitting in the tops of apple trees. It was a time when Guy and his friends could career about fields in an aged Land Rover on Cliff's family's Isle of Wight farm, and I could join Jenny and her soulmate Joanna in preparing songs, lines and costumes for their next amateur show. Time, too, for every mug we possessed to be left dirty on the table when the fledglings decided to fly off to someone else's nest. The house, crammed with camp beds one minute, became as quiet as Early Closing Day the next. Doors were beginning to open through which Cliff and I could imagine favourite chairs repossessed and a television showing something other than James Bond, then they would close again and we'd be back to huddling girls' and boys' size elevens on every floor. We were into the Between Years with a vengeance. Adjustment and readjustment. Endings and beginnings, some welcome, some sad. I was in two minds about everything.

When I was six I once had a bad splinter under my fingernail and rocked myself miserably to and fro for almost half an hour wailing, 'I don't want it in and I don't want it out'. That maddening child threatened to surface again in the seventies when alternating currents were running through the household, but even she was single-minded about one great improvement which had taken place.

Increasing numbers of Telepeople meant that strangers were less inclined to scream across High Streets. Every town now had its local Famous Face. As intrusions into private life dwindled to the acceptable, Cliff's career on television produced more pros than cons. Among these perks – invitations to First Nights, VIP Lounges, the Last Night of the Proms for example – two in particular can never be surpassed. The Wimbledon Tennis Championships were always the summit of our summers when we were first married. At least once in the fortnight we queued outside from early morning, waiting to join the stampede to the free standing enclosure on the Centre Court. There we stayed until the last ball was played, our fixed eyes occasionally glancing with envy at the hydrangea-rimmed box where the privileged sat and watched.

One day in 1974 an embossed card arrived inviting 'Mr Michelmore and Guest' (he wouldn't dare take anyone else, would he?) to join the spectators in the Royal Box. The secrets of life behind those hydrangeas were about to be revealed. There were cane chairs, ribboned programmes, rugs for the knees, and, behind the Box, on a shaded balcony, small tables set for tea with inch square sandwiches stacked like counters, folded doilies dividing cucumber from egg, fondant iced cakes, strawberries and cream, silver pots of Indian and China tea. Splendour upon splendour. Beyond bowls of mauve sweetpeas was the soundproofed 'Royal' Powder Room with every ladylike want supplied. Cliff reported that there was a pot of gentlemanly pommade in the Men's Room. There will never be another visit to compare with the first, when we went to Wimbledon in style and our very best clothes.

Finery too for all the family when Father went to the Palace to receive his CBE. It was March 1969. The children, begged off school for the day, Cliff and I were all dressed to the nines in good time when we noticed ominous flakes of white falling outside. I, who love snow, could have wished it away that day. The hired car failed to arrive, stuck in a snowdrift miles away, so Cliff pulled waterproofs and wellingtons over his hired morning suit and got my lightweight vehicle out of the garage instead. Rallying round bollards like a Paddy Hopkirk, he got us to the Palace Courtyard on the deadline of 10.30 and parked my dirty runabout, with its Kit Kat wrappers and toffee papers, among the limousines. Inside all was order and decorum, a military orchestra playing from the gallery, the Queen in blue and Cliff in a well concealed state of nerves. He is marvellous about wanting everyone to share good fortune. To this end he had arranged a luncheon party afterwards with friends and colleagues at the Hyde Park Hotel, where we arrived, still in my ramshackle car. The cockaded doorman had to squeeze among wellies, raincoats and rubbish when he drove it away to the car park. At home that evening, after a box at the Palladium pantomime had completed the day, Jenny showed us the souvenir she had smuggled from the Palace – a piece of toilet paper marked 'Government Issue'. I mentioned this later in a lecture to the women prisoners in Holloway and they bellowed 'We use that all the time, Miss'.

It was more 'con' than 'pro' that Cliff should have been working abroad when I broke my ankle at Bembridge. Nothing spectacular, just a foot turned on the edge of a flowerbed baked hard by the hot summer of 1974. Guy made his first 999 call in earnest and Jenny packed my bag. 'I've put your pearls in,' she told me 'and your false eyelashes. You may as well look your best.' Leaving them to fend for themselves I fretted that they would forget to turn the gas off and leave notes for the milkman. When Cliff returned, needless to say, he did not find the house burnt down nor was there enough soured milk to make a hundred scones. With a lurch as unpremeditated as the one which broke my bone, we had moved into the next phase of family life when doting parents realise that their children will not shrivel and die without them. Their world will not come to an end if either or both of you go under the proverbial bus. Relief on one hand, regret on the other.

I mentioned earlier that you can't 'cut down' in the media. It is an all-or-nothing world. After I left *Two-Way Family Favourites* occasional guest appearances came my way on panel games and discussion programmes, but nothing regular or absorbing. The producers I had worked for reached retirement age and were replaced by a new generation who naturally brought their young contemporaries into the limelight with them. The less you do, the less you are asked to do. I had no regrets. Cliff was working hard enough for six people and needed an un-tired person to unwind to and rely on. The children still needed me. I wasn't prepared to part with a fragment of this short and precious period of our lives. But after that fractured ankle episode it was clear that my maximum maternal phase was running out. That was the moment, in July 1971, when I was disinterred by the BBC to introduce a series called *If You Think You've Got Problems*. The dynamics of family groups and individuals had always fascinated me. This could be a way of channelling it productively before I turned into a lonely old net curtain twitcher.

It was an entirely new concept for radio. A broadcast therapy session which it was hoped would help any listener who could identify with the problem being aired. I was to be a sounding board for the 'clients' and a chairman for the experts. The go-between in other words. Thena Heschel was its first producer. She selected problems from listeners' letters and an appropriate panel of high qualified experts to discuss them. Then, on the morning of the recording, she and I met the various troubled correspondents over coffee in the quiet of a basement conference room. Our pre-programme sessions must have been unlike any previous meeting held there. To meet someone who had travelled a long distance to London, wearing posh clothes and a false chirpy smile, and then gently and gradually to reach the real person inside was a moving experience. I felt privileged that so many allowed me to do so.

Before our contributors arrived we had only seen their letters – intriguing, touching, sometimes wryly amusing – about a problem which was blighting their lives. Thena had the ability to read between the lines. When the writers walked in as living breathing people who sometimes laughed too much, sometimes cried, it was easy to feel unequal to the task of helping them extract the most from the considerable guidance which would be available that afternoon. It was up to me to make them feel, when they confronted the panel of distinguished experts, that there was someone on their side. Like a school teacher, in a way, encouraging them to do themselves justice. But not so well that their flaws and frailties did not show. It was also up to me to ensure that the professionals met the same vulnerable person the producer and I had seen earlier. No one is ever wholly natural the first time they enter a studio. We all try to appear confident. The kind of counselling a confident person can absorb would be useless to someone normally timid and shy. My job on the programme was to balance the see-saw and pass the Kleenex.

Having overcome nervous reticence or pretended *bonhomie* over the morning coffee, the clients went away with a secretary for a canteen meal, while the producer and I had lunch with the panel. We tried to fill in our layman's view of the backgrounds to the problems. I sometimes thought our untutored opinions might distort the picture but psychologists, psychiatrists, clergymen and therapists said this was not the case. They felt our reactions, even unfounded ones, all had a bearing on the 'client's' situation. If we got the impression they were, say, hoity-toity, the daughter-in-law who was giving them hell would too, even if it was not so. Every little detail helped to build up the picture. In the afternoon both sides of the fence came together, with me in the middle, in long, often tearful, recorded guidance sessions. These were edited down from hours of silences and verbal fencing to forty-five minutes of the most fruitful exchanges which rarely did justice to the patience, trust and genuine affection they often elicited between counsellors and clients.

I had been given the job of presenter, I was told, because people found me easy to talk to. I've certainly done my share of listening to troubles, and enjoyed it. But when the programme got into its stride and really intimate problems came up, I was shattered to discover I was as worldly as a sex manual written by Brownies. *Two-Way Family Favourites* was never like this. Excessive handwashing was symbolic of guilt about sex. A widow's nightmares full of furry animals demonstrated guilt about sex. Even pumping iron it seemed could relieve guilt about sex. There was a lot of guilt and sex about which, on Radio 4 in the 1970s was, to say the least, unusual. Before long I was using naughty words like 'orgasm' with scarcely a blush. More problems had their basis in sexual hang-ups it appeared than anything else, but there were many others, which had to do with unmourned death, hidden grief, fear of dying and unexpressed anger. One thing emerged on every programme. The problems laid out in listeners' letters almost invariably concealed another more complicated one underneath. Downtrodden wives turned out to be secretly dominating people using manipulation to

162

get their own way; truanting children employed school refusal as blackmail for attention; workaholic husbands made the office their excuse for ducking boring homes and demanding wives; 'problem children' were often the whipping boys for difficulties which the rest of the family would not accept as their own. We met agoraphobics by telephone, alcoholics before opening time, shy people – 'if you're bad at making conversation, keep asking questions' – and a transvestite who came to the studio as 'Alice' in demure old-fashioned 1950s clothes then went home to become 'David' again and a father to his children. It was enough to stretch one's eyes. Ordinary little women yearning to say boo to a goose sometimes brought the 'geese' in question with them to the studio and emotional reconciliations took place. We wept a great deal on *Problems*.

Not every session was searing and tragic. Once we discussed Father Christmas and James Hemming, the educational psychologist, caused me to examine my own motives when he said it could be a con-trick practised on children, fraught with lies and undermining trust. Wendy Greengross said, what I can see now is absolutely true, that no one is completely adult while a mother or father is still alive. It was disconcerting to discover that, whatever the problems we discussed, I seemed to have a bit of them too ... 'that could be me speaking'. 'If I hadn't done so-and-so, I would have ended up like this' ... but that, of course, was the point. Most of us had been through similar experiences to a minor degree. The people who came to us had them in unbalancing abundance. On Wednesday evenings when I returned from a particularly tormented recording, Cliff would have to sit and listen while I spewed it all out. Had he not been so willing I might still be worrying that his hatred of single socks emerging from the washing machine concealed a latent foot fetish, his abhorrence of cucumber had less to do with indigestion than fear of impotence ... a little learning can be a dangerous thing.

The enterprise, and it was a brave one, to offer listeners the opportunity of seeing themselves as the top experts saw them, showed signs of instability when a whole programme was consigned to a party of particularly strident lesbians. The new Controller of Radio 4 refused to put it out at its usual time on a Sunday evening. It was certainly very salty meat. Gay Rights protest demonstrations occurred in Portland Place and the skids were under our feet. Dr Wendy Greengross, our intuitive resident panellist, said 'Mark my words. They'll bring it back for one more season to save face, but that will be the last.' She was right. We did return for another series, but buried within it was a well camouflaged Last

Straw. A large, bluff, apparently uncomplicated, man volunteered to lay his financial incompetence on the line. The producer, eager to avoid anything dodgy this time round, thought the subject would be ideal. We discussed his chaotic household budget for some time, Dr Greengross saying little. She was good at lying low, then dropping in a quiet question which opened up a whole new can of worms. On this occasion her enquiry revealed that cash was the least of our client's problems. He and his wife operated a private group sex centre. At a time when we needed to be uncontroversial at all costs, when paedophilia was the sex shock horror in all the tabloids, we had stumbled upon a man who was heading towards intercourse with children. This was going too far.

That series ended *If You Think You've Got Problems*. In its seven years it had broken new and valuable ground. The great majority of participants said the counsellors had helped them to find their own solutions. One young woman, who came to us when she was a single parent struggling to bring up a son on her own, was helped by James Hemming to retrain as a teacher. Years later she married a schoolmaster, they had another son together and all four are now living happily, she tells me, in the West Country. 'Eileen' who was deeply depressed by the prospect of senility in old age appeared in the 1976 series. I heard from her two years ago, now living in Chester. Although widowed and in her seventies she wrote 'I write, paint, cook when I want to, watch what I like. I'm not afraid of senility any more. I play the tape of that programme from time to time and find it very comforting.'

There were many more cases like those which proved that the programme was not simply a voyeur's benefit, but a source of insight and information for anyone who chose to use it as such. Nowadays, of course, people can present their problems twenty-four hours a day on local radio phone-ins where, in a few minutes, they are less likely to have them turned inside out and revealed as uglier than they anticipated. It is not so comfortable to talk to someone who can see the whites of your eyes. But whether you choose to face a counsellor across an unfamiliar table or telephone from the security of home, one maxim comes through . . . don't just sit there. *Do* something. In 1979 I needed to remember that.

21/CLIFF

Magical Moments

Our signature tune was one of those which made dogs howl, cats purr and budgerigars fall off their perches. It also made viewers burst into 'tum–teetee–tum, diddly diddly doo' whenever they saw any of the *Tonight* people in the streets. The tune was called 'Tonight and Every Night' and it must have made its composer, Frank Spenser, a fair packet from royalties. Between February '57 and September '64 we had chalked up 1,000 editions and there were a further 800 to come before they pulled the plug on the series on June 18th, 1965. I had been with the programme before its birth and I was still there at its eventual demise. It was a long haul but along the way there had been memorable moments and forgettable ones as well. Most important of all, particularly in the early days, was the strength of the team. It was divided into three parts; the production team who were responsible for the content; the contributors and studio director for getting the whole thing on the air and third, there was a growing staff of film reporters. One sadness I have is that I see these former colleagues so infrequently these days now that they are scattered everywhere: but that is inevitable.

Fyffe Robertson went, with his new wife, to live at Eastbourne in retirement. When Robbie joined us he was a worrier. He worried only because he was such a perfectionist. His journalist training and practice with *Picture Post* had taught him that no detail was unimportant when getting the background to a story. Trevor Philpot brought that same attitude, and assets, to *Tonight*. Trevor shared Fyffe's ability to write concisely, accurately and with concern for the subject and for people. Slim Hewitt a former *Picture*

Post cameraman had made the transition from stills photography to film remarkably quickly and skilfully. Trevor and Slim worked as a team and enjoyed the freedom of the programme. 'We could go to places like Chicago or Miami, and we could look for stories until we found them. And when we found them we could chase them. We could chase Indians who hadn't yet signed a peace treaty with the United States into the Everglades and find them in an airboat. We could delve into the trash dumps of Lima, in Peru, and we could find people living in the rubbish and fighting with the pigs in order to survive.'

They were all grateful that so soon after *Picture Post* had folded they were able to bring their picture journalism into television. It was badly needed. They opened up for us, and the BBC, a rich seam of stories wherever they went. Commercial television with their 'Roving Reports' was but one of the many competitors for such stories. So there was, by now, a much livelier look to Current Affairs programmes across the channels. Another of our reporters, lovely Polly Elwes, had left an acting career behind her after a successful West End run in *For Better, For Worse*. She popped in her contact lenses and, at the age of seven, joined us. I should perhaps explain that Polly was a Leap Year baby and her first story, I think, was interviewing some of her fellow sufferers – from a birthday present point of view.

Macdonald Hastings was our elegant man about the country. No matter whether he was duck shooting in Norfolk, truffle hunting with hogs in Perigord or chasing a set of identical twins with a pack of bloodhounds, Mac was always dressed appropriately for the occasion.

Alan Whicker, a former News Agency reporter, was constantly complaining that he was always being sent to the wrong place at the wrong time of year. He thought that we sat in the office working out when hurricanes would happen in Haiti, or black rains would come to Rotherham before despatching him there. I have always wondered whether it's true that the interview which did most to set him on his way into tax exile in the Channel Islands was when, in 1958, he questioned very closely Dale Carnegie, the author of *How to Win Friends and Influence People*. I must read it, although it is too late for me to benefit.

Alan was always in a world of his own. In Alaska he stood his frozen ground when almost being run down by an ice-breaker; in Australia he sat under a tree in the Outback sharing a billy-can of tea with a former furniture buyer from Harrods. I *think* he was a furniture buyer anyway. The rest of us were, in the main, studio bound but even we were occasionally allowed out. One idea was to make use of the ever growing Eurovision network. That enabled us to have *live* outside broadcasts direct from other countries via the increasing number of links being set up and *Tonight* was not slow to see the possibility of getting out and about in Europe. This meant that a small production team was sent ahead of the main force to lay on the interviewees and other local performers as well as finding one or two good local film stories for our reporters to do in advance. There were other times, such as in Vienna, when we put the whole programme on film. This was something of a nightmare for the film editors who had to cut the film and have it dubbed in very short time. I think that even by today's standards those editors, under Tony Essex, performed a whole succession of small miracles. The viewers thought that our occasional excursions outside the normal confines of the studio brought a welcome breath of fresh air to the programme.

We took the programme to Copenhagen for a royal visit; to Venice for the Bienniale, Vienna for Christmas; Edinburgh for the Festival; Brussels for the opening of the Exhibition, and Paris and Geneva for no particular reason. Among our guests in the Piazza San Marco in Venice was Graham Sutherland, and we were all sitting around a café table when a smiley round-faced lady from Torquay came across and asked for our autographs. As her postcard went round the table for signing, Derek Hart suggested 'you should be asking for Mr Sutherland's, not for ours' and, taking the hint, she got out another postcard and asked 'would you do me a little drawing Mr Sutherland?' She got the autograph but no little drawing.

Those were the days when Programme Controllers could, on a whim, extend the hours of transmissions, and no sooner had we finished our first programme than Cecil McGivern was on the telephone from London to Alasdair Milne, our producer in Venice, telling him that he liked that one so much could we now do another, different programme later in the evening as well.

He who must be obeyed was obeyed.

The Christmas we went to Vienna it snowed beautifully. Robbie took himself off in search of Vienna torte and coffee topped with whipped cream; Magnus Magnusson was introduced to the more resistable delights of the Vienna sewer system in which the film *The Third Man* had been shot and scenes from which we intercut with Magnus's excursion; we discovered that whilst the Danube may not be blue the city of waltz and schmaltz was a baroque Christmas card of delight. The Vienna Boys Choir ended our programme with a carol.

In Copenhagen we discovered the singing duo of Nina and

Frederick who became, for a while, one of Denmark's famous exports; in Edinburgh that great Scottish poet Hugh McDiarmid (C. M. Grieve) talked about what the Festival *should* be doing for Scotland but was not (the Lord Provost declined to take part as he was playing golf); in Geneva Georges Simenon, ignoring the orders of his wife, talked interestingly and at length about his famous detective Maigret; in Brussels we nearly did not get on the air at all when they stopped everything from moving whilst the King declared the Exhibition open. At the time half our team were airborne in a cable car stranded far above the crowds and away from the cameras. We also went to Malta for their Independence celebrations and blotted our copybooks. Earl Mountbatten of Burma was due to hand Malta back to its rightful owners in the evening at the stadium in Valetta. For two days we had filmed stories about the grain stores, the past sieges of the island, we had brought with us one of the pilots of the famous three Gladiators, *Faith, Hope* and *Charity* which had helped save the island during the last war and Robbie had discovered some clandestine firework makers. It was a firework that caused us trouble. We had one of our very own made which read 'Goodnight from Tonight and Malta' and we erected it *outside* the walls of the stadium. We were going to let off our large setpiece before the main display in the stadium was due to begin because we had to catch an aircraft. The film had to be back in London for transmission the next day. So we gathered under our firework, said goodnight and lit the touch paper. The whole affair blazed away gloriously, happily shooting off rockets, spinning catherine wheels and spelling out our message. What we did not know was that at that moment the whole island had their eyes turned towards Valetta looking for the rockets that would signal that the Union Jack had been lowered for the last time. The whole island would then, from end to end, burst into light in one long fireworks party.

You are right. Our firework had prematurely signalled the start of the celebrations. We quickly packed our bags and ran into the night.

If we often envied our footloose friends their explorations the studio had its moments of excitement too. We brought the world to Lime Grove to enlighten, entertain and excite. One moment of excitement I did not enjoy, however, was when C. J. P. Ionides, one of the world's experts on reptiles came to demonstrate the way he had perfected the art of catching snakes. C. J. P. had thrown his watch away in 1927 and had never worn one since; the birds told him the time. He had spent many years in Africa, mainly Tanganyika (now Tanzania) and Kenya, hunting, catching and taming snakes. 'He looks like a faun,' someone had written of him and he did. His bent nose, hooded eyes and pointed ears framed beneath the battered remnants of an old felt hat. He brought with him a collection of snakes.

At this point I must admit that I am by nature a very timid man, cautious, lacking in adventure but filled with admiration for those who are brave or intrepid. In short I scare easily. What is more I do not like snakes, so I was more than apprehensive about the interview. C. J. P. Ionides variously known as Ironhides, the Greek, or Iodine, was renowned throughout East Africa as Bwana Nugo, the Snake Man. His reputation rested largely on his legendary skill as a herpetologist and his ability to catch snakes. He came to demonstrate.

In various bags he had a python, tree snakes, a boom slang, and a gaboon viper. The BBC insisted that a doctor stood at the side of the camera with a syringe and a selection of serums just in case we got bitten. The Snake Man was somewhat immunised against snake bites. 'I have been bitten by a number of poisonous snakes and I've never had any scientific treatment. I've had some treatment from an African who had a native remedy – a prophylactic. Presumably I've germinated a resultant number of anti-bodies in my blood.'

He spoke lovingly of his reptiles, how to handle them, how to milk them of their venom, and then he comfortingly assured me 'You are not wrong in being careful of snakes, some of which are highly poisonous and if approached too closely or frightened or made angry, can kill you. But snakes do not go about normally seeking those whom they may devour. In fact, all they want is to get away from the human being and go about their lawful occasions, either sleeping or catching their food.' We had arranged that when it came to the demonstration of his famous hat trick, he would warn us that he was going to take out a snake. He would then, with us at a safe distance, drop it on the floor and catch it. Ionides would wrap his battered old felt hat into his hand like a mitt and as the snake moved towards him he would catch its head firmly in hat and hand leaving the long body writhing outside. He said that the hat had more venom in it than a dozen snakes ever had.

'This is a tree snake. Its name is boom slang and this is the snake which killed Karl Smith in 1957. He was a great expert. A number of deaths have been recorded from them.'

The doctor by the camera put away his syringe and serums. The snake was a gorgeous translucent green. 'If it is fast enough you'll see it bite me, but I don't think it will – this time.'

Suddenly, and without warning, he dropped the death-dealing wriggling snake on to the studio floor.

169

I am not clear what happened next except that I took off in a flight of fright. Panic propelled me into vertical take off. I looked around from my eventual position of safety and there the Snake Man stood, holding up the old battered hat in which he had buried the business end of the creature, its tail twisting beneath. He was smiling. 'You see how simple it can be. I must put him away. They get damaged too easily.' What scared *him* I asked? 'Motorcars, traffic, heights and bright young women . . . but in the reverse order. Bright young women frighten me most.' He was a magical man.

There were other quite magical moments too. Ned Sherrin, our director, always had a creative eye to go with his persuasive manner. When Dan Dailey came, I interviewed him at the top of a flight of steps so that he could demonstrate the techniques of dancing up and down stairs. Even *I* did it, which is not bad going for someone with the rhythm of a three-legged elephant with gout. But my greatest dancing triumph was also engineered by Ned. This time it was with the assistance of Gene Kelly. Now I have been a life-long admirer of Mr Kelly's, so it was with some trepidation that Ned explained that he would like Gene Kelly to come into the studio, together with me, dancing to the signature tune. Seldom can so ordinary a piece of music have achieved such distinction. Mr Kelly agreed. He came up to the long thin Studio E. As Ned played him the music he walked from the door the length of the studio ending up at my chair. 'Right,' he said, and addressing me, 'all you have to do is to walk in time to the music, straight to the chair.' I did. He rehearsed the walk once more.

Came the start of the programme. The familiar bom, bom bom-bom beat out. Enter – Gene Kelly and me. He skipped and tapped, dancing the whole way and never missing a beat.

As we reached the chair he said, 'There you are. I told you anyone can dance if they try.' All I had done was to walk but for a while I enjoyed a quite spurious reputation as being something of a hoofer. Dear, lovely Bill Cotton could not believe it when I told him I could not dance a step when some of us appeared on his famous *Band Show*. He had seen me with Gene Kelly. It was later on the *Morecambe and Wise Christmas Show* that I was to prove what an awful 'mover' I really was when, in company with Mike Parkinson, Patrick Moore, Eddie Waring and a few others, I was one of the 'dancing boys' in a routine with Eric, Ernie and Glenda Jackson. Dressed in top hat, white tie and tails we looked a right lot of Charlies miming away to 'You were Never Lovelier', whilst falling over our far from dainty feet.

It is not on every programme that you can claim to have danced with Gene Kelly and Dan Dailey, played straight man to Bob

Hope and Jacques Tati and mimed to the songs of the Andrews Sisters. It is not often that you get the chance to meet a future super-star as a schoolboy, as I did.

> *CM*: It has all got to stop. They have had enough. The worms are turning, the rebellion of the long-haired men is getting underway. They are tired of persecution, they are tired of taunts, they are tired of losing their jobs, being sent home from school and college and they are tired of even being refused the dole. So, with a nucleus of his friends, seventeen-year-old David Jones had just founded the Society for the Prevention of Cruelty to Long-Haired Men. Well here they are and who can join? You've got to have your hair nine inches long I understand.
>
> *David Jones*: No we've passed over that now. We are fairly tolerant but for the past two years we have put up with taunts such as 'Darling' and 'Can I carry your handbag!'
>
> *CM*: Does that surprise you? Your hair is rather long.
>
> *David Jones*: Well we have long hair, yes, but its not too bad really. But I like it, we all like it and we don't see why people should persecute us just because of this.
>
> *CM*: How are you going to set about mounting the campaign?
>
> *A N Other*: We will get more followers behind us, we will march like the bomb marchers.
>
> *David Jones*: From Baldermaston.

David Jones changed his name to David Bowie.

Another of our guests to change names was the Honourable Mrs Gerald Legge who came, in November 1957, to give her personal reaction to the decision by the Queen to stop the Presentations at Court, the coming-out of young ladies of quality once they had been presented to the Queen at Buckingham Palace. Interviewed by Derek Hart she told us 'What I think perhaps nobody has quite realised, and I have certainly not seen it emphasised in the papers today, is that with one stroke of the pen the Queen has done away with Society. It is, in fact, a revolution because no longer will it be a social cachet for someone to have been presented at Court because such a thing will no longer exist.'

Now, almost thirty years later, Mrs Legge, is Lady Spencer and stepmother to the Princess of Wales.

We had the reputation of seeking out the off-beat story. The smallest piece of piping ever manufactured, the smallest parish church, the left-handed snails of King Lane, Leeds (the ducks got there before we did and ate them all).

In my notebooks I find some lovely moments recalled.

'Interviewed eighty-year-old Mr Wade, an all-year-round swimmer from Swansea who never dries himself. He says that the sea salt should be left on the skin. "Salt preserves meat, we are meat so salt preserves us." The veteran actor A. E. Matthews was having trouble keeping an old-fashioned lampost outside his house which the local authority wanted to move, so in protest he sat underneath it. We interviewed him. The unpredictable Matty was on form, "No I don't like that question have you got another one there? No don't think much of that one either. Look I'll tell you what I want to say then you ask the question afterwards."' It is an approach to chat show interviews I would like to see tried today.

Multimillionaire Nubar Gulbenkian (who had a fresh buttonhole orchid flown in to London every day) came to the studio in his latest acquisition. He had bought a brand new London taxi, gold-plated, with carriage lamps and whickerwork decor. Why had he wanted a London taxicab when he already had Rolls-Royces? 'They tell me that it can turn on a sixpence, whatever that is.'

If Gulbenkian was the most wittily expensive of our guests Mike Todd, the producer of *Around the World in Eighty Days* and husband of Elizabeth Taylor, was the most flamboyantly natural. Never ducked a question. Asked what it was like coping with the considerable egos of so many considerable cinematic luminaries, he admitted it was 'Hell, hell, hell. Every one of them reckoned they were a bigger star than the other. Half of them wouldn't talk to each other and the other half wouldn't act with each other. That is why it took so long to make and cost so much. Half the time and a lot of the money went in stupid squabbles.'

After his third appearance he thought he had been with us so often we ought to name the bit of our set after him. We did and for years it was the Todd Set.

Elizabeth Schwarzkopf, Thor Heyerdahl, Yehudi Menuhin and Dame Edith Sitwell all took their places in the programme which they shared with dogs who climbed ladders and stories of phantom horses in Birmingham. Mind you even the heavyweight sober-sided *Panorama* had its frivolous moments. One I noted was '*Panorama* had five minutes tonight on the Cult of the Bosom in advertising. James Laver, Barbara Cartland and Robert Robinson getting short time from Richard. Wonder if C. P. Tel raised an eyebrow at *this* sexiness. Doubt it.'

For a very short period I kept a notebook, rather than a diary, because I thought that if ever I missed a diary day I would then pack up writing in it. As it was I soon forgot to keep my notebooks up to date which was a pity. Here are a few jottings.

'March 12th Eric Fowlis and Ian Grant saw the Loch Ness monster. Seemed a sensible pair. Bet they make a bit out of the tourists. Must go to Loch Ness. Sure that *we* could see the monster with Jean's imagination and my eyesight.'

'Derek interviewed coutourier Emilio Pucci who had with him two models, two dressers, a pile of dresses. Models like peasticks. Where do they expect girls with bosoms to put them in those dresses. Looked ravishing.'

'Man from Wiltshire tried to charm rabbits out of holes. Failed. Wonder what he is like with warts?'

'Blind journalist Victor Reisel. Blinded by acid throwing mobsters talked about racketeering in labour unions in US. Sir Alexander Bustamente ex-Chief Minister Jamaica talked to G. J. Smith, Jim Mollison reflecting 25 years after he had flown Atlantic solo. Eamonn Andrews back from trip USA not much to say. Flanders and Swann marvellous. Say they are going to do West End theatre. Alan Whicker with cross Channel swimmers; Dieppe landings anniversary; Hornless sheep and boxer dogs; Australia with lovely commentary by Tony Jay.'

'Had lion tamer up from Olympia circus (Alex Kerr). Lions in courtyard. Derek H. did interview through window. Don't blame him. Left Bertram Mills to load up lions. After we went pub got frantic call hour later. They couldn't get the b★★★★y lions in to the truck. Donald B. said "That is their problem. We are not lion tamers are we?" Believe they missed performance at Olympia.'

The move back to Lime Grove where they had found a studio for us was not the only change. Reporters came and went as did my colleagues in the studio. In 1959 Geoffrey Johnson Smith achieved his ambition and became a Member of Parliament. He had served his apprenticeship as a Conservative London County Councillor and then he won the seat at Holborn and St Pancras. When he came to the studio in the General Election results programme we mischievously kept him waiting a while as he had often done to other people. Anyway Geoffrey proved that not all BBC Current Affairs people at the time were left wing pinkoes.

There were some people who found it difficult to tell what our politics were. On a number of occasions my name had been mentioned in connection with a seat in the House of Commons. A West Country newspaper reported 'Conjecture about the next prospective candidate for North Devon is now snowballing in the area. The latest name to be nodded over at the village whist drives is a famous one . . . that of Cliff Michelmore, the urbane compere of the *Tonight* television programme. . . . A dozen or more people are being tipped as the Tory Party's new candidate against the effervescent Jeremy Thorpe.' It so happened that the day upon which that was published I was having dinner with the effervescent Jeremy. He was better informed than the *Western Mail*. Then came this from a northern constituency. 'As a number of your television friends have stood for our party [Robin Day and Ludovic Kennedy had stood as Liberal candidates] we thought that you might like to break the duck and stand as our candidate.' From Crawley, just down the road from Reigate, 'I understand that a short while ago you were rather keen to stand for Parliament as a Labour Party Candidate. . . . I have been requested to write and ask if you would consider allowing us to nominate you. . . . The constituency is not an easy one but with the change in the political climate I feel it is a winable (sic) one. . . .'

And then this came from a Tory constituency which had just lost a by-election to the Liberals. 'I have been informed that you may be interested in considering standing for Parliament. . . . I have discussed this with the President of the Association and we feel that as a good local man is not available the name of a very well-known personality who is acceptable to a great majority of the population as a person who is pleasing to meet, whose company it is pleasant to be in, and who is so well known as yourself, is our ideal candidate.'

I had no intention of putting the sanity of the electorate to the test. It was impossible to see myself as an 'ideal candidate' for any of the asking parties so I never even contemplated attempting that giant leap across the narrow divide which separates a television hack from a party political hack. In later years others made the jump with ease and distinction. Only Geoffrey Johnson Smith of our number did it then.

Television was slowly being accepted as part of the opinion-forming process. There were many who expressed grave and real concern for some of the effects that it was having on the whole life of the nation. Its technology meant that, as a medium, it was becoming daily more flexible, more mobile and more immediate in this coverage. Within a very short period viewers were seeing pictures and reports of wars, revolutions, murder, riots and disasters as well as face-to-face, probing interviews with politicians on issues of the day. Sport and entertainment were somehow more readily accepted and expected. An enormous library of reports on the effects of television was about to fill the bookshelves and another industry was being born; watching the screen-watchers.

Television criticism began to spread with the speed of a Fleet Street rumour. 'The trivial masquerading as the profound.' 'So-called telly pundits with an inflated sense of their own importance and influence which is quite unjustified', 'Why should we accept these trite, banal instant opinions and judgements?' The knife-sharp tongues of the critics began to hiss.

The small screen was, by the late fifties and early sixties, stirring strong passions. Those who thought they were being offended were roused, not to complaining annoyance as they would be today, but to righteous indignation and all-seeing fury. The trivial often made national newspaper headlines. An item on weights and measures inspectors checking if pubs gave short measure (they did) brought a torrent of abuse from licenced victuallers everywhere. Asking holiday makers if they thought they were getting value for money in Bournemouth, Blackpool or Brighton would bring down the wrath of landladies, councillors and churchmen. Everything was blamed on television. It was responsible for closing cinemas, clubs, pubs, libraries and even a public lavatory in Leicester. The Stepney Registrar reported that 'every time we get a new successful programme on TV we get a crop of new names . . . Perry, Bronco, Gene. . . .'

Doctors weighed in with the new TV medical problems. Television has been accused of causing coronary thrombosis, because of slumping, pigeon toes, epileptic fits, glaucoma, fainting and even sudden death of budgerigars (*Evening Standard*). 'TV cuts Shetland Knit output' (*New York Herald Tribune*). 'Mr Bill Gibbs has installed TV in his fish and chip shop so that customers need not miss any of their favourite programmes' (*Grimsby Evening Telegraph*). 'A Physical Education expert today points to the dangers of "TV bottom and loafer's heart"' (*Daily Mirror*).

But one final quote from the *Western Mail* puts life in those early TV days into perspective: 'Television has *not* affected attendance at Women's Institute meetings in Radnor.'

So what television was *not* doing also made news. A local newspaper complained that 'The way television has treated Nuneaton is nothing short of monstrous. No chance has been given us to see ourselves as others see us.' *Tonight* decided to put that right by despatching Slim Hewitt and his camera to the town. He brought back a report typical of his lugubrious approach. 'The place everyone passes by . . . the lovely outlook on to its forty-two chimney stacks and three slag heaps . . . the street market that is Nuneaton's multiple store,' ran his commentary. Nuneaton was unamused. 'The BBC picked out only the worst spots and left out fine features such as the bus station and some of our flower beds,' complained

175

Mr Mayor. The whole affair ended up in the unwilling lap of the Director General with questions in Parliament for good measure. No grovelling apologies on that occasion, just a shot of Slim scrubbing the studio floor in penance.

Earlier a grovelling public apology had been made because of a *Tonight* interview in August 1957. 'TV's amazing 2 minutes with uncle' ran the headline. The story went on, 'BBC Television did an astonishing thing last night. In an "interview" programme a man was asked: "WHAT DOES IT FEEL LIKE TO BE A SUSPECT IN A MURDER CASE?"'

A man had been questioned by police for the best part of a week; they were inquiring into the murder of his seven-year-old nephew. He had been released and cleared of any connection. The *Daily Telegraph* accused us of broadcasting an item in bad taste and the BBC were quick to agree that it 'should not have been included' and the editor was rebuked for his lack of judgement.

No such treatment was handed out to us after Samuel Shenton had officially complained that he had been held to ridicule by an unfair report on the society which he had founded. It was the belief of the Flat Earth Society that if you walked in a straight line you would eventually come to a barrier at the edge of the world, a solid ice barrier over which thousands of people each year disappear. If one were to walk around the rim of the earth you came back to the place from which you started; the sun was a flat luminous disc, 32 miles in diameter; day and night were controlled by the sun's movements but the earth, covered as it was by a roof, never moved. The report brought Mr Shenton a lot of new followers.

It was into this round world that our son Guy was born on August 27th 1957. It was part of the nightly calypso. I had to stand like an embarrassed lemon whilst Rory McEwen sang:

> Cliff Michelmore's in a lather,
> He has suddenly found he's a father,
> A brand new Michelmore is on *Tonight*,
> Shoving his father out of the light,
> He weighs eight pounds this bouncing lad,
> Which is sixteen stone lighter than his Dad...

Two years later when Jenny was born there was no *Tonight* because we were in the middle of a General Election campaign. Jenny made a dramatic first appearance, delaying it as long as she possibly could. Not only did she keep Jean, the doctor, the nurse, me and everyone else waiting; she was also responsible for a BBC camera crew down in North Devon having a few days off because the reporter was still in Reigate hoping that she would be born before I had to drive down to join them.

When I made a guest appearance on *What's My Line* the following week-end they showed a lovely picture of Jenny and Jean. So her first television appearance was aged three days.

A five-nights-a-week programme with the occasional weekend sports commentary meant that I saw too little of the children in their early days. We did manage to spend Sundays together. We would drive Jean to Broadcasting House for *Family Favourites* and while she was doing that we would go off to the Zoo, Trafalgar Square or see the Changing of the Guard before all having a late lunch at a Corner House together.

To be honest I became a bit of a 'baby bore'. No faltering step or new word went unrecorded. I shot miles of cine-film and endless rolls of colour-slides. My colleagues were long-suffering.

Mind you they still are. Given a quarter of a chance I will still proudly tell them what they are doing. But Guy and Jenny had to grow up with two parents both of whom were well known. A handicap which, to their credit, they have both successfully overcome.

'Position of Privilege'

The twelve years which followed the start of *Tonight* were extremely busy for both of us. Jean had now, in addition to her radio and television programmes, a family to look after. I had more work than I could sensibly cope with but in such circumstances no freelance is ever sensible. With the constant threat of insecurity you store up all you can in the good times. Bad times, you are convinced, are only a week away. I averaged about three hundred broadcasts a year between 1957 and 1969. It was inevitable that some of my old ties would have to be broken. I was reluctant to give up my reports for the West Region which had been so helpful to me in my early days but I had now to take stock. A whole day away doing a two-minute eye-witness report for 5 guineas (including expenses) on a football match in Bournemouth or Bristol was just not worth it any more. My producing of children's programmes also ended, as did my football commentaries on the Light Programme. I got a tetchy note from Outside Broadcasts (Sound), 'In view of your increasing commitments elsewhere there now seems little point in scheduling you to do any more radio football commentaries in the coming season.'

There were compensations. We were able to move to a bigger house, to have Ernie part-time in the garden and his wife Nellie full-time to help with the housework. We also bought a small holiday place in the Isle of Wight and a boat so that the family (or at least the young members of it) could learn to water-ski. I was also able to take up golf on the shamefully thin pretext that my cricketing days were over and I needed exercise. Nearer the truth was the fact that my friends, Harry Secombe, Max Bygraves, Eric Sykes and others, were all starting to play golf and we enjoyed the fun of getting out together.

Another compensation was that I now joined the group of journalists who were on the very fringe of some of the important international events of the decade. One way or another I got caught up in the Cuban Missile Crisis, General Elections, Olympic Games, early Space Shots, Royal Investitures, Hungary and Czechoslovakia, Concorde's maiden flight, the Apollo Moon programme; I was also to introduce the first televised Grand National once Mrs Topham had agreed that television cameras could enter the hitherto forbidden grounds of Aintree.

Tonight was my regular commitment until *24 Hours* replaced it in October 1965. But, as has always been the case with the BBC, the more programmes you do the more they want you to do. Familiarity breeds content in some producers, although I suspect over-familiarity breeds resentment in some of the viewers.

One problem that excessive exposure does raise is that a number of viewers assume proprietary rights over those who appear, in their homes, on the small screen. They demand that you stop whatever you are doing – eating, playing golf, walking with your children or sleeping in a deckchair – and repay part of their licence fees by giving them your undivided attention for as long as they need it. Families in mid-mouthful find it difficult to deal with sometimes. Fortunately Jean is far less brittle than I am on such occasions. I am inclined to take on a case-hardening of aloof shyness, pretending not to hear the constant shouts 'The next *Tonight* tomorrow night then Cliff?' The tenth time in a morning that someone calls across the street at me my nerves begin to wear thin and fray at the edges. I know that, by now, I should have got used to the problems of recognition but I have not.

There are those who can cope with such attention with admirable grace and equanimity. Eric Morecambe was wonderful at giving himself to others unstintingly, even when he was not well. We were with him at Richmond ice-rink, shortly before he died, and he was having his photograph taken with the children and signing autographs right through the long interval. Harry Secombe, Larry Grayson, Rolf Harris and Roy Castle are others whom I admire for their ability to accept it all and never appear to be putting on a performance.

Sophia Loren when she was asked about the problems she had dealing with public adulation told her questioner that she found it difficult always being 'on parade'. When asked about being interviewed she replied 'What I would like is for Cliff Michelmore to come up to me in the street without warning and do an interview

179

there and then for which I was not prepared.' We did just that, in Park Lane. We waylaid her out shopping and she was as good as her word. 'The last time we talked in a studio you were wearing a sheath of shimmering gold. Do you really not mind us catching up with you on your way to the shops, unprepared to be interviewed like this?' I asked.

'It does not matter does it?' she replied, 'you can always throw the film away if it is no good. And as for not being prepared I get so scared on my way to the studios for interviews I prefer this way.'

What a lady.

And what a man James Mason was.

Walking in Terminal 2 at Heathrow to catch a plane to Geneva I suddenly found him at my elbow. 'Hullo, you won't remember me but we met at Lime Grove some time ago. I'm James Mason.'

You won't remember me – who could ever forget James Mason?

In those years I was to meet a lot of memorable people. I was fortunate enough to be given a series in which I could choose my own guests. It was called *With Michelmore* and my list included Matt Busby, Mrs Mary Wilson, Field Marshal Montgomery, Frank Cousins, Laurens van der Post, Ginger Rogers and David Niven. Typically David Niven sent me a hand-written reply saying that he would be delighted on the one condition that he would know the other guests would be.

David had lived in Bembridge, on the Isle of Wight, so we had a connection there. He told me that he was the first secretary of the Garland Club and still remembered the house in which his mother lived because the wind would whistle under the front door, straight through the house and out the back. I could assure him that they had fixed the doors since then. We had also met on a *Tonight* programme just after he collected his Oscar for *Separate Tables*. We finished the interview, I thanked him and turned to introduce a film story from Alan Whicker from the South Seas. 'What do you do if it breaks down now?' he asked as the film started. As if we had laid on a demonstration the film did grind to a halt. I turned to him, 'Now I can ask you the questions that I did not have time to ask you before,' and we went on talking for another few minutes until the film was fixed and we were off, once more, to the South Seas.

Our long interview was a huge success. It was in the days before he wrote *The Moon's a Balloon* or *Bring on the Empty Horses* and after we had finished I asked him if he ever thought of setting it all down in an autobiography. His reply was that whilst it had been suggested to him he thought that he would make an even worse writer than an actor. He went on to prove himself wrong, with both his books deservedly bestsellers.

His self-deprecating statements were already, of course, legend but I collected a few more in the course of the interview. 'I did a play and I'm a very bad stage actor; I'm a pretty bad movie actor but I'm a ghastly stage actor and Larry Olivier said "You have got to go on and do it. You will learn more by a disaster than you will from a success." I've done two plays. One was a great success and one was a disaster and I really don't know which I hated most.' He loved first nights because of what could go wrong, but after the first week he got bored and began to get fascinated by the audience. 'I love the theatre, I am never out of it as audience but I cannot *do* it.' There were many of us who disagreed. Our camera and studio crew were captivated by David Niven not least because of his enjoyment of telling the story of how he got out of the Regular Army when he sent the following letter: 'Dear Colonel, Request permission resign commission, Love Niven.' During the war he had returned to Britain from America and served with distinction.

Field Marshal Viscount Montgomery of Alamein KG GCB DSO provided me with the opportunity to sit and talk to him inside the famous caravan which he had used during the desert campaign against Rommel. I had previously met Monty in Germany and then later at the BBC in Bristol when he agreed to an interview for my newspaper column about being the President of Portsmouth Football Club. He gave me a few minutes between rehearsing for his television series and having lunch with the local tobacco company. When I told him I thought he was very much against smoking he said 'smoking was one thing, having shares in the company was another'. That rare twinkle lit his sharp eyes. As for Portsmouth FC, 'Football, Cliff, is just like war. You've got to have a plan; got to be trained ready for action; got to have the right people in the right places, and you've got to know your enemy. Must expect casualties and must have plans for that too. Just like warfare, must learn to adapt. Must have a good commander, must know who is in charge.'

His favourite television programme? 'Oh the one with all those pwetty girls in pwetty frocks dancing in formation. *Come Dancing*, that's it.'

At his home at Isington Mill there was no doubt who was in charge. It was to that beautiful house by the River Wey that I went, arriving as ordered at three o'clock very precisely. My open top TR6 gently crunched the gravel of his driveway and as I stopped a voice came from under the entrance porch, 'Only a former Woyal Air Force officer would dwive a motorcar as vulgar as that. Let me show you awound.' We went on a tour of inspection. He pointed out the three caravans which then stood in the grounds. That one he pinched from some Italian, that one was Rommel's and that one was his.

We went into his study to discuss the programme. Well perhaps *discuss* is not quite the right word. We were to prepare the *plan* of the programme. His desk was laid out with absolute precision; pens, pencils, papers and diary all lined up neatly as if on parade.

The first thing was 'I don't like being called Lord Montgomery, there are too many Lords about. Field Marshal, there aren't many of them. So call me Field Marshal, right?'

Right. Yes, he would answer questions about things other than his new book *A History of Warfare*. No, he did not want any advance notice of the line of questioning. Yes, we could do it in his caravan. We had a plan. After tea and a piece of Fuller's walnut cake I left him so that I could make the arrangements with my producer. On the day Monty was in cracking form

CM: What about growing old?

Montgomery: Some of my best commanders were young . . . you must be young. I felt rather old myself. When I fought the Battle of Alamein I was fifty-five, and in Normandy fifty-seven. But I've led a very abstemious life, you see. I don't drink, I don't smoke and I've never been mixed up with women.

CM: You were once married. Come on, Field Marshal.

Montgomery: I was married for ten years. Only one woman in my life.

CM: You were married late?

Montgomery: Forty. I hadn't time. I was studying my profession. I realised this was a life study and I got down to it. I gave up everything and I think the young officer of today has to realise it.

CM: The young?

Montgomery: Well I don't mind if they like to have long hair and mini-skirts. I remember the first time I saw a mini-skirt in Farnham. Put my spectacles on, looked round . . . the fact that boys wear long hair, a way of expressing themselves – let them wear long hair, I've a great belief in youth. If this country were ever in danger all these young people would turn out again.

CM: Politics?

Montgomery: In my mind war is a very rough dirty game. But politics, by gum, dreadful. I wouldn't ever do it.

CM: Eisenhower? How did you feel when he assumed direct command?

Montgomery: Well I always say I would prefer not to discuss my comrades in the last war but I would describe Ike as an extremely good supreme commander, but when he decided to come down off his lofty perch and take command . . . pity . . . you see he's never fired a shot in anger . . .

CM: Churchill with whom you had dinner at the Royal Beach Hotel after Dunkirk?

Montgomery: It was at that dinner that he said to me 'General what will you drink?' I said 'Water, I don't drink and I don't smoke and I'm one hundred per cent fit.' And in a flash the old man said 'I drink and I smoke and I'm two hundred per cent fit.' Then I knew we would win the war. We had got the man.

We had tea and Fuller's walnut cake after we had finished filming. 'Now Cliff bring that young son over here. He must go to my school at Leatherhead.' That is where Guy went to school, St Johns, Leatherhead.

Monty loved the hero-worship, liked taking over, liked still being in charge. After he died I missed going across to see him very much. We also missed the arrival of his Christmas card. It came, without fail, either on the last day of November or on the first of December.

Throughout the years I have been aware of the position of privilege I had, being allowed to talk at length to so many people I have admired. Matt Busby was one and he, surprisingly, told me of the day when he nearly chucked up football altogether. 'I had a form of inferiority, I thought the first team players were gods. One Sunday night I had my case packed and I said to myself I must get out of here. Phil McCloy came in and said 'Now don't be silly, give it a little more time.' Football should be grateful to Phil McCloy.

And RAB, Lord Butler, Master of Trinity on why he never achieved the highest of all Government position: 'I've been accused of having too placid a disposition and I think at times I haven't perhaps pushed as much as I might have done. . . . I left the Home Office at my own wish, I left the Treasury at my own wish.'

Laurens van der Post spoke of facing death by the Japanese during the war for showing 'the spirit of wilfulness'. 'I didn't want to be strangled, I didn't want to be hanged or buried alive. I didn't want to be bayonetted – all forms of execution I had seen. I wanted to be shot,' he said. How he avoided that is another story.

Laurens van der Post was an almost saintly man. Calm, deeply philosophical and full of insights into the African people. A bushman once told him 'We Africans do not need a telegraph service like you white men do because we have a tapping inside us that tells us what goes on at a great distance.'

In those pre 'chat-show' days there was often more time for the long, wide-ranging interviews. But styles were rapidly changing and so too were attitudes and programmes. On *Tonight* some tension was showing. Increasingly the production team would revert to 'The Book' in which were recorded the film stories and their dates of transmissions. We were repeating stories that had appeared elsewhere much more frequently than in the early days. This was because it was becoming much more difficult to get items exclusive to *Tonight* from outside London since, by now, every region and national centre was producing its own mini-version of *Tonight*. The ashtrays in the production office were filling with half-smoked cigarettes far quicker than they were in the fifties and the thrust had gone, much of it with the departure of many of our early pioneers. Some had gone to start their own series, others had moved across to *That Was the Week* and the strain on the remaining contributors were showing. Five nights a week for eight years had taken its toll. The final programme came not a month too soon for me. In October 1965 I was to move across to a new current affairs late evening programme, *24 HOURS*.

Whenever I am asked to recollect in tranquillity about the real fun days of TV the time up to the ending of *Tonight* must be my choice. I never looked upon them as the Golden Days of TV as so many of my contemporaries did. They were far from golden in terms of financial rewards but there were other compensations. For example I ended up in Madame Tussauds. My family thought that was *the* achievement of a lifetime. But there comes a moment when even in a waxworks you become dated, lose your appeal and get consigned (and retired) to the depths of a cave in Wookey Hole. There to this day my head sits on a shelf next to Eric Morecambe's. 'They look like identical twins don't they' said a lady when I once went there to do a programme. She didn't recognise me in the flesh. The head on the shelf was marked with a name tag to identify which was which. I could not have told us apart either.

I was also invited to switch on the lights of Blackpool in 1963. All had been forgiven for the earlier *Tonight* foray when we upset the landladies, mayor and council. It was something I hugely enjoyed. I was ushered out on to the Town Hall balcony with a vast crowd in the street below. Pull the switch, up go the fireworks and the whole town is set ablaze with dazzling lights. You almost feel the surge of the power. We still have the canteen of kitchen cutlery they gave me as a memento. The six-foot stick of rock has long since been forgotten by the local children's home. On my study shelf is another reminder of those days and one of the proudest of my possessions. It is a silver camera, like the one the Sportsview Personality of the Year gets. This was given me 'In appreciation' by my 'London Colleagues' after the 1964 Tokyo Olympic Games. I headed the back-up team in London and we had problems. The pictures reaching us from Japan arrived without a whisper of sound from our large commentary team out there on the spot. The McWhirter twins, Harry Walker, Simon Smith and Dorian Williams filled in magnificently from London commentating direct from the screen, half a world away from the action and no one could detect the difference. We were not best pleased therefore to hear the Head of Outside Broadcasts on a telephone line to Tokyo saying that 'the people back here are not sufficiently knowledgeable. They don't know what it is all about.' He was unaware that the line was open for us all to hear. Such ingratitude fired me into action. On the phone I told him that if there was not an immediate personal, public, apology the whole bloody lot of us would walk out then and there. Another team could work twenty-four hours out of twenty-four. Cliff Morgan, our London producer and one of the finest men television has ever persuaded across from a distinguished sporting career, was surprised by the ferocity of my attack. But he and the rest of the team got the apology which they all deserved.

My days as a sports presenter and commentator were now few in the land of television. But that year, 1964, I almost became one of the regular team of golf commentators. Being on speaking terms with Arnold Palmer, Peter Thomson, Kel Nagle and Tony Lema was something I found particularly rewarding, and interviewing Tony after he won the Open at St Andrews is an experience I cherish. But golf tournaments took up a lot of my time and, what is more, I talked too much when I did them, so I stopped. Then my great friend Peter Alliss tried his hand at it, found it both to his and the viewers' liking, and so started a long, and rightly successful, new career.

I had been in the studio in October 1957 when the Russians first sent up their Sputnik and also in May 1961 when the first American Alan Shepard was lobbed up into space. From then until 1970 I fronted the studio part of the space programme. Many thought that I was there to act as an interpreter for Patrick Moore and James Burke, or put a brake on them when they became carried away. We spent many long nights in that studio where I too was swept along on the enthusiastic wave crests created by Patrick and James. To be there in the studio at the receiving end, when man first stepped on the moon was an enormous thrill. To be there when Apollo 13 got into dreadful trouble was traumatic. We were not to know until the very last moment of splashdown if that mission would end in disaster, but even Apollo 13 provided one light moment. We had asked Bert Ford to come in and give us a weather report for the splashdown area in the Pacific. In great detail he forecast the cloud cover, windspeed, even the direction and height of the waves on the other side of the globe. I closed the programme saying that we would be back for the critical re-entry and splashdown. After that all night transmission we went out of the studio into the early morning air at Television Centre and, as we did so, Bert looked up and said without a trace of anything but surprise 'Oh, it's raining'. What was happening in the Pacific he knew about, not the rain at White City.

Years later I had the pleasure of meeting Alan Shepard, the man who hit the golf ball on the moon, in a match at Gleneagles. I played with Bruce Forsyth. His partner was Burt Lancaster. You can see the privileged company one gets to mix with in this business.

Jean meanwhile had decided to do less broadcasting (*retire* was not the word). At TV Centre I was approached and asked to help them put together a *This is Your Life* Jean Metcalfe. I had already helped trap two friends of mine, Donald Campbell and Stanley Matthews for the programme. For some reason I had reservations and said so. They did not pursue the matter but I was determined to 'make it up to my wife' because I had a sneaking suspicion, totally confirmed since then, that she would have enjoyed it. So in compensation, and to celebrate her twenty years of broadcasting, I arranged a special surprise *This is Your Life* type dinner. Peter Alliss and his wife were coming to stay and Jean knew that just one or two other people were going to be there too. Little did she know who was on that guest list. We had many surprises waiting for her. Richard and Dilys Dimbleby; David Frost; singer Mike Sarne her heart-throb of the month; Peter and Virginia May; David and Vivienne Nixon; the Milnes and Baverstocks; the Sykes, Secombes and Bygraves; Alan Whicker; Reggie Brook, John and Anne Webster and Maggie Hubble all from the Light Programme days and before; and Noel Iliff who had started her on her way. Kenneth Adam, her former Light Programme boss, had been digging into her early files and in his speech quoted from Jean's first annual report – 'Miss Metcalfe cannot spell'.

She may have regretted that she was not on *This is Your Life* but I bet they could not have laid on such a constellation as that. I believe that she has now forgiven me.

In 1965 a few of us learned that Richard Dimbleby was suffering from cancer. There was no outward sign that he was undergoing treatment that would have kept a lesser man away from work. Richard kept going and earned yet more admiration and respect from those who worked with him. He never did get his own late night talk programme he once told me he would have liked but he achieved everything else, notching up in the process a long list of 'firsts'. First BBC news observer, first BBC war correspondent, civil war reporter and first to reveal the horrors of the concentration camps to listeners. The Coronation, the State Opening of Parliament, the relay from Calais, Telstar across the Atlantic and through the Iron Curtain; Richard was there.

On Wednesday December 22nd he died at nine in the evening. At a quarter past ten we broadcast an obituary devoting the entire *24 HOURS* programme to tributes from many who had worked by his side through his long and distinguished career. Afterwards Paul Fox and I went down into one of the hospitality rooms at Lime Grove. We had been there but a few minutes when Paul answered the phone. 'I don't know' I heard him say. 'It has only just happened.' He then turned to me and said 'That was —— asking who was going to introduce *Panorama* now.' He named a *Panorama* interviewer. 'Well *he* won't,' said Paul. Later, however, he *did*. Such is the way decisions are made in television to this day.

Richard was unique, a man of his time who set standards he expected the rest of us to follow. His preparation for any broadcast was meticulous and his presentation faultless. He was quite simply irreplaceable. He had shown in his later days a courage which matched the integrity, devotion and discipline which he brought to everything he did. I was fortunate enough to work with him on many occasions; the BBC Tribute to Kennedy, General Elections, *Panorama*, and Specials on Suez and Hungary among them. No one could possibly assume his place and the BBC sensibly did not even try. His former roles were split, often having two people doing what Richard had handled on his own. That was the same with two General Election Results programmes I did in 1966 and 1970. When the round-the-world-by satellite programme *Our World* came along in 1967 I was to handle that one on my own. I began to realise then what a master Richard had been and what he meant when he said that there was no substitute for pre-broadcast homework. Fortunately I had done mine so that when the sound from Brazil went down and we had the great Pelé playing football on the sands with a group of youngsters I was able to take over the commentary. Incidentally it was on, and for that programme, that the Beatles recorded 'Love, Love, Love'.

The new late night programme *24 HOURS* which I introduced together with Kenneth Allsop was much more political than *Tonight* had been, which was understandable. *Nationwide* and a clutch of regional magazine programmes had taken over the *Tonight* time slot and loseness of style. *24 HOURS* came out of the much more heavily political stable which had previously housed such programmes as *Gallery* and and it was to become the late evening Current Affairs flag ship. Problems still seemed to be frequent. While Ian Smith, Prime Minister of Rhodesia was in London for talks, our invitation to him to speak about sanctions and the independent future of his country was withdrawn upon the direct orders of the Board of Governors. He was to be regarded as a rebel leader of an illegal regime. Billy Graham was upset when we confronted him with two of his 'converted followers' who had severe reservations about his evangelical methods. And we were constantly being accused of being too left or too right wing in our approach, but that is the accepted way of life in current affairs even now.

Our studio interviews and discussions were no longer bite-size. They ranged wider and longer than they had on *Tonight* but not, I always thought, necessarily deeper. Our reporters were on every continent and in every political hot-spot from the Far to Middle East, from Africa to South America. The programme itself got out and about much more, too. For a whole week I was in Montreal with programmes from EXPO '67 – the satellite was then on free trial offer; the Eurovision lines stretched into Hungary and we went up on the Citadel above Budapest; in the heady days of Dubchek's New Czechoslovakia I was in Prague finding out how industry, press and broadcasting, youth and housewives saw their future. We were there right up to the time when the Russians drove their tanks into the city. I went to Tunis hoping to present the first ever live transmission from the continent of Africa. We were for the first thirty-five minutes frustrated because a link went down somewhere in Italy.

Dick Francis, the producer, swears on his heart that a little Italian electrician was made to peddle his bike up the hill and hold the wires together so that Britain could enjoy a choir singing unintelligible songs from the steps of a café in Hammermet. The son of the President, Bourguiba Junior, had long since left us in a huff at not being interviewed.

23/CLIFF

Just Coming Up to the Angel

Back home there were some even more uncomfortable moments. In 1966 I had interviewed a Northern Ireland minister about the situation there. The following day, July 14th, we received a call in the office from a man claiming to be from the Ulster Volunteer Force. He was angered by what I had said. 'Tell him we are coming to get him,' said the caller. The threat was taken very seriously. It is little comfort to be told that if they warn you they are coming you are all right; it is when they do not tell you that you worry. After the programme that evening I was taken home in a police car. Entering the car in a backyard behind Lime Grove, I was told to get down on the floor, then we drove at speed out into the road and away. Very impressive. Very frightening I can tell you. It was past midnight and at home there seemed to be nobody about until our car came to a halt. From under the shadows of the trees stepped a man. A plain clothes policeman. I suddenly realised what it must feel like to have to live your life under constant surveillance. We did not tell the family until it was time to call off the watchful, permanent escort. We thought it might frighten them.

Later that same year I had to face another quite different emotional experience. In October I was called off the golf course at Walton Heath to learn of the tragedy that had happened that morning in the Welsh valleys at Aberfan. An aircraft was waiting at Gatwick and we flew to Cardiff and made our way up the valleys via Broadcasting House in Cardiff where they gave us the latest, and even more horrifying, news of the mounting number of children who were being brought out of the school. They had been killed in an avalanche of slurry which had slipped down from the tip overlooking the school enveloping the building in minutes.

We left the car outside the village and walked up through the narrow streets towards the school. From the coal pit the miners were coming off shift and going to join their colleagues who were already attempting to clear away the soft, filthy, murderous mud. That night from a low hill overlooking the grieving village we reported, as best we could, what had happened that day in Wales. One hundred and sixteen children and twenty-eight adults had died. There was not a family in the whole of Aberfan which had not lost a son, daughter, father, mother or friend.

From Hobart House, the Coal Board offices in London, officials were quick to criticise and condemn the amount and manner of the press and television coverage. We tried to separate fact from rumour and present an accurate and compassionate report. The people of Aberfan were left to their private grief.

Understandably the Coal Board may not have taken any comfort from what we had to report but the letters we received from the people in the valley and beyond were of some comfort to us all. I have kept them ever since.

'The slurry seemed to be about our feet and stifling our breathing. I do not know how you said a word. I want you to know that I felt for both you *and* Mrs Michelmore,' wrote a lady from Oddingley, Droitwich.

'My home is Merthyr Tydfil so I know how you felt. Your broadcast was one I will never forget, your face I will always remember.' Mrs Hussey, Dolgellau, North Wales.

It is an experience I shall never forget either. Even today I find myself hesitating before putting a piece of coal on the fire.

By its very nature television sweeps along from one crisis to the next; from tragedy to farce, from bloody wars to peaceful revolutions, we never knew what to expect except the unexpected. Each day, or each week, we reported and reacted to fresh situations. In December 1967 a military coup in Greece resulted in King Constantine being deposed. King Constantine, together with Queen Anne-Marie, Queen Mother Frederica, Princess Irene and the royal children, and accompanied by the Prime Minister, flew from Greece to Rome in two Army planes supplied by the Military Government. I was on my way to the Greek Embassy in Rome overlooking the Borghesa Gardens for the first filmed interview he had ever given. King Constantine was determined to return to his country and said so in a quiet dignified manner. He had failed in his counter coup against the Colonels but you had to admire his spirit and defiance, even though we doubted if he would ever see Athens again.

Some while later I was to go to Rome again, this time to interview Queen Frederica, King Constantine's mother, about her autobiography. She lived in a villa on the outskirts of the city with the entrance hall piled high with toys because the King and Queen regularly brought her grandchildren to see her. There was an unmistakable air of sadness about the villa. It was a small substitute for a palace and the Queen Mother knew it.

In Wales I shared another royal first with Brian Connell when we interviewed Prince Charles before his Investiture at Caernarvon. It was recorded in the BBC studios. We had a preliminary meeting and a palace briefing beforehand but when it came to the day of the recording Prince Charles was a deal more relaxed about the whole thing than some of the broadcasting hierarchy who had assembled to press the palm.

The investiture itself was an occasion I was delighted to have been involved in. The nearest I had got to the purple regal fringe before had been as Jean's assistant at Buckingham Palace. Later I was to act as the host at a televised party the BBC threw for the people of Great Somerford when Mark Phillips, who lived in the village, married Princess Anne. Then came commentaries at the Queen Mother's installation as Lord Warden of the Cinque Ports and at the Review of the Fleet at Spithead. So at least I marked up one or two royal moments to put with Jean's.

There comes a time, even in television, when you begin to feel that it has gone on rather too long for your own comfort. There are those who play the games of power politics and stay the course far longer, almost for ever. Wining and dining with Directors General, Controllers, Heads of Department and the like has never been something I enjoyed. So I seldom got asked. I left that to others. It was always said that at Lime Grove you never need worry about someone stabbing you in the back. In television they just stabbed you straight in the chest. The intrigue and plotting that went on in panelled rooms and upper offices had to be experienced to be believed. Those of us who were on the outer circle half-jokingly and half-seriously, used to say that *we* always learned what was going on in our lives through the canteen staff. Kenneth Allsop claimed that his source of information was the lift driver.

In my days, staff communication, particularly with freelance contributors, was not considered a priority so I kept to myself the fact that I was planning to move into industry and set up a company within the EMI group. By 1968 I had decided that I would give up nightly programmes and settle for a more predictable lifestyle which would allow me more time with the family. One critic, H. R. F. Keating, greeted my departure from the daily scene with 'What perhaps Michelmore more than any other performer stands for, and what he might represent, is something that could well do with being held up to the light of day all wriggling at the end of a pair of forceps.' Keating did just that. 'In fact the sheer weight of opinion that he and his like deluge us with, often obscures the issues on which it is profitable to exercise our minds in opinion-formulating. In the rush to comment on anything and everything that happens, provided that it has only just happened, the true moral dilemmas that confront us are submerged.'

That was written in 1968. Now in 1986 we face even more of that 'ceaseless wail of opinion' coming at us from all angles; out of the satellites in the sky, by cable, by video as well as four home channels. I have never regretted leaving the world of current affairs.

As well as setting up a company to make video cassette programmes in EMI there was still enough in television to keep me off the streets and on the screens. *British by Choice* gave those who had settled in this country an opportunity to explain why; *Across the Great Divide* allowed Britons who had gone across the Atlantic and made a success of their lives to tell how they had done it; *Wheelbase* gave me the chance to learn something about the motor industry and to get out on the East African Safari Rally. Then Tom Savage asked me if I would like to present the new *HOLIDAY '69* programme. Suddenly I was to become a traveller and get paid for the pleasure.

The *HOLIDAY* programme has taken me around the world. But even that halcyon assignment had its drawbacks. You can't come home leaving a camera crew without a reporter half-way across the world no matter how pressing the reason. I was away filming at the time of my brother Jack's death in 1983. When my sister Violet died, two years ago, it was like losing a parent all over again. But on the day of her funeral I had to be filming in Bermuda. I should have been on the Isle of Wight. I should have said goodbye. There will always be an unfilled corner of my memory which tells me so. It had been the same when brother Jack died a year earlier. Jean and Jenny went in my place and my daughter had the courage to sing 'God be in my Head' in the quiet crematorium at the end of the service, 'for you Dad' she said. At that moment I sat alone in an empty cathedral among alien palm trees, thousands of miles away. Nevertheless the Director General, Charles Curran, was to tell me 'You have got the best job in the whole of television'. 'Probably,' I replied. 'I would certainly rather have it than yours any day.'

There was also a brief, unhappy spell with Southern Television at Southampton where if it had not been for some understanding and marvellous colleagues on *Day by Day* I might have been tempted to jump into the river with frustration. Being away from home a couple of nights a week was not what was needed at a time when our children had so recently flown the nest and were away busy building their own lives. Even if Southern had kept their franchise I was not going to stay. It proved impossible to commute, as I had hoped, between our house on the Isle of Wight and the studios in Southampton because there were no late boats. The journey from Reigate was long and tedious. I needed to be at home a great deal more than I was.

When you set off in search of your past you obviously look back over your shoulder and ponder what might have been. That seems to me a reasonable thing to do. What seems to me both futile and unproductive is to go through the soul-searching exercise of examining what would have happened 'if only I had . . .' Unshackled by the sadness regret could put upon me I am able to smile when I look back at some of the chances I have avoided.

The offers from the USA and Canada which I rejected because I did not want to uproot the family were not in retrospect really all that attractive. In a country where they are only able to countenance winners and runners-up are disposable I cannot imagine that I would have been a winner. (I did not rate myself a Major League player.) Near to the end of Freddie Grisewood's days on radio's *Any Questions* Michael Bowen, the producer, came up from Bristol to London to ask if I would take over the chairman's job. It was something I would very much have liked to do but it would have meant more travelling. I declined with grateful thanks for even being considered as a replacement for Freddie. Then there was the turning down of *This is Your Life* after Eamonn Andrews had crossed the divide to Thames from the BBC. Bill Cotton has never forgotten, nor will he ever forgive, that it was on offer to me and because of my dithering the BBC lost the chance to keep the programme seventeen years ago or more.

And there are many more. 'Forgetfulness transforms every occurrence into a non-occurrence,' wrote Plutarch and I am aware of that thought as I note down some events of the past forty years of my broadcasting life. I am equally aware that many important moments have been forgotten or only half-recalled.

Was my homely face really cast in the role of Big Brother in a TV production of *1984*?

In 1966 did I really establish a world record (and get in the Guinness Book) for the greatest amount raised by a TV or Radio Appeal?

Was I really in mid-sentence when a voice came into my earpiece and said 'We are getting a report that President Kennedy has been shot. Say something and hand back to continuity'?

Was I really part of the 'Golden Age of Television' and was Jean part of the 'Golden Age of Broadcasting'?

And what is the next age to be called?

When I began broadcasting in Hamburg in 1947 the transistor had yet to make its appearance in the market place. Yet within nine years the 'tranny' was everywhere and the Russians had launched their Sputnik into orbit. Nine years later the first commercial communications satellite was in operation, man had walked and driven on the moon and we had seen all that on television in our own homes. I had been fortunate enough to be a member of the team which had brought those pictures to British screens. I had seen so much innovation, so many technical barriers pushed back and frontiers crossed, it was often bewildering.

Today there is a whole new cornucopia of technological advances being poured out upon us. It is hard to keep abreast of all the new delights the box has to offer these days but I shall go on trying. The technology many change but other things never will. Some viewers will still seek to exercise proprietary rights over those of us on their screens and tell us exactly what they think we should do. Take this from D. Antley of Brighton which came in the post last week:

> Dear Cliff, I wish you would not give your hair the Grecian 2000 – your face does not match it. Why not grow old gracefully and show your grey hair together with your wife Jean Metcalfe. So I beg you get your priorities right, as we all have to on becoming middle-aged. Yours truly, D. Antley.

I have a number of little vanities but neither Grecian 2000 nor the wearing of a hairpiece is among them. Long ago my forehead lengthened prematurely as my hair-line receded and the attempt to hide this shortcoming was to no avail. Now, having crossed the autumn equinox of life, I have come to terms with the fact that I can no longer keep up with, let alone get ahead of, the young

Turks of the eighties. So I do not even try to whether it is at work, play or at home.

Taking stock can be an unsettling experience. Long-closed doors must be opened and unattractive 'sleeping dogs' disturbed. It is tempting at the end of the enterprise to finish it off with a pleasing bow. No loose ends to spoil the symmetry. But an incident two years ago made me realise that personal stock-taking does not necessarily result in neatly balanced books.

At five o'clock one morning I collapsed on the bathroom floor and, in the five minutes it took for an ambulance to arrive, lost consciousness. Thanks to resuscitation equipment and the skill of the ambulancemen, I began to come round on the way to hospital at a point where the road passes a pub which has the golden figure of a winged seraph on its sign. 'It's all right Mr Michelmore,' said one of the attendants, 'we're just coming up to the Angel.' My worst fears that I was dying were immediately confirmed. It came as a considerable relief shortly afterwards to find myself alive, if not kicking, in the Intensive Therapy Unit of the East Surrey Hospital.

Anyone who has shared the experience of a suspected heart attack will confirm that there's nothing like being wired up to all-seeing monitoring screens for clearing away the mind's excess baggage. That was when I began taking stock. My introspection lasted well into the second day when a phone rang on the Sister's desk. The nurse who took the call answered evasively – 'I am not in a position to tell you that. You must put your enquiry to the Hospital Administrator' – then firmly replaced the receiver. Her pretty little face split with laughter as she came over to my bed. 'I don't know how he got through to the ward,' she said 'but that was a *Sunday Times* reporter and all he asked was "Is Mr Michelmore *dead* yet?"'

No, by God, I wasn't. And I was feeling stronger by the minute.

The hospital's investigations fizzled out inconclusively as, I'm told, they often do in these circumstances. But I was lucky. Months later the puzzle was resolved. The heart attack symptoms seemed to have been caused by a mysterious blood condition which had now cleared up. I was enormously relieved and so, if they had any sense, were my family for I am not a mutely suffering invalid. A head cold has me counting life insurance. Anything more troublesome and I find myself imagining obituaries, usually along these lines:

Michelmore found criticism hard to accept and could be intolerant even when proved wrong. His temper was combustible, on a short fuse, but, to be fair, he would as quickly forget the cause of his anger when it had passed. He was a voracious reader, rapidly absorbing and retaining information, forming opinions and taking decisions. But slow to make friends. Popularity was not important to him. He was not afraid of losing favour in what he considered to be a good cause. At times he lacked concentration and the persistence to see a project through to its conclusion. Direct rather than subtle, he never claimed to be a patient man.

They might also say that I had been extremely fortunate to have achieved a measure of success in broadcasting in spite of lacking the intellectual powers and education of some of my contemporaries and the physical attributes of others.

Hopefully they would add that I was greatly blessed by the love of a wife and family who, with good humour and tolerance, overlooked, and even ignored, the deficiencies in my character.

If, by the time those obituaries are written, there are grandchildren to be mentioned among my descendants, I hope they will be able to say that Michelmore found unexpected resources of patience with them – matching speeds with tottering toddlers, curbing his frustration as they began to outstrip him, flattered when his exaggerations, so despised by their parents, held them in fascinated awe.

I mentioned earlier the unease it causes when you have to disturb 'sleeping dogs' as you look back and take stock. It was painful to remember growing up without a father and the insecurity that brought when I became a parent myself; the recollection of children which might have been, and the deaths of my mother and older siblings; above all, the unhealed grief of that missed farewell to an irreplaceable sister. But there can be no shadows without light.

Nothing can ever dull the brightness of the moment when I met an auburn haired announcer in 1949 and bought her a cup of coffee at a boxing match. The years we've spent together ever since continue to shine. She says it would be only 'airport insurance' to return to her childhood religion at this late hour. But my faith?

Whilst it has often wavered and sometimes faltered, it has never really left me and I pray it never will.

Rhubarb Chutney?

When it came to the crunch in 1979 that 'dress rehearsal' with a broken ankle a few years before did nothing to soften the children's departure. Guy was at Oxford. Jenny was at the Guildford School of Acting and Cliff was working for Southern Television three days a week staying in Southampton. It all came nastily and suddenly together.

No matter how many test flights they make in preparation, there is no mistaking the moment when fledgling children are finally buoyantly on the wing. True, there will be vacations and holiday jobs based near home but the role changes from doting parent to infrequent landlady. This after all is what you've worked for over the past twenty years, to see them able to set off, head high, to take what they can from life and replace it with whatever they have to give. Nevertheless, I can't have been the only mother whose upper lip lost its starch on those empty days in the middle of the week when I was the only person in the house. I wandered aimlessly about plumping cushions – which I deplore – doing a little desultory housework – which I detest – but what was it for? All this could be done swiftly and painlessly just before I heard Cliff's returning key in the lock, only allowing sufficient pause to adopt the appearance of a fully stretched housewife. I'm not complaining. Confessing.

There was much to celebrate in 1979. Guy had been discouraged from aspiring to Oxbridge by his housemaster at school but others there agreed with us, and him incidentally, that he had a good chance. In the event he was offered two places at different Oxford colleges and chose Pembroke. It really had a lot of style ... all those punts and May Balls which none of us had experienced at closer quarters than the printed page. Cliff opened an account at Blackwell's to give him a toe in that venerable door as well, and I labelled things and made extra rhubarb chutney to see him through the first term. I also wrote out recipes of particular home-made favourites but these proved to be more Look-and-Say than Make-and-Eat. His living allowance was by no means elastic so he worked out his own *modus vivendi*. One good restaurant blow-out now and again to keep the spirits up, baked beans the rest of the time until the craving for meat grew so strong that he bought the cheapest stewing steak to frizzle in a pan, then chew without swallowing. The smell and flavour he said were enough to keep the carnivorous wolf from the door until the next beanfeast. He was reading English so the name we had chosen for him might yet turn up in a by-line in *The Times*.

Jenny enjoyed her last bit of school intensely, dancing, acting, singing at a high level, and leaving at sixteen with a fistful of O levels. She was still determined on a stage career but drama schools expressed a preference for students who were over eighteen. Her grandfather's ghost must have smiled when we suggested that a secretarial course after leaving school might be a wise precaution. She wasn't overjoyed but toed the line using the subsequent shorthand and typing in tedious spells of temping while she auditioned for a place at college. We had 'Rosalind' slapping her *As you Like It* thighs in the kitchen and 'Nina' crying real Chekovian tears all over the bedroom by the time Webber-Douglas accepted her and she too was off and away, to melancholy digs in London. There wasn't enough song and dance for Jenny at Webber-Douglas. After a year they redirected her to the musical theatre course at Guildford School of Acting and there she fitted happily for the rest of her training. Oxford, London, Guildford, it all came to the same thing. The fledglings had flown, apart from occasional pit-stops for refuelling at home. Then Cliff went off to Southampton to fulfil his two-year contract with Southern Television and the house was empty on Tuesdays, Wednesdays and Thursdays.

There had been times, many of them, when a bit of peace was all I longed for. Admittedly the yearning was for limited peace, with the presence of the family propping it up on either side like bookends. Such large amounts of sudden solitude were as hard to handle as a very small but very sharp bereavement. Compared with many, I was fortunate. Compared with some, I was downright in clover. It was shaming to discover how quickly depression breeds self-preoccupation. Cliff was finding his life divided between home and Southampton a minor hell of travel and hotel rooms.

Jenny's digs were abysmal. Even Guy among the dreaming Oxford spires had his problems. But all I thought about at the time was *me*. The hollow days in the middle of the week chafed like new shoes which needed breaking in.

It was the thought of 'breaking them in' which did the trick along the lines of 'Don't just sit there – *do* something'. I made a start by tidying Guy and Jenny's things away then moved on to my own long neglected drawers. I must have filled several rubbish sacks with a lifetime's collection of 'might-come-in-useful's by the time I reached the boxes of old photographs which had for years been swelling, bulging and threatening to force the lid off the chest in which they were stored. Those old photographs provided a trigger.

In the introspective atmosphere of suddenly feeling old and 'putting my affairs in order', it occurred to me that the sort of life led by the people in the sepia snapshots had not at that time been recorded. There were books about Bright Young Things dancing the night away at The Embassy Club, and plenty of plays set in poverty-stricken areas of back-to-back housing in the twenties, but the people in between, my people, keeping up appearances at the front while a tin bath hung on the wall at the back, had not received much attention. It was time to get out my old paintbox and set down the pictures we all have stored at the backs of our minds, mental snaps of what it was like when we were children.

The more I painted the more it came back to me – the *smell* of soapsuds on washing day, the *feel* of faded voile in a Sunday dress. The small detailed sketches this 'comfort painting' produced were never meant for other than family viewing. I thought I might keep them secretly for the children's children to discover one day. It was all so enjoyable I began to feel guilty. Beside the paints, brushes and cartridge paper on the kitchen table I kept a handy ironing board to which I could spring if someone, even, I regret to say, my husband, arrived unexpectedly and caught me at it. Old skills became more fluent day by day – pools of water in washes of sky, bold blocks of shadow – and the drawings poured out. Day trips to the seaside in stockings and hats, children in winter scarves crossed and tied behind their backs, old sewing machines, wireless sets and mangles. In most cases the memory muscles exercised well. The further back I dug the better they worked, except for that mangle. There was a particularly fine example hoisted like a barber's pole above a Redhill antique shop so one wet early-closing afternoon I sat in the car park opposite making notes of the cogs and rollers. 'My 'comfort painting' was becoming serious. Inevitably, in the end, Cliff caught me with my paints down. Good therapist that he is, he didn't scowl and run a finger along a dusty mantelpiece but admired and encouraged and insisted that the pictures should be linked with a narrative 'then I'll show them to a publisher I know'.

Until then the drawings had been random dips into memory without a sense of direction. With difficulty I managed to shake them into some sort of shape and concocted a flimsy text. The day came to buy an artist's folio like the ones I had seen art students carrying around – I felt younger every minute – and the collection went off to the publisher. It was accepted. In my mind I had called the book 'House Without a Bathroom' much as one might call a pet Spot or Bonzo, but the publishers, Michael Joseph, feared that with such a title it might land on bookshop Do-It-Yourself shelves. 'Why not use the house name?' they suggested. 'Call it *Sunnylea.*'

Gestation was protracted. Printing watercolours is a complicated business it seems. There were high points of excitement along the way; the first transparencies, specimen cover designs and proof-reading. It would not have surprised me if we had prepared a layette by the time publication day arrived. The 'birth' was painless in September 1980 although postnatal depression set in with the ten-day publicity tour which followed. This I didn't relish. What to do about the hair for a start? No time to heat a roller or visit a hairdresser. When 'Superwoman' Shirley Conran first faced this problem she splashed out on a wig but they always make my head itch. It wouldn't look too wholesome to scratch the scalp with a Biro on *Pebble Mill at One*. A hat was the answer, a spectacular crushproof cartwheel to cover hair and minimise face. For its debut I put it on carefully in the loo of an Inter City train to Bradford. Sweeping out to meet my public I discovered that, being considerably wider, hat through doorway did not go. That millinery was made for carrying. By the end of the tour it was a much-travelled, much-carried hat. This, for example, was the first day's itinerary:

22.9.80
After publication party at 8.00pm travel to Wolverhampton.

23.9.80

8.30am	Beacon Radio, Wolverhampton
10.00am	*Wolverhampton Express and Star*
11.30–1.45pm	BBC TV *Pebble Mill at One*, Birmingham
2.15pm	BRMB Radio, Aston
3.00pm	Radio Birmingham
5.00pm	*Evening Sentinel*, Stoke on Trent
7.00pm	*Derby Evening Telegraph*
	Overnight stay, Manchester

Repetitive interviews and waiting in deserted shops to sign copies were as nothing compared with Literary Lunches. These are bookish Baby Shows with suppliant authors holding out their progeny to be kissed. The paying guests leave the dining room, after lunching and listening, past tables piled with speakers' books which it is hoped they will be tempted to buy. On one of these occasions I was sitting next to Sir John Mills. At the end of the room and the height of her fame was Barbara Woodhouse, head-high in paperbacks. We fixed bookselling smiles on our faces while the ladies – Literary Lunchers are usually ladies – filed past smiling back. Few paused. Most headed straight for Barbara, money in hand. After some minutes of non-productive grinning Sir John, wearing an uncharacteristic snarl, muttered 'My teeth have dried out'.

Dry teeth or not, it was all worth the effort if only to receive the readers' letters which continue to dribble in to this day. From Mrs Joyce Sumner in Australia: 'I still remember the Wall's Ice-Cream man calling "They're Luvly" and the muffin man who came round on winter Sunday afternoons with his tray on his head, ringing a bell. I too had a "Sunny Jim" doll and washing day was just as you described.' From Oscar Heim in Moseley, Birmingham: 'Yes, yes, and yes again to bull-nosed Morrises, men and women with hats, solid-tyred buses with open tops and aprons, paddling drawers, Stop Me and Buy One, non-electric toys, organ grinders and milk from little carts.' For Dorothy Dycher in Vequeville, Alberta: '*Sunnylea* was a little bit of home', and Janet Martin in Quebec said 'It was almost my own story . . . the shadows of the fire in the grate, liberty bodices and stone hotwater bottles, curling tongs and Carter's Little Liver Pills.' Margaret Kneebone explained that her 1920s childhood home was in South Africa. 'Even so everything you described and drew rang a bell with me . . . the joy of having baths in the kitchen and shadows cast on walls by candles.' By the sound of it we all lived in a *Sunnylea* at some time in our lives. My most treasured letter came from Molly Stacey in Gorleston, Norfolk who wrote with such flourish. 'How you have cheered my heart, dear lady. Oh, that we were still in that lovely land. Yet, thank God, we have been there, eh?' Spot on, Molly Stacey, spot on. You made me thankful too. There would be no more looking back with regret at that world's passing. Or to the part of my life when the children were young. I had been there and I was glad.

Two years ago one of the book illustrations was made into a Christmas card and last year three more paintings were commissioned to complete a set of four. It is not the way to make a fortune but the sight of people buying the cellophane packets, the thought of something of mine being posted all over the place, was like being reborn. There was nothing picturesque about my renaissance. I was no Aphrodite rising from the foam. This had been a clumsy clamber out of the doldrums, but who cared? I was one of the lucky ones who are allowed a second wind. What a suitable way to go into my dotage, as the Michelmore's answer to Grandma Moses.

That is how I painted my way out of my withdrawal symptoms. But Grandma Moses? No, not really. For a start there are no grandchildren yet. 'In your sixties and not a grandparent?' The pity and surprise people express is quite embarrassing. We are in no hurry. Guy and Jenny have careers which they are reluctant to unsettle until they have discovered how far they can go. Guy writes and records film music when he is not working on television and has put in many hours with the Special Constabulary. He has never told us much about it but we know he once received a Chief Constable's commendation for courage and resource so his early ambitions have not been entirely unfulfilled. Jenny left drama school with a Best Actor Medal and has given us hours of delight ever since as we travel the country to see her perform; from *Blood and Ice* in Edinburgh to *Antony and Cleopatra* in Chichester, Principal Boy in Nottingham to Weill, Eisler and Brecht in Salisbury. No need to 'Make tar-raa' now, it's all paid for and genuine. Cliff and I are comfortable on the sidelines appreciating the finer points of their game.

They do not have a high regard for my potential as a grandparent. Neither do I for that matter. I have never liked *all* babies, *all* children, *all* old people, *all* dogs. In my day a grandchild sat at its grandmother's knee marvelling at her knowledge of wild flowers and wise old saws. Mine will I fear be restless and boisterous. Shall I be able to retain the Yeastvite smile when favourite china goes crashing, when piping voices drown *The Archers* or paint is daubed on pale blue walls? Send for me, dear children, when your young are ill and I will read them into the ground. Bring them to us when they are poetically asleep or charmingly talkative, but don't leave them for weeks while you swan off into the sun. With any luck I shall be divertingly eccentric by then. Nothing unsavoury you understand, just mildly interesting. Part of The Plan which began with a swooning Norma Shearer seduction was to end my days wandering daffily among bluebells, *sans* teeth, *sans* girdle, grey hair flying, wearing purple. But the moment to 'turn' has so far eluded me. There was always an imminent audience to face or a dinner to attend. When my hair decided to go on ahead it became, not wild and grey, but a disappointingly dull and ambiguous beige. After years of following suit and feeling boringly beige all over I decided to dye it. Now I am artificial auburn and don't care who knows it. Defiance has come to the old dogsbody at last.

Growing old I find has less to do with policemen looking young than watching your words when you hear of someone's death. It seems only yesterday that the response to a seventy-year-old's departure was a carefree 'Oh well, he was a good age'. Now I hear myself saying 'How sad. So young.' On the principle that wills should be made when you are youthful and in the pink, this may be the right chipper moment to write myself an End of Term Report:

Jean could make a valuable contribution if she was more honest, less tactful. She must realise that she cannot go through life avoiding commitment or hurting the feelings of others. She shows great appreciation of colour and form but should learn to curb her love of the familiar and take more risks. She tends to be cautious. All activities are over-prepared.

Cookery: Good, although her knowledge of calorific values is not always applied.

PE: Poor. She should take more exercise.

Housework: Could do better.

Reading: Requires attention.

Progress: Good. Since dyeing her hair, Jean is gaining confidence in expressing opinions and no longer sets too great a store by popularity.

Remarks: Jean is sympathetic, understanding and tolerant with her peers. A useful member of the form who has yet to fulfil her potential for personal involvement and leadership.

In other words – too much *laissez*, not enough *faire*. But I'm learning.

If I could choose, I would like to die with one last golden autumn under my belt, remembering the best of the thousands of wonderful days we Michelmores have had together. Times when the children in their first yellow macs and sou'westers looked like small jaundiced mushrooms, when Guy asked to see the zoo's nocturnal animals in the 'Mock Turtle House' and Jenny carolled 'Ding Dong Merrily on High, Suzannah is next Chelsea'. The days when Cliff arranged a huge surprise party for my fortieth birthday and called it diplomatically 'a celebration of twenty years in broadcasting', when we rode together on a Canadian train, spellbound by the majesty of the Rockies, then laughed to tears as a scratchy recording of 'Rose Marie' came over the intercom. Cliff buying expensive winter flowers 'because we both like them about the house', sending yellow roses every anniversary, phoning from the other ends of the earth and hurrying home at the first possible moment.

Those are the things I'd like to remember when the time comes, and what I wonder will they remember about me. My father left behind the word 'Fry-pan-chum' which he invented to fill an impossible crossword clue, and the phrase he used to deflate pretentious prose, 'Come, let us lean over against the deep river'. Aunt Norrie's malaprop play titles linger on – *The Rains Came* is still to me 'When the Weather Broke', and *You Can't Take It With You* – 'You Can't Get In Without it'. When anyone says admiringly 'Good enough for the Queen' I remember my mother, and at other times catch myself saying as she did 'Finish it up. It'll only go to waste'. Facing our brimming Christmas dinner someone always quotes Uncle Tom's annual response, 'I enjoy turkey much better cold'. I wonder what they'll remember about me. Rhubarb chutney? The Toothbrush Syndrome? 'She always wanted the electric blanket on High when I wanted it on Low'? Cliff, the modest and realistic man, has always said 'No fuss when I die. No unnecessary expense.' To be honest I have to admit to a vulgar hankering for a positive fiesta of a funeral, with flowers coming out of my ears. Does that sound eccentric? I do hope so.

Meanwhile, as I write, there is promise everywhere in my own personal world. Hedgehogs are back in the garden and the goldfish in the pond have survived another winter. Cliff and I are learning to spread ourselves luxuriously into space which used to be filled by others and, do you know, we *like* it. The kitchen is free of chip smells and the garden clear of motorbikes. Cliff has more time to read undisturbed and walk on the heath in low afternoon sun. When this book is finished I have 'Son of Sunnylea' to complete which takes us into the thirties. This time there will be no ironing board as an alibi, no guilt. We cannot guess at the delights Jenny may have in store for us as her career goes steadily onwards and Guy, with his brains and originality, continually surprises. A ninety-year-old once told me 'The nicest thing about being extremely old is that you can wear your good clothes everyday. There is no point in saving them.' Significantly, Cliff and I still have a number of 'Sunday Best's in the wardrobe. There are buds on the old tree yet.

If one day, later rather than sooner, a voice should call 'Come in Mrs Michelmore. Your time is up. Any last words? Any regrets?' I hope I shall say 'Thank God for a marvellous husband and children. And I wish I had dyed my hair *years* ago.'

Postscript

Invited to provide the last words in this book, our son and daughter produced the following uncensored assessment of their parents. At the time they had not read the preceding pages. Their combined conclusions have been written by Guy. Additional material by Jenny.

Every Mother and Father is a celebrity in the eyes of their children. To Jenny and me however, these two celebrities have always been, first and foremost Mum and Dad. As a family, we Michelmores are spectacularly ordinary in a domestic sense. Triumphs and disasters, love and anger, snakes and ladders have come to our family in the same random proportions as to everyone else. Despite the exceptional pressures and demands of their chosen profession, family life has always been the highest priority in our house and the fact that Mum and Dad popped up with monotonous regularity in the homes of millions of other people around the country, made little difference to our family relationships when they popped up in our own. Some concessions to a busy working life were inevitable however and within the space of a few months, my sister and I became connoisseurs of fine nannies as they flowed thick and fast through the household. An intoxicating succession of young women were engaged and discharged with astonishing speed until finally one was found who could deal with the considerable demands of both parents and children with equal diplomacy and tact. Patty was surrogate mother, *sous chef*, agony aunt and ACAS all rolled into one. When professional demands were at their greatest, Patty stepped into the parental breach admirably. When Dad worked until late into the evening every day on *Tonight* and Mum disappeared to talk to BFPO 49 every Sunday on the wireless, it was seldom that we came together as a family. I suspect at one point we saw as much of Dad on the television as at home. It's a peculiar experience sitting in the kitchen having tea and watching your father on the television but one which, if you're brought up with it, even very small children get to grips with remarkably quickly. Until we were five or six it didn't dawn on us that grown ups did anything else; children watch television and adults appear on it. It's only now that I work in the industry that I've discovered it's probably more true the other way round. In spite of, or maybe even because of, the demanding nature of the job, when we were together as a family they really earned a gold star for effort and never more so than on holiday.

While growing up with well known parents makes no difference to the way you look at them, it makes a big difference to the way other people look at you. On holiday we could rely on the undivided attention of our parents and they could rely on the undivided attention of just about everybody else. Had my father and mother been handing out free money it's hard to imagine that they could have attracted more attention from our fellow holiday makers. Things came to a head in the West Country. Even Father's wheeze of removing his spectacles didn't deflect his admirers. 'There goes Cliff Michelmore without his spectacles' they would say to each other as he walked into lamp-posts and other bits of roadside furniture. Father never has been terribly good with over-enthusiastic viewers. He has more than once threatened to push back the frontiers of medical science by offering to place comparatively large autograph books where no autograph book has gone before. Mother on the other hand was remarkably tolerant. She would stand for ages being harangued by elderly listeners even when it became clear that they thought they were talking to Judith Chalmers. Even my mother's endless patience came to an end however when on one notable occasion in Cornwall she discovered some woman offering my two-year-old sister and me half a crown each if we would let her take our picture. We were whisked away just as I was entering negotiations along the lines of 'Make it a quid and I'll throw in the world rights...' Thus a promising career as an entrepreneur bit the dust. From then on we always went on holiday to the Isle of Wight where my father was born and people who remember him delivering their milk still call him Arthur. With commendable presence of mind, the family was installed at Bembridge, which boasts one of the most blue-blooded beaches in Britain. Only there will you see a nanny in full uniform careering though the shallows to prevent one right honourable six-year-old hitting another over the head with a spade, threatening irreparably to disrupt the line of succession. Compared with such ridiculously distinguished company, a television personality was far too tacky to warrant any serious attention. Thenceforth, we enjoyed our holidays in peace.

My mother is totally obsessed with Christmas. The moment she hears a weather forecast offering an outside chance of a little sleet she gets a wild look in her eye and starts whistling carols. The scale of our Christmas decorations at their peak would have put most major civil engineering projects to shame. The ageing beams of our home would creak under the weight of garlands, colossal gold balls and bits of holly. If Father takes the initiative on holiday, leaping into boats and hurtling around on the beach, Mother is very much in charge of Christmas. I don't know what's got into her. I think she must have been hit on the head with a copy of The Complete Works of Dickens *when a small girl. In any event there's no stopping her now and nor would we wish to. Christmas has always been a major event in our family with roaring log fires, towering Christmas trees and plenty of festive spirit. Both our parents have a phenomenal sense of occasion. Birthdays and Christmasses were the best days of my childhood. Once I woke on my birthday morning to find that somehow, during the night, they had managed to replace my old bedroom furniture with all the teenage things I'd longed for, including a kidney-shaped dressing table topped with roses and a bowl of sugared almonds to match the draperies. How I had slept through such wholesale removals I shall never know. They also surpassed themselves at parties. Father was always inventing games. One involved bandaging members of your team with reams of coloured toilet rolls, and Mother once arrange an entirely Pink Tea – pink sandwiches, pink cakes, pink milk to drink.*

To paint a picture of a blissfully happy family smiling inanely as though we're auditioning for a detergent commercial would not be completely honest. We have arguments from time to time although my mother and father both approach them in a totally different way. Mother will avoid them at all costs, partly because she is phlegmatic, calm and philosophical by nature but mostly because she's chicken. Father can be quite explosive and will not shy from a fight whether it's over a point of principle or going bonkers over something trivial because he's feeling crotchety. Our parents don't have rows, or rather they've had three in living memory and they're so bad at them its not surprising they don't have more. Mother, a past master at giving in gracefully and retreating swiftly, will occasionally stand her ground. Father rises to the occasion and a short skirmish ensues. In the bloody aftermath, Mother will mope around for days telling herself not to be so foolhardy as to join battle again whereas Father's temper is as swiftly regained as it was lost. Our Mother has no aptitude to argue and this is both one of her greatest strengths and her weakness. Always the diplomat, her ability not to rise to even the most obvious bait could be very frustrating as a child. *When I was a niggling teenager I often 'rattled her cage' trying to get a good row going without success. It was like fighting with cotton wool snowballs, to have a mother who refused to argue back.* If there was a domestic Nobel Peace Prize, Mother would win it hands down. There are alarming signs that this is going by the board in her old age, probably as a consequence of dying her hair. She is beginning to develop the ability to sniff out battles which she can win and goes in all guns blazing much to the astonishment of those of us who had learned to rely on the fact that she was a dead loss if confronted. New tactics are clearly called for to deal effectively with her dotage.

If Mother is the arbitrator of the family, Father is very much the leader. Decisive, courageous, inspirational. *Pa's inspirational streak is wonderful. Like a sparkler when it's not November. Our childhood was ordinary and conventional most of the time but once in a while, quite unexpectedly, he'd have a firecracker of an idea. One weekday the four of us found ourselves unusually at home together, our days off having coincided. Without warning he bundled us all into the car and took us to Boulogne for lunch.* He is witty and wise yet unpredictable, occasionally temperamental, never one to suffer fools gladly. He would like to be good at absolutely everything and finds it hard to admit that there are things he can't do and is not averse to a bit of bluff from time to time. High on the list of things he can't do are sing and put on an American accent. The former he does mercifully infrequently and the latter rather too often for the good of the family and the Western Alliance. He becomes amazingly angry at inanimate objects and can occasionally be found in a Basil Fawlty style dispute with a domestic gadget. For a chap with a degree in engineering he is astonishingly bad with machines. He has a good mind and a genuine love and knowledge of books and literature. He enjoys earning money and spends it selflessly. He once attempted to explain to his nine-year-old son how, because of supertax, he had to earn a hundred pounds to pay for the ten-pound garden plant I had just obliterated with a football. Needless to say, the explanation, like the plant, was a lost cause. After a particularly profitable patch he found he could afford either a swimming pool or a Rolls-Royce. He went for the pool and he can't even swim.

Mother on the other hand is infinitely good-natured, calm, patient, prepared to see the best in anyone, sympathetic and considerate with a remarkable reliability and attention to detail. *I don't believe she's as calm through and through as she appears. Better at biting her tongue than we are perhaps, but inside she's probably as angry as the rest of us. She smooths things out with a kind of optimistic pessimism. Assume the worst, says Ma, and it won't happen, hence her Toothbrush Syndrome. This often works but when it doesn't, well you've only spent money on a toothbrush. If I fail to get a Lead at an audition she's sure to say 'At least you've met the director'. Fall over in a dance routine. It could have been worse. 'After all, you didn't break your leg.'* She has far too little confidence in her own ability and has a tendency to put herself down and give up, lacking the obstinate arrogance to achieve anything which does not come with comparative ease. However, once goaded into action, she is equally hard to stop and has hidden reserves of determination and single-mindedness which she employs infrequently but to great effect. Whilst the unreliable nature of these qualities has meant that she has never realised her full potential, it has undoubtedly cemented a marriage in which one pioneering spirit is more than enough. Her most annoying habit is commencing lengthy and enthralling tales of domestic incident and supermarket folklore just when you are walking out of the room. She is a good listener however and does a good line in common sense and solving other peoples' problems. We were somewhat disconcerted to discover that Mother could, on occasion, be more broad-minded and liberal than her children. This came as quite a shock to Jenny who has always contended that she would have thrived on having a rebellious, drug-taking, meth-swigging daughter with an illegitimate child and a penchant for shoplifting in Tesco's on Saturday afternoons. Posterity will remember my Mother for the phrase 'Bumper Bundle', which she invented, and her rhubarb chutney which is so good that were it to be liberally distributed on both sides of the iron curtain it would make a lasting contribution to world peace, East and West united in a common passion – 'Make rhubarb chutney not war'.

As small children we made frequent trips to Broadcasting House or Television Centre to see Mother and Father earning our living. Consequently many a childhood illusion was shattered at a tender age. Once you've stepped inside the Tardis to discover that, if anything, it's smaller than it looks from the outside, and seen little men clambering out of Daleks and going for a pee, it's never quite the same. When producers hired either my mother or father they certainly got value for money. My sister and I were occasionally thrown in as part of the package rather like Green Shield stamps or the glasses you get at petrol stations – three Michelmores for the price of one. Jenny and I made our broadcasting debut when I was seven and she was five, chanting chorally 'Supercalifragilistic-expialidocious' to an ill-prepared public on *Two-Way Family Favourites* one Sunday. Now my sister is an actress and I work in television, which some have observed is as predictable as winter following autumn. The charge of nepotism is frequently levelled at those who follow in their parental profession. For many years I avoided it, then I confronted it and gave great philosophical reposts, then I became a bit more whimsical and now I just tell people to get stuffed. Jenny was far more practical about the use of the family name. 'What will you call yourself when you go on the stage?' a family friend asked her when she was only nine. 'I think I'd like to be called Jenny Oliver, but I'll definitely keep the name Michelmore at first just to help me get started!' *Since then I've wished a hundred times that I had chosen 'Jenny Redgrave' or 'Jenny Giel-gud' for a working name so that I could reply 'No relation' whenever someone asks. People who spot the Michelmore always continue 'Oh yes, I can see the likeness'. When you are trying to be alluringly feminine it feels like an insult to be told you resemble a bulky man in his sixties with glasses, chins and disappearing hair.*

Unlike a Smith or Jones, there aren't many of us Michelmores about and even the most incompetent sleuth seems to be able to put two and two together.' Any relation to THE Mr Michelmore?' they ask with a sheepish, knowing grin. I'm frequently tempted to reply 'Yes I am the son of the famous Reginald Michelmore of Stoke-on-Trent. Tell me, which of his romantic novels is your particular favourite?' Stunned silence. But if the name is instantly memorable to some, it appears to be instantly forgettable to others. I once introduced myself to a gentleman while out filming who immediately turned to his Managing Director and introduced me as Guy Dimbleby. There is still one chap whom I have been bumping into regularly, if not frequently, for some years who calls me 'Mr Wolstenholme'. But if Jenny and I get a bit frazzled at constantly being associated with our parents, imagine how it must be for the select few who share our name but not our family. Michelmores of Britain you have our sympathy.

Now to be honest, our parents are getting on a bit and whilst *senile dementia* hasn't taken a firm hold of either of them yet, it's clear that it's only a matter of time. We're very worried about Mother. Once a gentle and calm adult, she's rapidly becoming a revolutionary geriatric. She always confessed to Jenny that her real ambition in life was to dress in purple, not to wear a panty girdle and to be eccentric in her old age. The first sign of change was when she began to dye her hair. 'Highlights' to start with but getting bolder and more outspoken with every furtive visit to the hairdressers. We aren't down to the turquoise mohican yet, but there are those of us who believe it's only a matter of time. The hairstyle is merely a reflection of a more aggressive approach to life in general. If it keeps up this rate she'll be establishing cells of the Militant Tendency at WI coffee mornings before we can stop her. On the other hand Father is, if anything, becoming more benign and patient in his dotage. A symbol of this is his attitude towards the cat. When it first arrived seventeen years ago he was quite happy to have it around the house, as long as that house wasn't his. If television presenters had hackles, he would have raised his every time he saw 'the bloody animal' as he was wont to call it in moments of stress, tension and honesty. A decade and a half later I think it's no exaggeration to say he actually likes the animal and when he foretells its demise these days it is more out of regret than wishful thinking.

So how will they spend their twilight years? Mother will become more and more extraordinary as every month goes by. She will pass her time painting, at which she is already extremely talented, and being artistic and temperamental at which she is getting better all the time. Father will play golf and read. He will cease to try and understand any form of new technology. He will relate fascinating stories to those who come to listen, at increasing length and with decreasing fidelity. His tales will suffer from a strange kind of compound inflation, every aspect of which will assume greater and greater proportions, increasing exponentially until they pass into the realms of myth and fable. If he suffers from any kind of infirmity, he will become completely unbearable, although recent trends have been towards a more tolerant and tolerable little old gentleman than at one time we had reason to believe we would get.

I don't expect either of us were particularly easy children to bring up, and to contend with the everyday dramas of domestic life and deal with the repercussions of being well known at the same time, must have placed exceptional pressures on the family. Once our parents are trundling around in their bath-chairs, living off warm milk and rusks, I only hope that Jenny and I will be able to look after them in their senility with the same love and common sense that they looked after us as small children. How successful they've been as parents, what kind of people they have helped to mould, only time will tell. Perhaps the true verdict can only be given by our own children in years to come if we've got the courage to ask them what it is. But should I ever be tempted to write the story of my life, I wonder if I'll be foolhardy enough to give my children the last word?

Index